PETE HILL MIC FRGS

Pete has climbed in many continents and countries across the world, including first ascents in the Himalayas. He has a Mountain Instructor's Certificate (MIC), the highest UK instructional qualification, is a member of the Alpine Club, an honorary life member of the Association of Mountaineering Instructors, and a Fellow of the Royal Geographical Society. A lack of common sense has found him on the north faces of the Eiger and Matterhorn in winter, as well as a number of other extreme routes climbed in extreme conditions in the European Alps, Africa, Nepal and India. Pete lives in Scotland and has two daughters, Rebecca and Samantha. He runs skills courses from introductory level through to advanced. He can be contacted through his web site at **www.petehillmic.com**

Endpapers: *Glacier d'Argentière, France.*

Facing page: *The author on 'Alice' 7a, St George, Switzerland.*

THE INTERNATIONAL HANDBOOK OF

TECHNICAL MOUNTAINEERING

PETE HILL MIC FRGS

A DAVID & CHARLES BOOK

David & Charles is an F+W Publications Inc. company
4700 East Galbraith Road
Cincinnati, OH 45236

First published in the UK in 2006

A catalogue record for this book is available from the British Library.

ISBN-13: 978-0-7153-2166-9 hardback
ISBN-10: 0-7153-2166-8 hardback

Printed in China by RR Donnelley
for David & Charles
Brunel House Newton Abbot Devon

ALL ILLUSTRATIONS BY ETHAN DANIELSON

Commissioning Editor: Jane Trollope
Art Editor: Sue Cleave
Project Editor: Chris Bagshaw
Desk Editor: Jessica Deacon
Production Controller: Ros Napper

Visit our website at www.davidandcharles.co.uk

David & Charles books are available from all good bookshops; alternatively you can contact our Orderline on 0870 9908222 or write to us at FREEPOST EX2110, D&C Direct, Newton Abbot, TQ12 4ZZ (no stamp required UK only); US customers call 800-289-0963 and Canadian customers call 800-840-5220.

DISCLAIMER

Whilst every effort has been made to ensure that the instructions and techniques in this book cover the subject safely and in full detail, the author and publishers cannot accept any responsibility for any accident, injury, loss or damage sustained while following any of the techniques described.

Contents

Opposite title page: *Logie Head, Scotland.*

Following pages: *Part of the Mont Blanc massif in France – superb technical climbing territory.*

Introduction

This book has been inspired by frequent trips away from my home in Scotland to an assortment of overseas locations across the years, from the sport climbing venues of Europe through to the more remote pleasures available in Africa and Asia. A huge variety of techniques is needed to deal with the situations that these venues demand, and suggestion was made to me that an encyclopedic collection would be the best way of dealing with this. Never one to back away from a challenge, the contents of this book are the result.

Most of the entries are unashamedly pitched at a level that assumes the reader has at least a basic knowledge of movement on steep ground and simple technical procedures, even though reference is made to a few fundamental subjects such as tying on and a number of knots.

It should be remembered throughout that the techniques described will rarely be stand-alone. There will be many peripheral skills to be performed and considerations to be made when dealing with any given situation such as, for example, the safety of your group if instructing or the summoning of extra help if encountering a problem whilst lowering or hoisting. These 'add-ons' will have to come from personal experience, practice and consideration of individual situations.

I hope that you find the entries useful. I would encourage you to practise any new technique that is likely to be of use to the extent that it becomes second nature, well before it may need to be deployed. To be faced with the prospect of having to abseil into a crevasse in order to set up a hanging hoist from a twin ice screw placement that needs linking before escaping the system, and not having tried the skills, at least separately beforehand, would be a tall order. Enjoy!

Pete Hill. Scotland, 2006

Opposite page: *Minimalist climbing in the Swiss Alps.*

Following pages: *Langtang Lirung, Nepal.*

A–Z

ABC A = anchor, B = belayer, C = climber

The ABC is fundamental to climbing, and checking it should become second nature. It is essential that the anchor, belayer and climber are all in a straight line. If the belayer is off to one side of the line between the climber and anchor and the system is loaded then there is a high probability that they will be pulled sideways from their stance, especially if standing up. This is relevant in a vertical as well as a horizontal plane. The belayer also needs to be tight on to their anchor. If there is slack in the system between the belayer and their anchor, the inevitable result will be that any loading of the system will cause them to be pulled forwards, possibly resulting in them being pulled over the edge of the crag or, at the least, being pulled off their feet if they are standing.

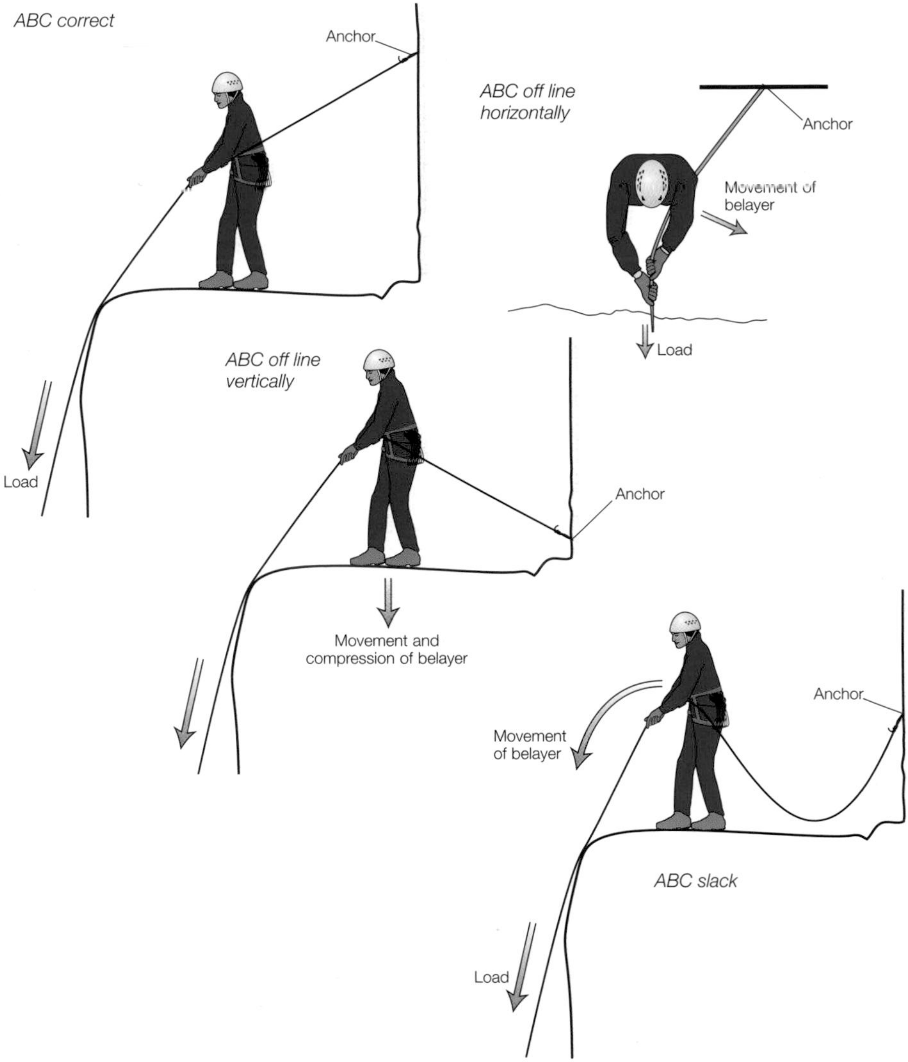

ABC correct

ABC off line horizontally

ABC off line vertically

ABC slack

Abalakov thread

See also: ice screws, kiloNewtons, tat.

The Abalakov thread is a very strong method of anchorage on ice and has the advantage that, in a retreat situation, it leaves no equipment behind. Having said that, the thread will only be as good as the ice into which it is constructed, with the depth at which the holes are drilled also being instrumental in determining the overall load bearing capabilities of the system. It also takes a little time to construct.

As well as being useful in a retreat situation where retrieval or retention of equipment is paramount, it is also suited to use on ascent. Should the loading on the system have the potential of being severe, or if the ice is of questionable quality, then two or more threads can be constructed and linked so as to share the load. In this instance, the threads need to be in the region of not less than 50cm (20in) apart.

The ideal tool for manufacturing the thread is a long **ice screw** with a moveable hanger, one that tilts back at 45 degrees from the tube and is thus designed with Abalakov construction in mind. A screw with a diameter of around 15mm is ideal.

METHOD

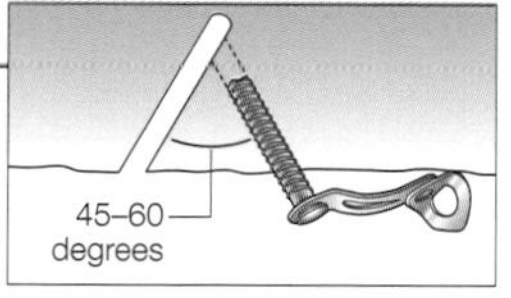

The angles for constructing an Abalakov thread.

- Two holes need to be cut in the ice that will eventually meet at an internal angle of between 60 and 90 degrees. To start, place the screw at an outside angle of 45–60 degrees to the ice and wind it fully in. Withdraw the screw and wind it in from the opposite angle, so that the teeth finally cut into the first hole. These holes need to be arranged at 90 degrees vertically to the slope.
- With the screw removed, a piece of **tat** readied for the purpose is threaded through the tunnel system and knotted together to give an attachment point. The apex of the tat, the point at which the load is applied, should give an angle of not more than 90 degrees.
- If a second thread is required, it should be placed at a 45 degree angle from the first, with the nearest holes no less than 50cm (20in) from each other. If a third is needed, the same criteria apply.

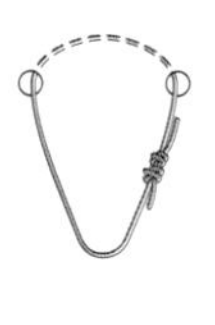

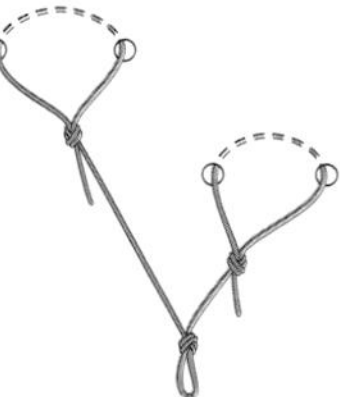

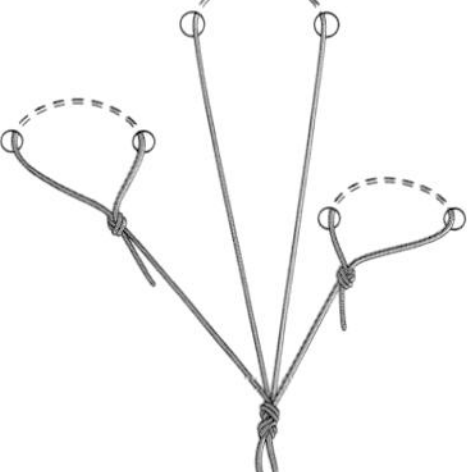

The positioning of adjacent Abalakovs.

notes

The distance between the two holes being drilled is important, as it will affect the overall holding capabilities of the anchor. In good ice, the holes should not be less than 10cm (4in) apart. Although the quality of the ice is obviously a major influencing factor determining the strength of the anchor, as a rough guideline a thread made with a 10cm (4in) gap between screw holes will have a holding capability of 6–7 kiloNewtons, a gap of 20cm (8in) will increase this to 11–12 kilo Newtons.

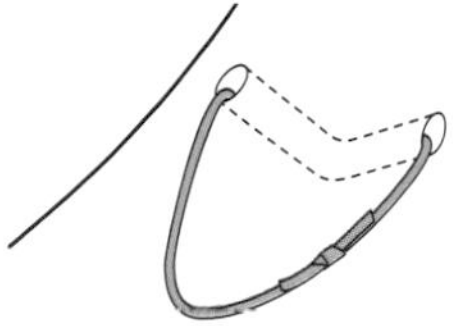

The completed Abalakov thread

tip

It can be tricky threading the tat through the ice if you are not prepared. Moistening and bending the tip of the tat can help in some instances, but if multiple Abalakovs are likely to be used a purpose-designed multi-hook should be carried. Alternatively, one can be fashioned from a wire coat hanger and could be manufactured prior to the trip.

Abseil: changing from ascent to descent from a stance

See also: abseiling, abseil rope – deploying, abseil rope retrieval, cowstail, Italian hitch, Italian hitch – locking off, multi-pitch climbing, slings, spike anchor.

The process by which an ascent is turned into a retreat is relatively straightforward, but can potentially cause a number of problems if not carried out in a logical manner. The reasons for having to descend are legion, and include a deterioration in the weather conditions, having climbed off route, being on ground that is too difficult or dangerous, fading light, illness of one of the party, and so on.

The method given below is for two climbers using a single rope on a **multi-pitch** rock route. It is assumed that the leader has taken a direct belay, using an **Italian hitch** on a **spike anchor**. Obviously, many variables exist and it is up to each climbing team to come up with a process that is slick, safe and appropriate.

METHOD

- Once the second arrives at the stance the **Italian hitch** is locked off, rendering both climbers safe.
- If retrieval of the rope from directly around the anchor cannot be guaranteed, an anchor system that can be sacrificed should be arranged. This will most likely consist of little more than a **sling** or **tat** around the spike.
- Both climbers need to secure themselves to the new anchor point with a system that does not use the climbing rope. This may best be done using a **cowstail**. At this point, however, they should not untie from the climbing rope.
- Once they are safely attached to the new anchor, the original anchor system can be dismantled in order to salvage the gear.
- One of the pair now unties from the end of the rope, and threads it through the new anchor, stopping at the middle mark.
- The same climber now holds both sections of rope together at the anchor, whilst the second climber unties from the end. By doing it in this manner, there is no chance that the rope can be accidentally dropped down the cliff.
- The rope is **deployed** in an appropriate fashion.
- One of the pair unclips from the anchor and descends using an appropriate **abseiling** technique. It is important that they have the majority of the spare equipment with them, as they will need to construct the next abseil point. For security, if the next stance is small they can stay attached to the abseil rope whilst carrying out the work.
- Once they have completed the anchor they can clip themselves into it using their cowstail and remove their abseil device from the abseil rope. If needed, they can protect the second during their descent by holding on to the ends of the rope.
- Once the second person has arrived at the new stance, they clip themselves into the anchor and remove any abseil device from the rope.
- The knot, if one has been tied for security, should be removed from the end of the rope that will be pulled up and through the anchor.
- The other end, the one with a knot still tied in it, is threaded through the new anchor. One person can continue feeding this through as the other now pulls down on the rope from above, releasing it from the original anchor.
- With the middle mark in place, the rope end knot re-tied and the rope deployed down the next section, the pair can repeat the process as required.

Abseil descent: changing from descent to ascent

See also: abseil devices, abseil loop, clove hitch, French prusik, HMS karabiner, klemheist.

There may be a situation where it is necessary to change from an abseil into an ascent of the rope. Perhaps, for instance, the abseiler has descended over a cliff to find that the rope they are on is hanging free, and re-ascending is their only option.

For the purposes of the following description, it will be assumed that the abseiler is using a standard **abseiling device**, protected by a **French prusik** back-up.

METHOD

- Stop on the descent at an appropriate point, and let the French prusik back-up take the weight.
- Clip in an **HMS karabiner** with a **clove hitch** tied in the rope below the French prusik on to the **abseil loop** as an extra safety.
- Using a second prusik loop, tie a **klemheist** on to the abseil rope above the abseil device, and clip this to the abseil loop. This may need to be extended a little to reach above the abseil device.
- Releasing the French prusik, descend until body-weight is being taken by the klemheist. Take care that the clove hitch back-up has sufficient slack between it and the French prusik, otherwise the system could jam.
- Remove the abseil device.
- Attach a sling to the French prusik and place a foot in it incorporating the appropriate amount of wraps to get the length correct. Now unclip the prusik from the karabiner connecting it to the abseil loop.
- It is now possible to **ascend the rope**, taking in the slack at the clove hitch at intervals to ensure continued safety.

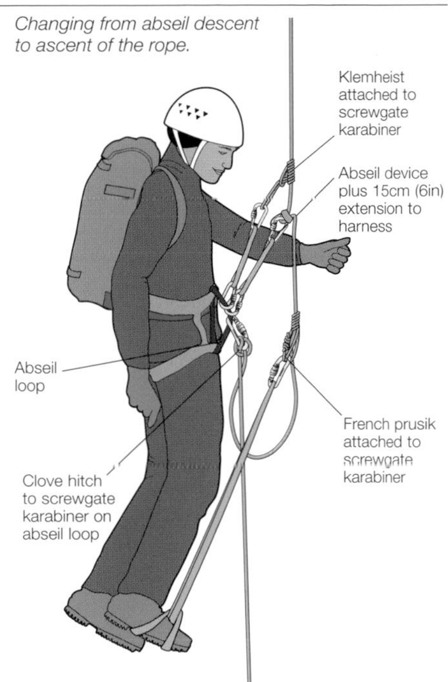

Changing from abseil descent to ascent of the rope.

Abseil devices

See also: belay devices, Italian hitch, karabiner brake.

There is a wide range of devices suitable for abseiling, and these can be categorized as those that are designed specifically with descent in mind and those that can perform other tasks as effectively, usually as a **belay device**.

The decision of which device to choose will usually depend on the activity for which it is to be used. Standard figure-of-eight descenders are excellent as devices for abseiling, giving good control and a lot of surface area over which heat can dissipate during long or fast descents. However, they are not particularly efficient as belay devices, as they tend to be heavy and can twist the rope. For this reason, the figure of eight is seen by some to be the preserve of abseiling groups and specific abseiling-related activities and not as a general-purpose tool for mountaineering.

Modern belay devices are often designed with descent in mind as well as the protection of someone ascending, and they do both jobs well. The only drawback of using a standard belay device as a tool for descent is that, due to the relatively small surface area, heat can build up during a long or fast descent, with the possibility of rope damage occurring. For that reason the speed with which descent is made when using a belay device as a descender should be carefully controlled.

There are various other devices suitable for controlled descent. The Grigri is designed for protecting a leader as well as for abseiling, although it can only be used on a single rope and care should be taken that the correct rope diameter is used and the descent is well controlled.

Abseil descent may also be made using an **Italian hitch** and a **karabiner brake**.

Abseil loop

See also: belaying, bottom rope, harnesses, shock loading.

This is the sewn loop at the front of a **harness**, designed as a strongpoint and is primarily for holding a static load. This load could be the weight of the climber when abseiling, or perhaps as a connection point when performing an emergency technique. It is sometimes referred to as a 'belay loop', which is something of a misnomer as **belaying** at the harness should always be done on the rope loop created by tying on. Belaying should only take place with the load passing directly to the abseil loop in a situation such as when belaying a climber in a **bottom rope** scenario, where the abseil loop would not be **shock loaded** at all, should the climber's weight come on to it.

For most climbing and mountaineering situations it is not worth purchasing a harness without an abseil loop, although some designs, primarily aimed at the lightweight end of the market, do exist. Leading a route when clipped in with a karabiner to the abseil loop is to be greatly discouraged.

Abseil position

notes

If **abseiling without a harness**, the position for descent with two ropes is the same as if a harness was worn. When descending with a single rope, the position is with the controlling hand, the one holding the dead rope, turned downslope at an angle of about 45 degrees. This helps alleviate a little of the discomfort felt by the rope running under the groin and over the shoulder.

See also: abseil protection, free abseil, abseiling without a harness.

The position adopted when abseiling is crucial to a successful descent. Leaning too far back can cause the feet to slip upwards inverting the abseiler, who may injure themselves. Standing too upright can cause the toes to slip off the rock or ice and cause the abseiler to bang their head forwards on the surface. When using a harness, the weight should be taken by the harness itself, with the only grip on the rope by the abseiler to be one that controls the rate of descent. They should be squarely facing the rock with their legs straight, feet approximately hip width apart. A good way to prompt novices is to have them feel their heels in contact with the rock or ice, which in turn means that they are sitting back enough. The upper body should be relaxed, in an upright position, and not leaning forward.

Free abseil

The body position for a **free abseil** (one where the abseiler's feet are not in contact with the rock or ice for some or all of the descent) is similar to that above. Maintaining a sitting position with knees bent loads the harness correctly and will give a comfortable descent. If the abseil becomes free at the lip of a roof, care should be taken not to bang the head as the lip is passed. It is possible to kick back away from the lip, at the same time as releasing some of the abseil rope, so that the return swing is completed underneath the roof. Care should also be taken that enough distance is descended during the time of the swing, otherwise the abseiler will meet the lip with some force. It may be prudent simply to push the body slightly away from the lip as it passes, using the free hand, or to lean back more than is normal and fend off the obstruction with the feet.

Abseil protection

See also: abseil devices, abseil loop, cowstail, French prusik, group abseiling, klemheist, Y-hang abseil.

Abseiling is an activity with inherent risk, and anything that can be done to reduce this risk should be considered. The simplest form of abseil protection is by using a **safety rope**, and this is the method favoured for pure abseiling activities that take place in a controlled **group abseil** environment. This safety rope is controlled by a supervisor at the top of the crag and is there as a back-up should the abseiler need assistance.

Away from a group scenario, it may be possible to rig a safety rope to protect someone descending a short distance, perhaps for the retrieval of **protection** on a **single pitch** crag and left in place by a second. In this scenario it would be fairly easy to achieve, with the person on top of the crag providing security to whoever needed to descend.

When faced with an abseil due to retreat or in emergency in a multi-pitch or mountain environment, personal abseil protection is a very important factor. It would be very unlikely that a second rope would be deployed to be used for safety, not least due to the time delay caused by setting it up at every stance. There is a method that is very quick to set up and extremely safe in operation, requiring only a minimal amount of equipment.

METHOD

- The **abseil device** is clipped to the **abseil loop** on the **harness**, but is extended by around 20cm (8in). This can be done by using an **extender** with screwgate karabiners replacing the normal snap gates, or by threading a 60cm (24in) **sling** through the harness next to the abseil loop and clipping the ends together.
- A **French prusik** is then tied around the **dead rope** and clipped to the abseil loop. This should be attached with a separate karabiner to that holding the abseil device. The amount of turns on this prusik depends on whether one or two ropes are being descended: with the norm to be two ropes, about four turns of the loop will be sufficient. It is important that the prusik loop is of a length that it can in no way touch the top of the abseil device, otherwise it could fail and the system could be rendered useless.
- The abseiler may now step over the rope, which can be held centrally in a relaxed manner. One hand holds the French prusik in the released position whilst the other hand controls the descent with the dead rope. Should there be a need to stop, the French prusik is released and will travel up the rope, pulling itself tight as it does so and preventing any abseil rope from running through.

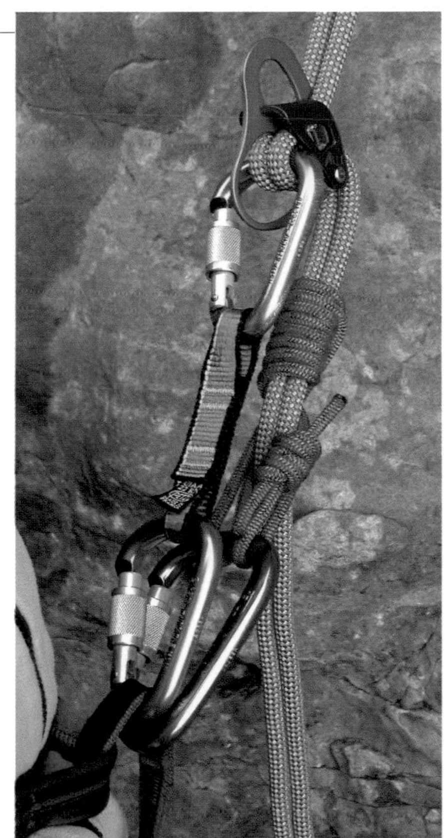

Centrally loaded abseil protection, using a French prusik.

Abseil protection

tip

A useful technique, if multiple abseils are to be encountered, is to clip the abseil device to the harness using a 120cm (48in) sling divided into thirds. The first third is used to extend the abseil device away from the harness, as mentioned above, the other two thirds can be used as a **cowstail** which can be clipped into the next belay point when it is reached. The connection of the abseil device to the sling can be in the same manner as is used for a **Y-hang** abseil.

tip

If it is found that the descent is jerky, this can be solved in most cases by the addition of a karabiner clipped through the rope between the bottom of the abseil device and the connecting HMS karabiner. This has the effect of keeping the belay device a little above the HMS, allowing the rope to run in a smoother manner.

notes

- The positioning of the back-up prusik below the abseil device means that the system is mechanically very sound. The device takes the load of the abseiler when hanging, with the French prusik simply holding the dead rope in the brake position and in fact taking very little of the load at all. However, it is sometimes seen that climbers arrange the prusik knot above the abseil device, and this has a very different effect on the loading of the system. If the prusik is above, the entire weight of the person is suspended by the prusik, with the abseil device not being loaded at all. If this is a French prusik, there is a chance that, should it be knocked, it could fail and slip down the rope, possibly burning through. If a **klemheist** were used instead, to stop the possibility of it slipping, once the weight of a person is on it, it would be impossible to release and would have to be cut in order to continue the descent.

- A place that is convenient to clip the prusik loop is on to a leg loop, and this practice has continued for many years. However, anyone considering using this method should be aware of two major problems. Firstly, if the abseiler is rendered unconscious by stone fall or similar and is hanging in their harness, their bodyweight will cause them to rotate slowly until the prusik touches the top of the abseil device and fails. Secondly, should the abseiler tilt to their side when using the system in the lock-off position, such as when retrieving gear or assisting an injured climber, the French prusik could touch the top of the abseil device, causing it to release.

An abseil back-up, clipped in to a leg loop.

Abseil rope

See also: dynamic rope, fixed rope techniques, group abseiling, low-stretch rope.

This is the name given to any rope down which a descent is to be made. It can be either **dynamic** or **low-stretch** in nature, usually depending on the activity that is taking place. Dynamic rope will often be used when descending single or multi-pitch climbs in either summer or winter, as it will most likely be the same rope as used for the ascent. Low-stretch rope is often the first choice of those organizing **group abseiling** activities, as it is less prone to elongation that could cause damage to the rope and rock, and to bounce, causing concern to novice abseilers. Low-stretch rope may also be extensively used when abseiling from routes in the Greater Ranges, where it has been necessary to **fix ropes** on various sections of the mountain.

Deploying the abseil rope

The deployment of an abseil rope can be either easy or difficult, depending upon the prevailing weather conditions and the type of terrain to be descended. In calm conditions and with the line of descent vertically downwards, there should be little problem in letting the rope snake out from the hands in a controlled manner. However, in situations where the wind is cutting across the line to be descended, and the route to be taken is more diagonal than vertical, problems can arise if the task is carried out without some thought going into it beforehand.

Once the abseil anchor has been set up in the appropriate manner, the rope can be readied. It would be a good idea to tie a knot in the end of the rope, in order to negate the chance of abseiling off the end. If the rope is plenty long enough and easily reaches the ground or a large ledge then this may not be necessary. However, if there is any chance that the abseiler could continue down the rope and off the end, such as on a multi-pitch retreat, then knotting it would be a sensible precaution. The best way to do this for most situations will be to tie a single overhand knot into each of the ends independently. This means that any kinks in the rope can twist themselves out as the abseiler descends, and they will not be faced with knots in the rope as may happen if the ends were tied together.

The best method by which the rope can be deployed, in most situations where conditions are less than perfect, is by throwing it overarm. Leaving a couple of metres slack, start flaking the rope from the anchor end of the system by wrapping it backwards and forwards across the hand. Coiling the rope in preparation for deployment is almost guaranteed to result in a tangle whilst it is in flight, whereas flaking the rope will

tip

It is extremely useful to have the centre of the rope marked. This is often done by the manufacturer with either a tape or coloured ink marking. However, should you need to mark the centre yourself, the purchase of a specially formulated rope-marking ink should be considered. This is easily applied, and is designed not to affect the rope's fibres in any way. If choosing to use coloured tape as the marker, care should be taken to ensure that the adhesive on the tape will not react detrimentally with the rope. Do not use a fibre-tip marker pen.

notes

When deploying the rope on a short route, never throw the whole thing off so that it hits the ground with force. This can cause grit particles to become enmeshed in the fibres of the rope, possibly causing future damage.

Whenever there is a possibility of other people climbing or walking in the area below your abseil point, it would be courteous to shout 'rope below' before deploying. If an abseil is required at a busy crag, careful choice of the descent route will help avoid both tangles and irritating other crag users.

make subsequent tangling far less likely. Once all of the rope has been flaked, divide it into two sections, one part in each hand. The rope in one hand is then gripped in the middle and thrown overarm at the destination, taking into account any wind that may push it off course. The weight of the rope will pull the flakes off from the other hand, and the result should be a line directly to the destination.

A second method, and one that works well when deploying the rope on slabs or snow slopes, is the 'rope bomb'. To arrange this, the rope (dealing with just one length at a time when using doubled ropes) is coiled around the hand a few times. Slipping it off, a few more wraps are made around the initial coils. The angle of coiling is then changed again and the wrapping continues. This process is repeated until the desired amount of rope has been readied. The finished article will resemble a large ball of knitting wool, and will roll down the descent route when deployed with great accuracy and little chance of knotting.

Joining the abseil rope

See also: abseil rope retrieval, double fisherman's knot, overhand knot, reef knot.

Two sections of rope may need to be joined in order to achieve an abseil. This could be the joining of two separate ropes, or the mending of a rope damaged by a rock-fall.

The standard method is to use a **double fisherman's knot**. This allows a secure union of the ropes, but can make them somewhat problematical to untie after loading. To counter this, a **reef knot** can be tied on the rope prior to tying the double fisherman's. This arrangement allows for good security, allied with the fact that the knot cannot pull itself tight together. This does, however, result in a fairly bulky knot that may catch on uneven ground when retrieving the rope. If this is a concern, then it may be prudent to secure the ropes together using a simple **overhand knot**, tied with both rope ends as one. This method will allow the knot, when the rope is pulled for retrieval, to present a flat side to any obstruction and lessen the chance of the rope becoming stuck. When tied, the overhand knot should have tail ends of at least 30cm (12in), and it should be pulled fully tight before the abseil commences.

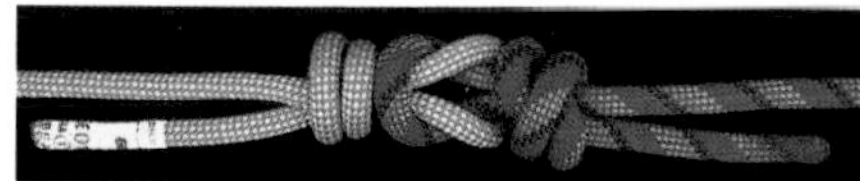

A double fisherman's knot with a reef knot to stop it over tightening.

An overhand knot.

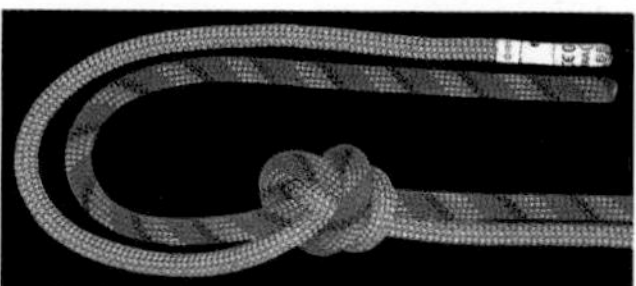

Abseil rope retrieval

See also: abseil rope, accessory cord, figure of eight, Italian hitch, tat.

The retrieval of the **abseil rope** is crucial under most circumstances, and great care and skill is needed to complete the task with the minimum of difficulty. The length of the abseil, the equipment to be used and the anchors from which the abseil will be made, will dictate the system to be used.

Routes that include abseils as an expected part of the ascent or descent will often have dedicated abseil stations. These can vary from a collection of **tat** left by previous climbers through to bolted and chained abseil points. Often, however, the rigging of the abseil point will be left up to the individuals concerned.

A plan of action needs to be thought through, and many factors taken into account. These would include the availability of anchors, the distance to be abseiled in relation to available rope length, direction and destination, and objective dangers such as loose rock or potentially avalanche-prone ground.

If abseiling from a purpose-made station, such as a bolt and chain set-up, most of these considerations have been dealt with for you.

The rope is simply threaded through the appropriate part of the system. Retrieval should be fairly straightforward, as this is what the bolted stations are designed for.

In-situ tat

If abseiling from a collection of tat that has accumulated over the years, caution should be exercised before committing weight to the system. Fabric slings and off-cuts of rope can deteriorate rapidly, from ultra-violet degradation, exposure to elements such as rain, snow and freezing, abrasion from wind action and by abrasion or burning-through caused by rope retrieval. If there is the slightest doubt as to the integrity of the anchor then it needs to be reinforced. It would often be prudent to carry lengths of flat tape or spare slings if it is known that abseils will have to take place from a non-equipped station. If the worst came to the worst and it was necessary to cut a length from the end of the climbing rope in order to fashion an anchor, having a knife to hand would make the process easier. Alternatively, and in an emergency, pounding the rope with a rock on a hard surface will also cut it without too much effort.

If the anchor is a sling, there does not need to be a karabiner attached. The action of the climbing rope running through would generate enough heat to melt it, but as the rope would, in most circumstances, be doubled for the abseil there would not be any rubbing occurring. It is only when the abseil is completed and the rope end pulled through for retrieval that there would be significant abrasion of nylon on nylon, and by that time the abseil is completed. It is because of this mechanical deterioration that any slings found in situ should be treated with the utmost caution and are best discarded.

Direction of pull

When retrieving the abseil rope from a sling anchor, for instance a spike, it is important that the rope is pulled in a manner that will ease the process and will not enhance any friction inherent in the system. Pulling on the rope coming from the side of the sling closest to the anchor will allow for a reduction in friction, as this action will have the effect of lifting the sling slightly away from the anchor instead of pushing it tighter on to it if the outer rope were pulled.

Expedition abseiling

In many situations in the high mountains or on an expedition, there may be only one rope being carried by two or three climbers. Should an abseil retreat have to be made, this means that only half of the rope length can be abseiled at any time, more than doubling the time that it would take to make the full descent. There is a method by which the entire length of the rope can be used. It requires the carrying of a length of cord to the same length as the abseil rope. This cord needs to be strong enough to allow it to be pulled on, allowing for the friction of the main rope against the surface of the rock or ice, and as such a thin **accessory cord** is recommended.

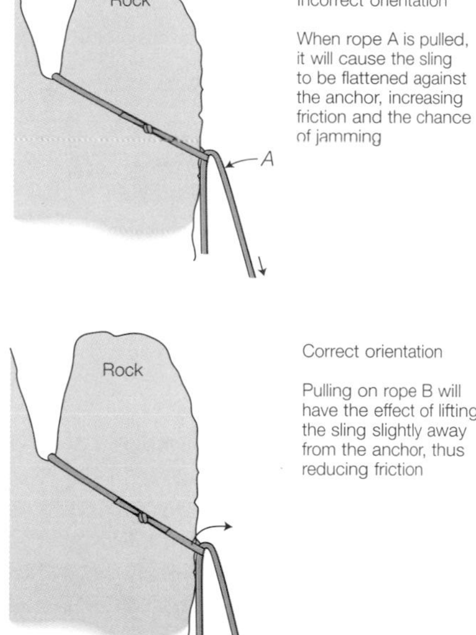

The correct and incorrect orientation when retrieving the rope from a sling.

Abseil rope retrieval

notes

As accessory cord is quite thin, care must be taken to ensure that it does not tangle when being deployed. A major problem can be the wind, as the lighter cord will tend to blow around more easily and either jam somewhere off route or be damaged through abrasion. If this is a possibility, it is sensible to have the cord stowed in a manner by which it can pay itself out as the first person descends. This is best done by flaking it into a stuff sack that can then be clipped on to the harness. Once the first person is at the end of the abseil, they can hold on to the cord to ensure that it does not blow out of reach.

tip

Abseiling using an **Italian hitch** can twist the rope, making it awkward to retrieve. Care should be taken to remove any of these twists because if the rope jams with one end out of reach above the stance it is very difficult to get back. To help solve this problem, a karabiner can be clipped on to one side of the abseil rope before descending. When at the bottom, it will be known when there is no tangle as the free-running karabiner will slide down once the correct number of twists have been removed from the rope, which can then be pulled through as normal.

METHOD

- Tie a **figure-of-eight knot** on the abseil rope and the accessory cord.
- Connect them together using a screwgate karabiner.
- Clip the abseil rope into the anchor. This should be through the smallest possible aperture, for instance a small screwgate karabiner. If the abseil anchor is made from a sling, tie an overhand knot in it to reduce the diameter at the end and ensure there is no chance of the knot being pulled through, which makes rope retrieval difficult.
- Clip the screwgate connecting the two ropes back into the main abseil rope below the anchor.
- Descent is made on the main abseil rope. Once the ground or next stance has been reached, the accessory cord is pulled and the abseil rope will be retrieved.

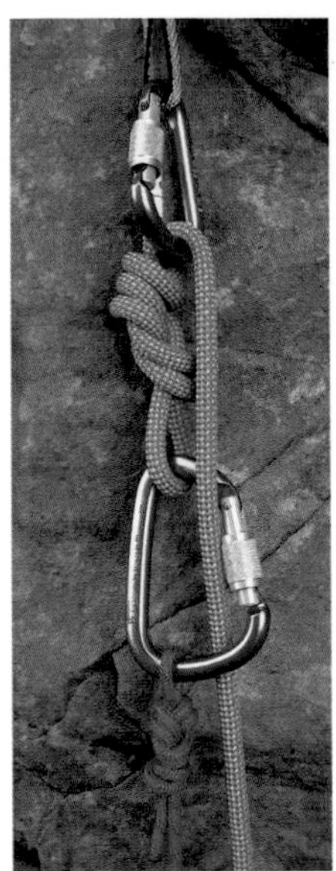

The set-up for a retrievable abseil, suitable for lightweight expedition use.

Abseiling on a single rope

If abseiling with a device that can only be used on a single rope, such as a Grigri, and the rope has to be retrieved, the following system is recommended. This is assuming that only one rope is available and it will be used doubled.

METHOD

- Pass the abseil rope through the anchor, ensuring that it runs smoothly. The diameter of the anchor, be it a screwgate or sling, is important, as laid out in bullet point 3 for the previous technique.
- Tie a figure-of-eight knot in the rope on one side of the anchor.
- Clip a screwgate karabiner into the knot, and then clip it across on to the rope coming out of the other side of the anchor.
- The descent is made on the rope that does not have the knot on it.
- When the ground or next stance is reached, the Grigri is unclipped.
- Pulling on the rope with the knot in it will allow it to run freely through the anchor and be retrieved.

It is also possible to use the previous abseil method for Grigri descent and rope retrieval.

Abseil – stacked

See stacked abseil.

Abseiling

See also: group abseiling.

Abseiling is the controlled descent of terrain using the security of a rope in order to minimize risk. However, abseiling is potentially one of the most dangerous activities undertaken by the climber or mountaineer, and many well known and high-profile mountaineers have died in abseiling accidents, both on small crags and in the Greater Ranges. It cannot be stressed enough that any system to be used must be checked and checked again before committing bodyweight to it.

It is one of the facts of mountaineering that very long abseil descents, sometimes lasting several hours or even days, have to be completed to get down safely from some peaks, after a tiring day of ascent, a time when errors can creep in due to fatigue no matter how much care is taken during rigging and execution. As always, familiarization with the methods in a safe environment before needing to use them in anger will be time well spent.

Why abseil?

There are many reasons as to why an abseil may have to take place. Getting to the start of an otherwise inaccessible route on a sea cliff is one example, making the decision to abseil off a multi-pitch route due to difficulty or time considerations is another. Descent may be necessary in order to get down to help a colleague who is in need of assistance, or it may simply have to happen in order to retrieve some equipment left on the route by your second.

Cleaning a route is often done by abseil, as is the placing of bolts and, more surreptitiously, the pre-inspection of a route prior to making an ascent. Many multi-pitch bolted routes will incorporate abseil stations for descent. As well as all this, it is important to remember that many enjoy abseiling in its own right and pursue it as an activity purely for pleasure.

notes

There are a number of factors that have to be considered when setting up an abseil of any kind:

- The ability of those within your group.
- The equipment available: are there safe anchors that can be used, is the rope going to be used singly or doubled for retrieval and, if so, does it reach to where you need to get to?
- If the rope is to be retrieved, as is usually the case, is there anything that can be done before leaving the stance to help the rope run freely?
- Which direction are you abseiling in, does straight down do the trick or would aiming to one side or the other of vertical allow a better stance to be gained?
- Who goes first, who goes last, who rigs the next stance if a multiple abseil is taking place, and finally, what about the objective danger: is your descent route taking you across areas of unstable rock that could be dislodged by the rope, or will you be travelling across potentially avalanche-prone terrain where your extra bodyweight may trigger a slide?

Only when all of these factors have been considered can the preparation for the actual descent take place.

Abseiling past a knot

See also: Abseil loop, abseil protection, abseil rope, anchor, clove hitch, French prusik, harness.

This technique is of use in a mountain situation, should you have a knot in the rope for some reason. This may be because you have tied two ropes together to increase the distance that can be abseiled from a stance, or the rope may have been damaged by stone fall or a similar incident, perhaps having the core showing through. In this case, the damaged area of rope will have been isolated and a suitable knot tied in order to bypass the weak section.

Abseiling past a knot

Abseiling in contact with the surface

If the descent is down terrain where it is possible to keep in physical contact with the snow, rock or ice, then the entire process is reasonably straightforward. It may simply be a matter of cutting a suitable ledge in the snow or utilizing a useful rock ledge to un-weight the rope whilst the knot is passed. Pull up a length of rope from below the knot and clip yourself in using a **clove hitch**. This will safeguard you whilst you remove the **abseil device** and any back-up **abseil protection** and replace them below the knot in the rope. Once they have been replaced and the system checked, the safety clove hitch can be removed and the descent can continue.

In the situation where you could unload the abseil rope, especially during a long descent in the Greater Ranges, it would be very easy to let your concentration lapse and end up in a position where you are on very steep ground, completely unclipped from the descent system at some considerable risk to yourself. An extra moment spent running over the logical progression, and constant monitoring of your own security, would be time well spent.

Should you be in a situation of having to pass a knot whilst hanging free and being unable to un-weight the abseil rope, the process is slightly more awkward but still should not take a lot of time, providing it is well practised prior to being required for use the first time.

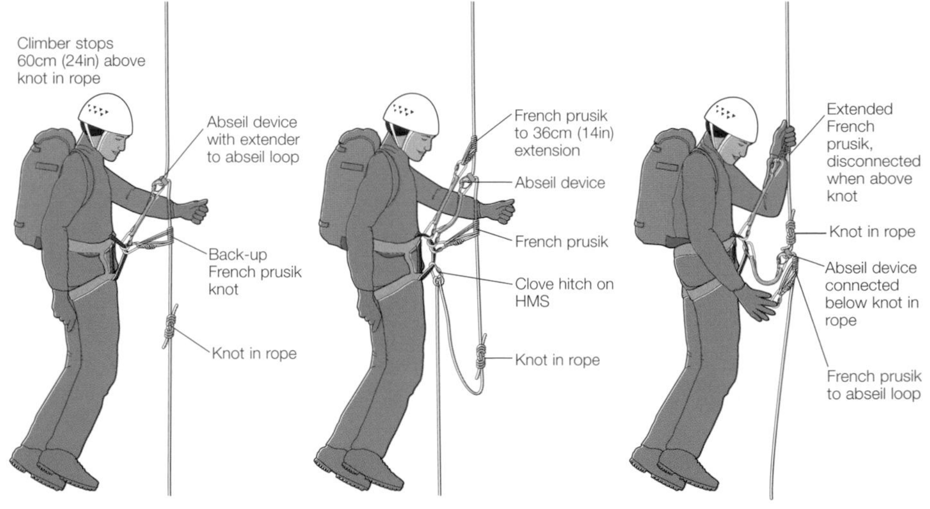

Abseiling past a knot.

METHOD

- It is important that you stop well before the knot, approximately 60–70cm (24–28in) would be fine, to allow you time and space to organize the system.
- Attach a French prusik to the **abseil rope**, ensuring that it is above your abseil device and its back-up.
- This should then be clipped into the abseil loop on your **harness**, with the distance between prusik and harness in the region of 50cm (20in). You need to have your bodyweight taken by the prusik, so abseil down a short distance so that the load is on it when your abseil device is around 30cm (12in) above the knot in the rope.
- To be suspended by a French prusik with no back-up is not recommended, so to protect your-

self when taking off the abseil device pull up a length of abseil rope from below the knotted section and tie a clove hitch in this, and clip it into a karabiner on your harness **abseil loop**.

- You may now remove your abseil device and back-up, replacing them below the knot in the rope. Extreme care must be taken at this point to ensure that nothing is dropped, and it would be prudent to carry out this procedure carefully and with minimum haste.
- Once the abseil device is replaced, ensure that it is pushed up hard against the underside of the knotted abseil rope and that any slack between it and the back-up is removed.
- Once the system has been checked over, the safety clove hitch may be unclipped from the harness.
- The requirement now is to transfer your weight from the French prusik above the knot to the abseil device below it. This can be achieved by pulling down on the top of the prusik and allowing it to slip slowly down the abseil rope, transferring your weight as it does so. It is extremely important that practice has shown you exactly how far above the knot you must initially load the French prusik, as if you are too close to it the load will not have been taken off the prusik before it jams down on to the knot in the abseil rope, which would then necessitate the cutting of the prusik to release it. This would not only involve the unfortunate loss of an important piece of kit, but also would shock-load the **anchor** system, which may not be desirable.
- Once your bodyweight is transferred to the abseil device, the French prusik can be removed or replaced below it, and the descent continued.

Abseiling with a harness

See also: anchor, abseil devices, abseil loop, abseil position, abseil protection, dead rope, Italian hitch, live rope, Y-hang abseil.

Abseiling with a **harness** allows a good deal of comfort during the descent, as well as an increased level of security over methods without a harness where the rope is wrapped in a specific manner around the body. This comfort will have a lot to do with a more relaxed body position, as well as the support that a well-designed harness will provide.

Abseil loop

Most harnesses these days have a small sewn loop at the front centre. This is known as the **abseil loop**, but is sometimes erroneously referred to as the belay loop, a purpose for which it was not designed. Some lightweight Alpine harnesses do not have an integrated abseil loop so these are either best avoided or, alternatively, an attachment point for an abseil device can be made by threading a short sling around the harness strongpoint at the front, usually around the same section that the rope would thread through when tying on.

The abseil loop of a harness is designed to take a static load, which is what the weight of an abseiler would be. The **abseil device** is clipped on to the abseil loop using a screw-gate karabiner, ensuring that the **live rope** from the anchor enters the top of the device and that the dead rope exits from the bottom. Either one or two hands can then hold the dead rope and control the rate of descent. It should be noted that, in the event of the abseiler letting go of the dead rope for some reason, possibly due to carelessness or perhaps because of being hit by stone fall or similar, they will simply end up in a free-fall situation with the rope running easily through the abseil device. For this reason, it is strongly recommended that the abseil is **protected** by some means.

Abseiling without a belay device

There may be a time when using a belay device to abseil is not practical: maybe it has been dropped and lost, or perhaps the ropes are starting to freeze up and are difficult to manipulate. In this situation an **Italian hitch** may be used very effectively. It is important that an HMS karabiner is used to aid a smooth descent and to greatly reduce the chance of the system jamming. The Italian hitch may be

> **notes**
> The maximum braking effect with an Italian hitch is evident when both the live and dead ropes are held parallel to each other. In an abseiling situation, though, this is quite difficult to achieve as the weight of the rope hanging down the cliff behind you makes it awkward to bring the controlling hand up high. However, as the hitch is usually tied on two sections of rope and the knot itself is quite bulky, keeping a tight hold on the dead rope is usually sufficient for a controlled descent to take place. Be aware that as the end of the rope is reached there will be little mechanical help from the weight of the rope and a firmer grip may have to be taken.

used on either one or two ropes. In an abseil situation the latter will be the norm, and in this case one large Italian hitch is tied and clipped into the karabiner. If two separate hitches were tied the differential of movement on each section of rope would cause the knot to jam after a very short distance.

Controlling the descent

Care should be taken to ensure that there is no possibility of the dead rope of the hitch running across the gate of the karabiner, with the possible effect of the sleeve being unscrewed and the rope unclipping itself. For people who favour holding the dead rope in their right hand, the karabiner should be clipped into the abseil loop, with the gate opening to the left and the larger rounded side away from the body. For those wishing to control the descent with their left hand, the gate should be opening to the right, again with the larger curve of the karabiner to the outside. Clipping the karabiner to the harness and then the Italian hitch to the karabiner in this manner ensures that the dead rope is running across the back bar of the karabiner, keeping it well away from the gate side.

Abseiling without a harness

It is quite possible to abseil without a harness or other technical equipment. There are two methods that can be efficiently used, one that allows an abseil to take place on a single length of rope, which may be the case if one end has been tied off around an anchor, and another method that is excellent for using if the rope has been doubled for retrieval and two lengths are available.

The method for use with a single rope is as follows, and can be altered to suit a left- or right-handed person. The description here is for a right-handed abseiler.

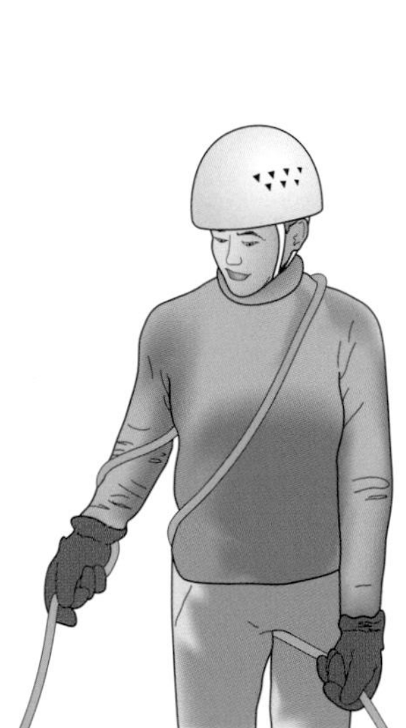
Abseiling with a single rope.

METHOD – With a single rope

- Facing the anchor, step over the rope and pick it up from behind you.
- Bring it in front of the right hip, across the chest, over the left shoulder and diagonally down across the back under the right armpit, taking a wrap around the right arm and holding it in the right hand.
- The left hand needs to hold on to the rope where it disappears under the crotch, as the centre of gravity is very high and if this lower section of rope was not held it would be easy for the abseiler to twist out of the system.
- The body should be turned with the right shoulder about 45 degrees downslope to help with comfort, and descent is made by allowing the rope to run slowly through the right hand.

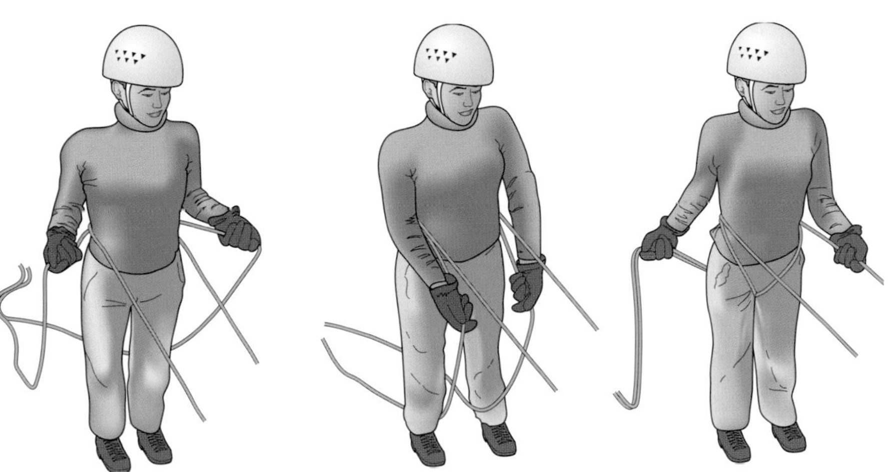

Abseiling with doubled ropes.

METHOD – With a double rope

- Step between the ropes and hold one in each hand.
- Cross them over behind your back and bring your hands forwards.
- There is now a loop of rope running down from each hand. Step the left leg over the left loop and the right leg over the right loop, grasping both ropes together with one hand behind you once you have done so.
- The two ropes, still being held together, can be brought up to the right-hand side of the body if you wish to control the descent with the right hand, or to the left hand side if you prefer that side.
- The ropes are held palm up, with no twist needed around the arm.
- Descent is controlled by feeding the ropes through with the hand holding them; the other hand may loosely hold one of the ropes in front, but this is not necessary.

The advantage of this technique of descent is that, apart from being considerably more comfortable than the single rope method, the body is well supported in a criss-cross of ropes and has a much better centre of gravity with much less chance of twisting out.

notes

It should be remembered that for use on less steep or less technical ground, a simple hand-over-hand descent may well prove to be the quickest and simplest form of descent. A good example would be if a short distance of easy-angled but slippery slabs is encountered and full bodyweight doesn't have to be placed on to the abseil rope at any time.

tip

It is important that you wear gloves when abseiling, in particular for the method used on a single rope. Plenty of clothing with a high collar and long sleeves is also highly recommended.

Accessory cord

See also: Abalakov thread, prusik loop.

Accessory cord is the name given to load-bearing rope used for a variety of general purposes. Usually short in length, it can be used to tie **Abalakov threads**, create **prusik loops,** and for many other purposes.

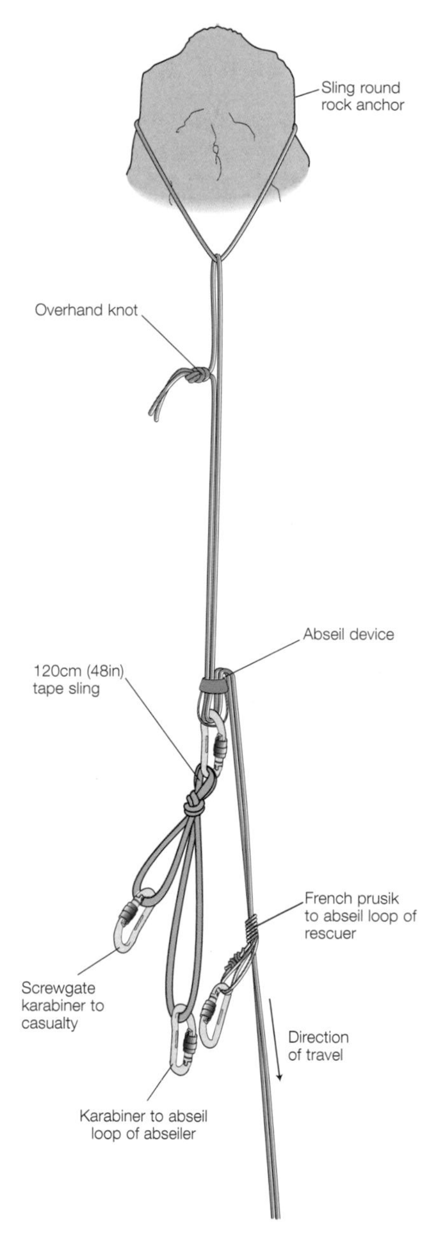

An accompanied abseil set-up.

Accompanied abseil

See also: French prusik, Parisian baudrier, Y-hang.

An accompanied abseil is one where two climbers descend together, with one taking charge and operating the system. This may be, for instance, if the other of the party is inexperienced in abseil techniques, or perhaps it is a companion who has taken sick on the ascent and is unable to continue.

Before rigging the system, they must decide on the most appropriate position for their partner to be in whilst descending. If they are feeling well and they are able to look after themselves to a certain extent, then organizing the system so that both people are next to each other would be the most appropriate. However, if they are unwell or injured then it may be more appropriate to have them suspended horizontally at waist height of the abseiler, supported at 90 degrees to their body position.

A 120cm (48in) sling is ideal for the system, and should be prepared in the **Y-hang** manner. The sling should be adjusted equally for a fit and able companion, or into thirds for someone needing special care on the descent. Should the system be needed to help an injured or unconscious party member down, they may need the assistance of a **Parisian baudrier** around the chest to keep them upright.

Checking the system

Taking a moment to check that the system runs smoothly is time well spent. For instance ensure that the **French prusik** is on the side that is most comfortable for control, and that the rope is running smoothly.

In some instances, it may be advantageous for the horizontal climber to be clipped to the abseiler by means of a short extender to avoid them swinging around excessively and either injuring themselves further or simply getting in the way whilst the person in control deals with the mechanics of the descent.

Aid, point of

See also: protection, sling.

Aid climbing is a huge subject, although pure aiding on a route is a dying art in many parts of the world. However, some routes still require points of aid, although this is often just for one or two consecutive moves.

The use of aid can be described as the (normally) temporary manufacture of a hand- or foothold that is used to assist progress up a route. This hold can be formed in a number of ways, from simply standing on the shoulders of another person through to a second pull on the rope. However, for the majority of situations a point of aid will consist of a piece of **protection** being placed and then clipped into with a sling. The climber's foot will then go into this sling to create a foothold, possibly with them also using the placement to pull up on with their hands. Once the awkward section has been passed, climbing will continue as normal. The second climber will usually remove this aid as they follow up the route. In some cases, this point of aid will be in situ, left there by previous ascensionists, and as such will normally be left in place for subsequent climbers to use.

Alpine butterfly

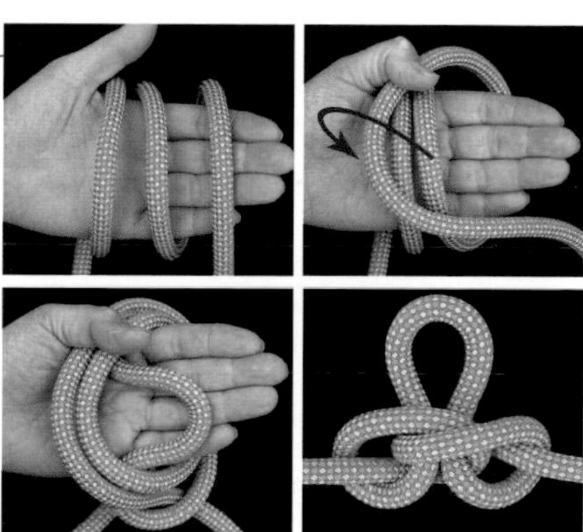

See also: fixed rope techniques.

This is an extremely useful knot, in particular in relation to rigging **fixed ropes** and tying on to the middle of the rope when moving together. Its main advantage is its ability to cope with a pull equally from either direction, without the knot distorting. For many uses, and with modern ropes, the overhand knot may be seen to be more convenient, but for the purist and those rigging or working in the Greater Ranges, the Alpine butterfly is a most useful tool.

Alpine clutch

The Alpine clutch.

See also: abseil loop, ascending the rope, autobloc, HMS karabiner.

The Alpine clutch is a method of using two karabiners jammed against each other, to grip the climbing rope. Examples of its use are as an attachment to the **abseil loop** when **ascending the rope** or as an alternative to an **autobloc**. Avoid using it as either a belaying or abseil method, as the clutch only works in one direction and as such no slack can be paid out should the need arise.

There is a lot of friction generated within the clutch, so if it is used as part of a hauling or hoisting system, some degree of the mechanical advantage created by the set-up is lost. It is best used on two **HMS karabiners**. If it is used on other types, without such a gentle curve at the base of the back bar, the clutch tends to jam. For the same reason, any karabiners on to which it is clipped need to be identical.

Anchor

An anchor is the generic name given to the item to which the climber or a rope is attached. An anchor could be a large boulder, around which the rope has been tied, a complicated system of slings and modern protection equipment, designed to take the loading of a fixed rope, bolts and chains, or a buried ice axe being used on a winter climb.

Angle pitons

See pitons.

Ascenders

See also: ascending the rope, fixed rope techniques, prusik loops.

There are a variety of types, shapes and makes of ascenders, from a basic passive type such as a Tibloc, through to more complicated devices such as handled jammers and swing-cheek pulleys with in-built cams designed to grip the rope.

The most basic mechanism for ascent will be a pair of **prusik loops**, and these are normally carried as standard on any climber's rack. However, small devices such as the Tibloc are light enough that they would make little difference to an everyday rack, and so are often included.

Should the need to ascend a rope be known beforehand, a climber would do well to carry a more substantial method of doing so. Handled jammers are the most popular, and they are excellent at providing not only a good grip on the rope, but also at being comfortable to use. Although heavy compared with smaller devices, if a lot of rope ascent is to be made, such as when following **fixed ropes** on an expedition, they are a sensible choice. Handled jammers are also easier to grip when wearing gloves at altitude, whilst many of the lighter-weight devices are awkward to use with anything more than minimal hand covering.

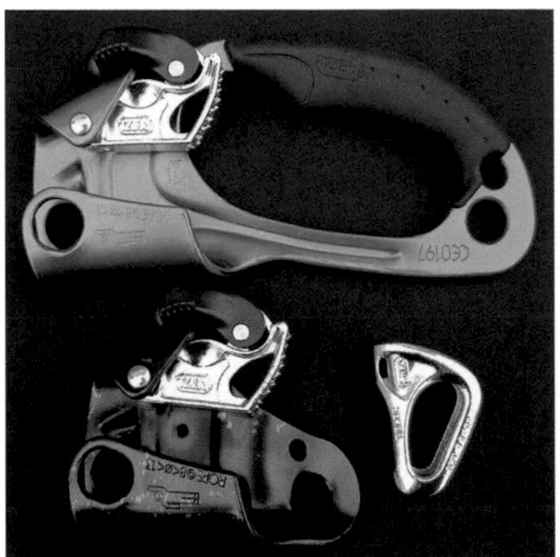

A variety of ascenders.

Ascending the rope

See also: abseil loop, ascenders, fixed rope techniques, French prusik, jammer, klemheist, lark's foot, prusik loops.

There are a number of occasions where ascending the rope may be necessary. This could include self-rescue from a crevasse, following a fixed rope on an expedition-sized peak, or being alongside someone when teaching them to climb. The ascent of a rope can be categorized as follows:

- Ascent with feet in contact with the surface.
- Ascent without feet in contact with the surface.

There are also subdivisions:

- Use of basic multi-purpose ascent equipment.
- Use of purpose-designed ascent equipment.

The carrying of two **prusik loops** is to be encouraged in most climbing and mountaineering situations, as these not only work well for ascending the rope but can also perform other tasks, such as extending equipment, constructing belays etc. The carrying of specifically designed ascent equipment is normally reserved for the realms of big wall or high mountain climbing.

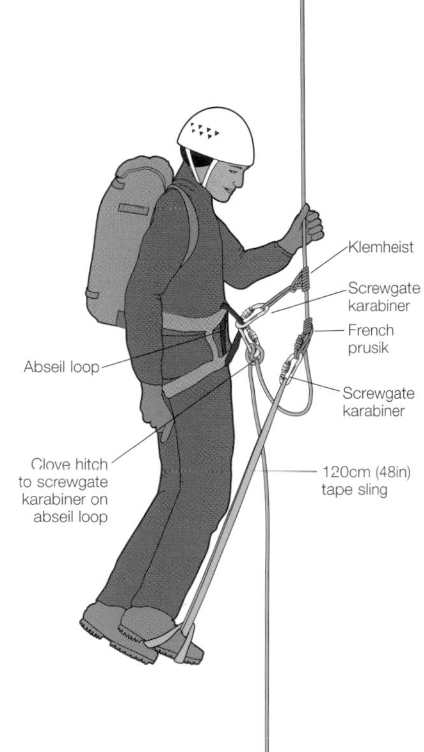

Foot contact possible

The first category, ascent with feet in contact with the surface, usually makes ascending the rope relatively easy. This includes situations such as ascending a fixed rope on snow during an expedition, or walking up a slab climb next to a novice being taught climbing skills. The former is covered under the entry **fixed rope techniques** and is quite specific to expedition skills, as the rope being ascended will probably have a number of intermediate attachment points that need to be negotiated. For the purposes here, we will assume that the rope has a solid attachment point at the top of a cliff, and that a single length of it is hanging down.

Great care should be exercised if ascending a rope on moderate terrain simply using a knot such as a **klemheist** as the safety. As the knot will not be constantly weighted, should a slip occur there is a danger of the knot running down the main rope for some distance before it locks, and as such it could burn through and fail. For this reason, the use of a simple prusik loop knot should be discouraged in these situations. A mechanical jamming device would be far more secure, with a handled **jammer** being perfect. This should be attached to the harness abseil loop with a sling, the length of which should allow the device to be pushed out to full arm's reach but no more. The attachment of the sling to a handled jammer can be with a **lark's foot** through the handled section. The jammer should be kept ahead of the climber and care taken that at no point would shock loading occur, which may cause damage to the rope. If travelling any distance, it would be prudent to tie a series of **overhand knots** on the bight at intervals on the ascended rope, in case the device should slip.

No foot contact possible

Ascending a free-hanging rope may be completed with either prusik loops or mechanical devices. The decision is normally based on the situation in which it has to be performed. If it is known that some free-rope ascent will need to be made, then mechanical devices will probably be carried. However, the impromptu ascent of a rope is most likely to be accomplished with prusik loops or at the most a small device such as a Tibloc, as these are the items usually carried at the back of a harness. The following describes the ascent of a rope using two prusik loops.

Ascending the rope

notes

For most forms of rope ascent, it would be a sensible precaution to have a connection from both devices to the harness. One would obviously be connected directly, but the one being used for the foot could have a secondary sling coming from it, clipped into the abseil loop of the climber's harness. This would be prudent for two main reasons. Firstly, it would stop the loss of the foot device should it become detached or slide down the rope for any reason. Secondly, it would serve as a back-up should the device to the harness fail. As a minimum, overhand knots should be tied at regular intervals during the ascent, so that there is no chance of the climber sliding any great distance, should the ascender fail.

METHOD

- A klemheist is tied around the rope and clipped to the harness **abseil loop**.
- A **French prusik** is tied around the rope below the klemheist and a 120cm (48in) sling is clipped in. This acts as a foot loop and, once the foot is in place, a couple of turns around the boot will most likely be necessary to get the length correct. As a guide to its length, with the French prusik just underneath the klemheist, the thigh of the person ascending needs to be about parallel with the ground.
- An **HMS karabiner** should be clipped into the harness abseil loop and a clove hitch attached to it, taken from the rope below the lower prusik. This will act as the safety back-up in case one of the prusik knots slips or fails. It should have the slack taken up through it at intervals during the ascent.
- Ascent is made by alternating between loading and moving the French prusik and the klemheist. The knots need to be completely unloaded in order to move, and it assists the lower knot if the abseil rope is held firmly below whilst moving it upwards.

Ascending for instructors

A common reason for needing to ascend a rope is when teaching others to climb. An instructor may routinely ascend a rope alongside the novice so that they can offer help and advice, but at the same time be safely out of the climber's way. The following method is an efficient set-up as it not only makes the most of a mechanical advantage in the rigging, similar to that seen in a hoisting system, but also, if set up as described, the instructor has the ability to descend swiftly to help the climber should they be lowered off or fall. The equipment needed, apart from a couple of slings and screwgates, is a Grigri or similar device and a handled jammer with a karabiner hole at the lower end of the handle.

METHOD

- A handled jammer is clipped on to the rope at about head height.
- A sling from this runs down to create a foot loop. The length of this sling is important, and it should be just long enough to reach from the feet up to the position of the jammer when it is pushed up to just less than arm length.
- As a back-up, a shorter sling may be placed from the jammer to the abseil loop on the harness.
- A D-shaped screwgate karabiner is clipped into the hole at the lower end of the jammer.
- A Grigri is put on to the rope below the jammer, and connected to the harness abseil loop.
- The **dead rope** coming out of the Grigri is taken up, clipped through the karabiner on the jammer, and allowed to hang down.

➲ A foot is placed in the foot loop, and the dead rope from the Grigri is pulled in tight. The harness is sat in, with the Grigri taking all of the weight, and the jammer slid up the rope. As the foot loop is stood up in again, the dead rope is pulled in through the Grigri, both safeguarding the person and easing their ascent due to the mechanical advantage inherent in the system.

Descent for instructors

Should there be a need for the instructor to descend, the process is quite simple. They sit back in their harness, allowing the Grigri to take the load, reach up and unclip the karabiner on the jammer, removing that as well, then simply abseil to whatever level is required using the Grigri as an abseil device.

Ascending the rope using an ascender and a Grigri.

Ascending the rope – changing direction

See also: abseil loop, abseil protection, ascending the rope, clove hitch, French prusik, klemheist, prusik loop.

The requirement to change direction from an ascent of the rope to a descent is not quite as common as the reverse, that is, the change from an abseil to a rope ascent. However, it can occur and is fairly uncomplicated to carry out. It is assumed that the ascent has taken place on a rope using two **prusik loops**.

METHOD

➲ Having stopped ascending, place an abseil device underneath the **klemheist**, quite close to it, and clip it into the **abseil loop** on the harness, extended in the normal manner for a protected abseil. This connection to the abseil device will most likely be slack for the moment.

➲ Keeping the **French prusik** on the rope and your foot in the sling, place a second karabiner into the prusik loop and clip it to the abseil loop. Now push the French prusik up the rope as far as possible. This will shortly become the abseil back-up.

➲ Stand up in the sling and unclip the klemheist from your abseil loop. Slowly let your weight back down on to the abseil device, and remove the klemheist.

➲ Ensure that the French prusik is in the abseil back-up position, remove the sling and back-up **clove hitch** placed for the ascent and descend as normal.

Assisted hoist

See also: belay device, belay device – locking off, crevasse rescue, French prusik, hauling, hip hoist, live rope, multi-pitch, semi-direct belay, single pitch, unassisted hoist.

The assisted hoist is one of the most basic of all rescue procedures, and provides the root for techniques such as **crevasse rescue**. It is a fairly simple procedure to master and, once understood, can be used in a variety of situations. It has a parallel in **hauling**, which is covered elsewhere. It is used where a person following a climb is unable to complete a certain section, maybe because of tiredness, or simply because the section is too hard. In some situations, it may be the norm to lower the person to the ground, but if on a **multi-pitch climb**, or maybe even a **single-pitch** sea cliff, it would be quicker and more effective to have the person at the top with the belayer. The term 'assisted' means that the person who is in difficulty helps with the procedure, making life a lot easier for the belayer. Should the person on the climb be unable to assist, perhaps due to injury or being more than a third of the available rope length away, then the **unassisted hoist** would be the more appropriate.

The following explanation of the procedure assumes that the climbers are vertically aligned, that the second is not too far away, and that a **semi-direct belay** using a standard **belay device** has been set up.

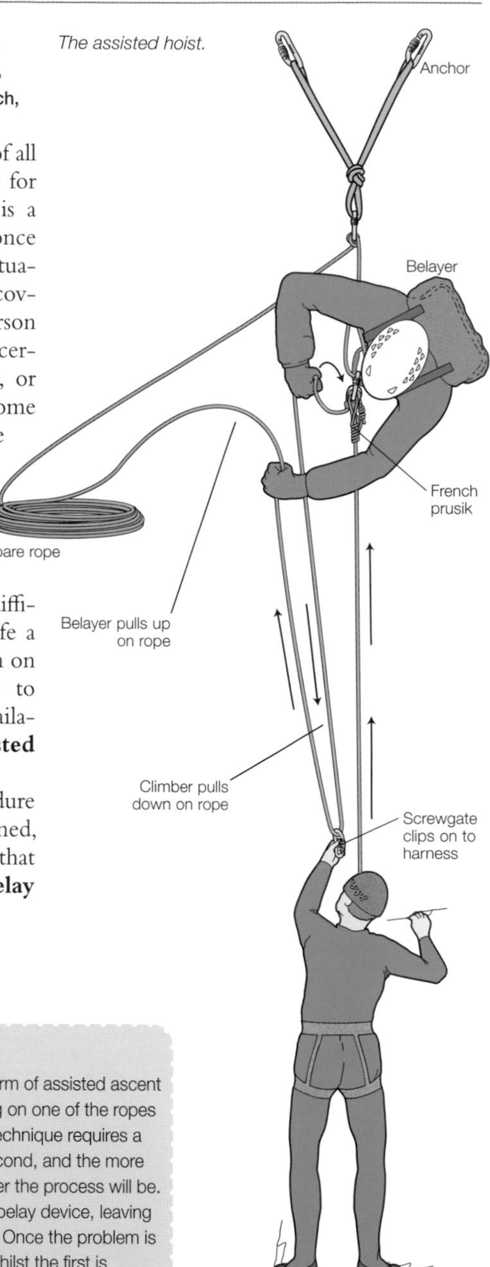

The assisted hoist.

tip

If a pair are climbing with **double ropes**, a simple form of assisted ascent can be quickly set up. This entails the second pulling on one of the ropes whilst the belayer takes the other one in tight. This technique requires a reasonable amount of strength on the part of the second, and the more purchase they are able to get with their feet the easier the process will be. The rope being climbed up can be locked off at the belay device, leaving the leader free to assist by pulling on the other rope. Once the problem is overcome, the climber is held on this second rope whilst the first is unlocked and taken in. Climbing can then continue as normal.

METHOD

- The belay device needs to be **locked off**.
- A **French prusik** must be attached to the live rope immediately in front of the belay device, with sufficient turns to enable it to hold the weight of the climber. Although metal-to-metal clipping of karabiners should normally be avoided, in this situation it is acceptable to clip the French prusik directly into the belay device attachment using a second karabiner. Once the prusik is attached, push it well down the rope until it is tight.
- Using a bight of rope from the **dead-rope** side of the locked-off device, lower or throw this down to your second, who will clip the bight into their abseil loop with a screwgate karabiner. It is best if they use a karabiner from their end, as if you threw the bight down with a karabiner already on it you could hit and injure your second. It is important that they take a moment to ensure that the rope is running smoothly and that there are no twists in it, otherwise the friction created will make the hoisting difficult to manage.
- Holding on to the rope now coming up from the second, best done with a couple of wraps around the wrist, carefully untie the locked-off belay device, pulling through the slack rope as you do so. Care should be taken when undoing the last part, the 'slippery hitch', (best done by pulling the tail of the rope through), to not shock-load the French prusik, otherwise it could slip and fail. The final section of the release might be eased by clamping one hand around the outside of the belay device as you pull the rope through the slippery hitch, and by doing so squeezing the dead rope in the locked off position.
- The system is now set up. The second pulls down on one side of the bight that you lowered to them, you pull up on the other. This gives a mechanical advantage that allows you to pull the second up with reasonable ease. As hoisting takes place, the French prusik will ride up and sit below the belay device in an unlocked position.
- If you need to stop hoisting, perhaps for a rest or whilst the second takes out a piece of protection, first push the French prusik down the rope as far as it will go, then slowly release the weight on to it. It is important that you do not let go of the rope completely, as there is a chance that the French prusik could release and burn through.

Although this system makes the most of a 3:1 mechanical advantage, it works for the best when both the belayer and second are coordinating their efforts and pulling together.

Auto-locking karabiners

Auto-locking karabiners were designed to provide an automatic system whereby the sleeve covering the gate of a karabiner would secure itself of its own accord, and not need to be screwed shut as normal. There is a variety of auto-locking karabiners available, although climbers are quite often suspicious about their security and reliability. The better versions have a two-part mechanism for unlocking them, which goes a long way in preventing the accidental opening that had previously occurred in simple pull-back designs. The use of auto-locks is really up to personal preference.

Autobloc

See also: Bachmann knot, French prusik, klemheist, Penberthy knot, prusik knot.

An autobloc is the generic name given to a family of knots that will grip the rope when a load is applied. It is also sometimes given to a number of mechanical devices that perform a similar function.

Bachmann knot

See also: French prusik, klemheist.

This knot is similar in design to the **French prusik** and the **klemheist**, although not quite as efficient in operation. The main advantage is that a karabiner is used in the system to provide a handle that makes the manipulation of the knot when wearing gloves somewhat easier. The disadvantage is that the shiny back bar of the karabiner is presented to the rope, lessening the amount of friction created by the knot when loaded. It may be chosen over the other two for use when ascending the rope, but extreme care must be taken, due to the reduced friction and the fact that, should the knot start to slip, it would not have to travel very far to generate enough heat to possibly melt through the loop with which it is tied. It is also extremely poor at gripping on icy ropes.

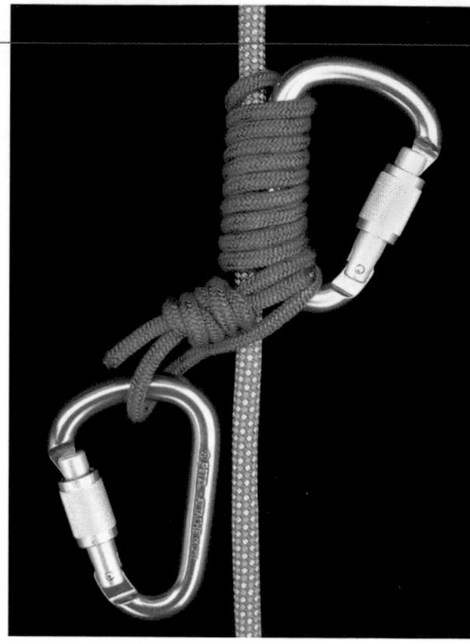

The Bachmann knot.

Belay devices

See also: abseil devices, bolts, dead rope, self-locking belay devices, shock loading.

There is a vast array of belay devices available to the modern mountaineer, and selection of a suitable device should be done carefully. There are several factors involved in deciding which device may be suitable for your particular needs, or you may end up buying more than one as your requirements are so diverse. For instance, someone who spends a large proportion of their time clipping **bolts** on hard routes may choose to purchase a mechanical belay device such as a Grigri which, with its semi-automatic (but not hands-off) locking system is often favoured over a traditional plate for ease of holding a partner working a route. However, that same climber may also enjoy the delights of winter mixed routes, so would also need in their armoury a belay plate that is non-grabbing and allows a certain amount of slick action before the rope is arrested, as well as allowing the ability to abseil on two ropes simultaneously.

Factors in choosing a belay device

Many factors such as style and season of climbing, type and diameter of rope to be used, whether single or double, if the ascent is low level or weight is an issue such as in the Greater Ranges, all have to be considered before obtaining a device that will perform at the required level. It is also important to think ahead and decide if the device will also have to perform as an **abseil device**. The best modern equipment will deal with both ascent and descent with ease.

Categories of belay device

Belay devices can be conveniently categorized into three types: slick, stiff and grabbing. At the 'slick' end of the market are devices consisting of a plate or tube with two large diameter slots through which the rope can easily pass. Controllable in experienced hands, these devices are very slick when used with ropes of less than 10mm (⅓in) diameter and practice is needed to arrest a fall efficiently.

However, this property is most convenient for climbers using belay systems on ground utilizing snow or ice anchors. As a **shock-load** of any sort is best avoided when using snow or ice belay systems, the slick devices allow a little slippage of the rope through the device as a fall is arrested, thus taking away a lot of the loading from the anchor system itself. It is also easier to use when ropes are frozen, as a bight can be pushed through the wide opening without too much problem. Its simplicity and lightness also lends its use to travel in the high mountains.

notes

The days of carrying a large figure-of-eight descender as well as a belay plate are gone, and the figure of eight is now primarily the preserve of group abseiling sessions due partly to its size and weight, and partly because of its propensity for twisting the rope should it be used to belay. The habit of running the rope through the large eye and then straight into a karabiner, as sometimes seen with indoor climbing, is to be discouraged.

Stiff belay devices

A 'stiff' belay device could either be one that has smaller diameter holes than the slick version or, more likely, one that has a controlling slot or slots for the rope to run into that assist the belayer by providing extra friction to the braking hand holding the **dead rope**. These are often ribbed to assist with braking. The device may also be turned round so that the slots are not brought into play, should there be a need for the device to work in a slick manner.

Grabbing devices

A grabbing device is one where the rope is held firm almost immediately in the event of a fall. In recent years the Grigri has been the classic example, although there are other devices on the market that perform in a comparable manner. In the event of the system being loaded, the device reacts in a manner similar to some automotive seat-belt systems, in that the force of the rope moves a cam into a position where the rope is held firm. The pressure is released by a lever on the outside of the device that allows the belayer to move the cam away from the rope, thus letting them pay out as usual. This is an active camming system; an example of a passive camming system is found in devices with no moving parts that rely on the loading of the rope to rotate the device in such a manner that the rope is held in position by pressure between the device itself and the retaining karabiner connecting the system to the harness of the belayer. Pulling back on the relevant section of the device will allow the pressure on the rope to be released and the belayer to control the movement of the rope once more.

Self-locking belay devices

It is important to mention here a specialist device that can cause problems if used incorrectly. Self-locking belay devices have found much popularity with guides and instructors, as they allow for the belaying of two clients at the same time when bringing them up on steep ground. These devices generally work by the weight of a climber pulling on the rope that in turn compresses around a karabiner clipped at the back of the device. This method is very popular but has one drawback

An active self-locking belay device (Grigri).

for most of the device types available. It is very difficult to release the device and feed rope through whilst the system is loaded. This could be a major problem on, for instance, steep rock, where a second has fallen and has loaded the system with no chance of getting their bodyweight back on to the rock. In this situation, and if the device has not been designed to be released when weighted, the belayer must go through an awkward sequence of techniques in order to slacken the dead rope and pay out to the person below. One or two devices are a little more user friendly than a flat plate, some use a rib running along between the rope slots that allows a certain degree of slack to be introduced into the system, others have a handle attached that allows the belayer to press down and use the leverage to pay out the rope. As with any belay device and system, plenty of practice is essential if one of these devices is to be used on technical terrain.

Belay device – locking off

See also: belay device, French prusik, live rope.

It is useful to know how to lock off a **belay device**, and imperative if any one of a number of emergency techniques is to be employed. Of the variations possible, the one demonstrated below has much to recommend it as it is not only fairly simple to tie but, because it is tied around the back bar of the karabiner, it leaves the **live rope** directly in front of the belay device clear, essential should a **French prusik** be used for hoisting or for a similar purpose.

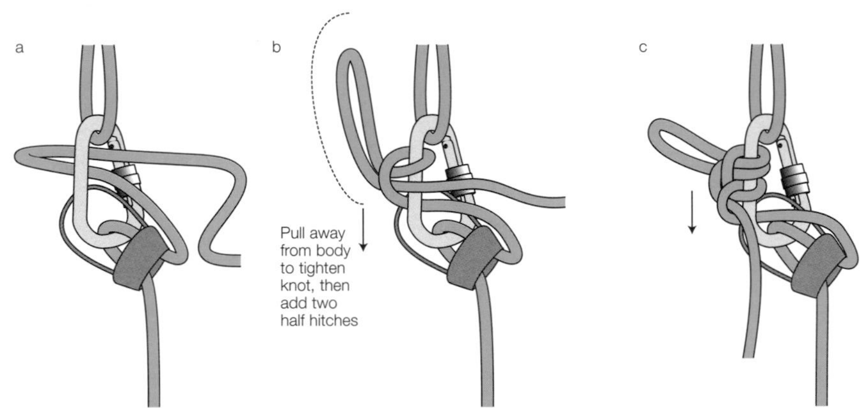

Locking off a belay device.

METHOD

- Holding the load, use the thumb of the holding hand to push a small loop of the dead rope through the centre of the karabiner. Grip this with thumb and forefinger of the other hand and pull a small amount through. This is the point at which the system is at its most vulnerable.
- Now place a bight of rope through this loop and pull on the bight so that the resulting knot (a 'slippery hitch') slides up to the top of the karabiner next to the belay device. Practice of this part of the manoeuvre is essential before needing to use it in anger, as care must be taken that no rope is let slip through the fingers at this point.
- Pull about 40cm (16in) through on the resulting bight of rope.
- Tie two half hitches around the back bar and the dead rope coming out from the slippery hitch. When completed, the tail loop left over should not be less than 10cm (4in) long.

Belay device orientation

See also; ABC, abseil loop, anchor, belay device, dead rope.

The orientation of the **belay device** is important, as it is through the device that any load will be transmitted past the belayer to the **anchor** system. To have an incorrectly set up system could cause a number of problems, including the loading of the belayer instead of the anchor, the twisting of the device causing it to jam and become awkward to operate, and problems when leading through on multi-pitch climbs.

As a general rule, when tied in to the end of the rope the belay device should always be clipped into the rope loop created by tying on, and not on to the **abseil loop** of the harness. There are a number of reasons why this point of attachment is superior, in particular the direct transfer of load along a dynamic system to the anchor point. It also eases the execution of advanced techniques such as escaping the system.

If the belayer is to pay out rope to a leader, the karabiner holding the belay device should be clipped in to the top of the tie-in loop. The **dead rope** in this instance will be coming out from the bottom of the device. If the leader is belaying a second, they should have the belay device clipped in to the bottom of their tie-in loop with the dead rope coming out from the top of the device.

It is important to ensure that the rope runs smoothly through the device, whichever position the belayer may be in, and that the braking hand is not inhibited in its movement in any way by rock or ice.

notes

As the body position that you take when belaying will vary, due to the nature of the stance and the direction from which the anchor rope reaches you, it is important to be able to operate a belay device efficiently with both your left or right hand. Using the incorrect hand will result in a decreased ability to lock off the device efficiently, and may also result in a severe twisting action, pivoting you from your stance when a shock load is applied. The simplest way to remember the correct orientation for most single pitch routes is that if the rope from the anchor runs on the right hand side of your body, you should hold the dead rope with your right hand. If the anchor comes round to your left, your left hand should be used. However, this may well vary when, for instance, a multi pitch route involves leading through. In that case, the orientation needs to be carefully thought out especially when the anchors, often arranged above the second, will not give a direct line of pull when loaded.

Belay devices – self locking

See self-locking belay devices.

Belay methods

See also: ABC, belay devices, direct belay, indirect belay, Italian hitch, semi-direct belay.

A variety of methods exist for belaying a climber, whether they are a leader or a second. The technique chosen will largely depend upon the circumstances in which it is to be used. For instance, the method chosen to protect a second on a single pitch roadside crag may well differ markedly from that chosen to protect a second on a technical step when moving together in the Greater Ranges. The table over the page demonstrates some of the belay methods, along with a number of their merits and drawbacks. It should be remembered that this table is not exhaustive and other methods also exist.

Belay methods

METHOD	PROS	CONS
Direct belay: around a rock spike or boulder	Quick to organize; fast take-in of rope.	Exceptional judgement needed to ensure anchor is sound; suitable anchors not always available; belayer not secured; impossible to lock off should a problem arise; climber possibly not protected when they are next to the belay; usually only for belaying a second on moderate pitches; high wear and tear on rope.
Indirect belay: waist belay	Simple to use; fast to organize; no equipment needed; controllable braking action; takes a percentage of loading away from the anchor system; can be only option with frozen ropes; easy for second to lead through; could in some circumstances be used without other anchors such as when belayer is in a bucket seat and system will not be shock loaded.	Escaping the system is awkward and requires some extra kit; can be extremely painful for belayer when loaded; gloves and long sleeves essential; ABC critical; careful consideration of rope direction needed when belaying leader.
Direct belay: Italian hitch	Can smoothly take in and pay out; belayer secured; belayer can be next to edge of stance for communication with hitch well behind them; system can be locked off; belayer out of system thus is not loaded in the event of a fall.	Can twist rope; should only be used to belay a second; exceptional judgement needed with anchor selection; difficult to use with frozen ropes; difficult to use due to excess friction if hitch is more than 3m (10ft) behind belayer.
Semi-direct belay: belay plate operated from harness	Can hold substantial falls; smooth to take in and pay out; relatively easy to lock off in an emergency; variety of different devices available for different situations and rope diameters; simple to arrange stance for leading through; belayer being in system can take some force away from anchors; ground anchors do not have to be used if belaying leader on technical route with poor protection as dynamic lifting up of belayer may be beneficial in reducing loading on runners.	Awkward to completely escape the system in an emergency; belayer pulled forwards on rope stretch as system loaded; ABC critical.

Belay position

See also: ABC, belay methods, direct belay, ground anchors, multi-pitch climbing, stance management.

Allied to the **ABC**, so important to the security of both belayer and climber, is the position that the belayer takes in relation to their chosen belay method. For instance, it would be pointless for a perfect ABC to have been attained if the climber, belaying from the top of a crag, was 5m (16ft) back from the cliff edge and communication with their second was almost impossible.

When belaying from the top of a climb, line of sight with the second is preferable. Although this cannot always be the case, it does ease communication problems and allows the leader and second to talk to each other, an important consideration if the second is a novice. However, to be too close to the edge of the cliff would not be advantageous, as the loading caused by a second slipping could be sufficient to cause the belayer to be pulled a short distance over, causing injury and possibly some difficulty in regaining the stance. Care should also be taken if there is any objective danger to the second, such as debris that could be dislodged by the rope. In this case it may be better to use a **direct belay** system, as the load would be straight on to the anchor allowing the belayer the ability to position themselves carefully and not be in danger of being pulled around in the event of loading.

The position of the person belaying a leader is critical. They should ensure that they are in as good a position as possible in relation to the run of the rope, but care should be

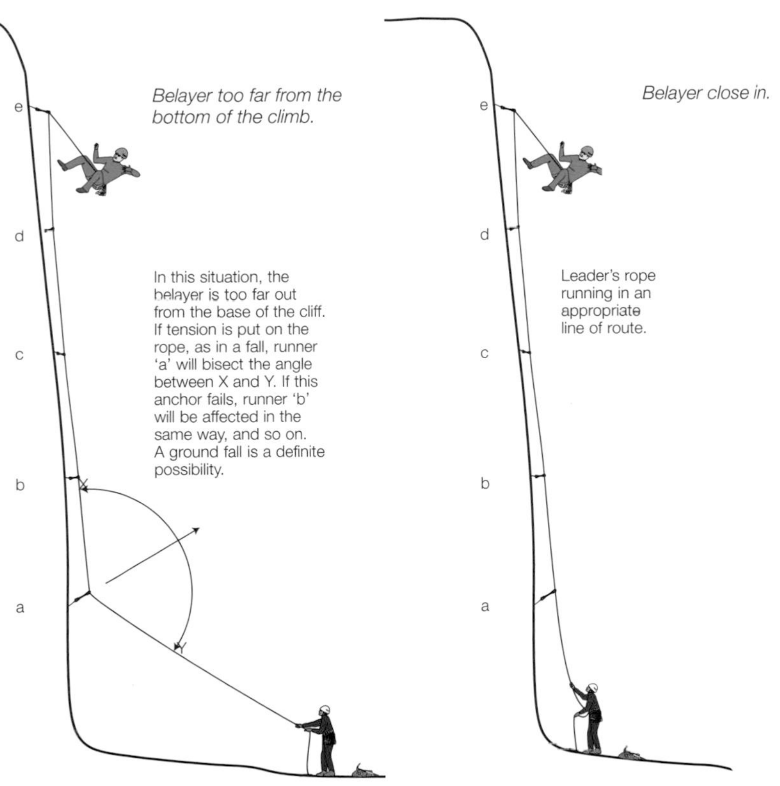

Belayer too far from the bottom of the climb.

Belayer close in.

taken that they are not in any danger from falling debris. This can be quite a problem on winter routes and at altitude, with chunks of ice creating a particularly dangerous hazard, as well as rock being dislodged. Consideration of the direction that the leader is to take will dictate the positioning and organization of the stance, and this may have to be some way to the side of the line that they are to take if falling debris is a problem.

Another extremely important consideration, particularly in relation to single pitch routes, is the distance from the bottom of the climb where the belay is adopted. If the belayer stands too far away, the effect of a falling climber will be for the rope to pull upwards on the first running belay. If this has been placed to take a downward load, as it would normally have been, it could fail. The second anchor would then be affected in the same manner with possibly the same outcome, and the problem progressively passed up the route from runner to runner. If the top runner, the one that is holding the weight of the leader, fails, there would be nothing to stop them from hitting the ground.

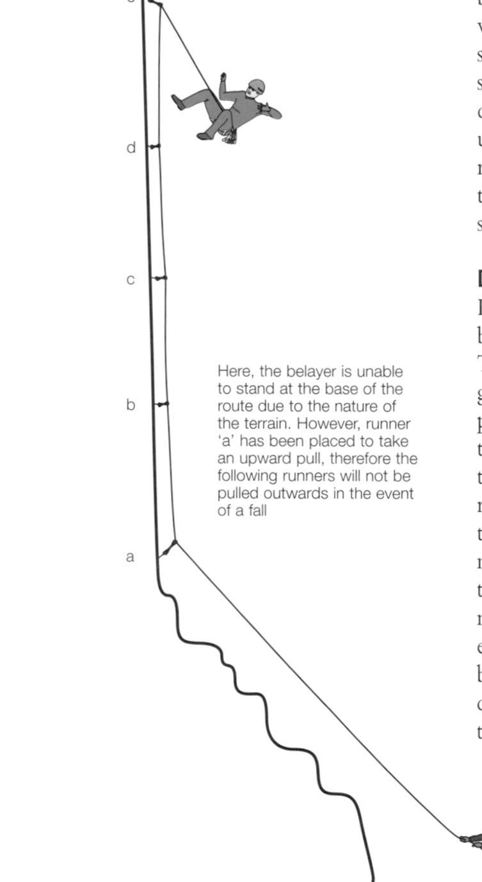

Bottom runner redirecting the rope.

Directional runners

In some situations it is impossible for the belayer to be right at the base of the route. This may be because there is very rough ground at that point, or even vegetation that precludes a close position being adopted. If this is the case, the leader needs to ensure that the first runner is working as a directional runner, that is, one placed in order to align the rope with the direction of the route. This means that it would most likely be placed to take an upward pull, with all subsequent runners being placed in the normal manner. The effect of this is that, in the event of a fall, the bottom directional runner keeps the rope close to the route and avoids any chance of the others being stripped out.

Bent gate karabiners

See snapgate karabiners.

Bolts

'Bolts' is the generic term given to any permanent rock anchor that has been drilled, glued or screwed on to the rock face. These can be of various types and designs, but the most common will be the expansion bolt, ringbolt and staple.

The expansion bolt is designed and placed in the method that its name suggests. A hole is drilled into the rock and an expansion bolt equipped with a hanger (a scooped or bent metal plate that fits over the shaft of the bolt and allows a karabiner to be connected) is tightened into it. This action of tightening the bolt head forces the expansion part of the anchor to fit tightly into the hole.

The ringbolt is also placed into a pre-drilled hole. This time, however, the bolt is secured in place by the addition of an ampoule of resin, which glues it into position.

A staple is placed in a similar manner to a ringbolt, except that two holes have to be manufactured for the two arms of the staple to locate into. This is then secured in place with resin.

Variations do exist, such as an expansion bolt that is hammered into the rock instead of being screwed in, but once placed they should all give good security. This will only be apparent, of course, if installation has taken place as per the manufacturer's instructions and the device has been drilled, placed and seated correctly.

Other factors may also affect the security of bolts, such as the amount of use that they are subjected to. For instance, a key bolt on the lip of a roof of a hard but popular sports route may be the recipient of frequent loading as climbers attempt to make a hard move past it. This can weaken the expansion or resin placement and also, in some extreme cases, compromise the strength of the rock into which the protection has been placed. Corrosion, caused by placement on sea cliffs, is also a consideration.

Bolts – clipping

See also: bolts, double rope techniques, extenders, snapgate karabiners, wires.

The clipping of **bolts** should be considered in relation to the run of the rope and the direction the karabiner faces when placed on the protection, as in some circumstances it would be possible for the rope to become unclipped from its retaining karabiner. It may also be possible for the entire extender to unclip from the bolt, or the extender to unclip from itself.

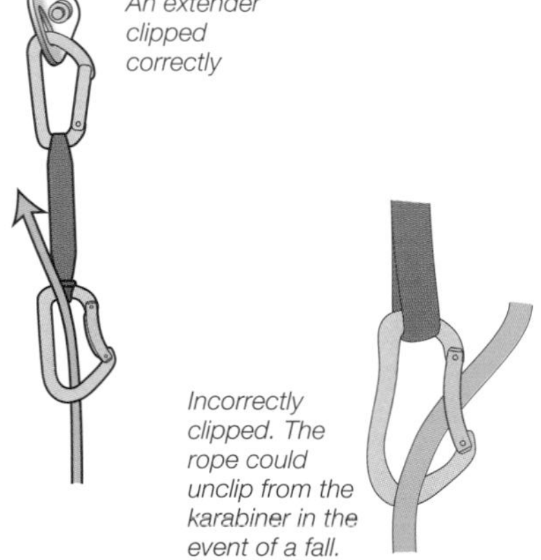

An extender clipped correctly

Incorrectly clipped. The rope could unclip from the karabiner in the event of a fall.

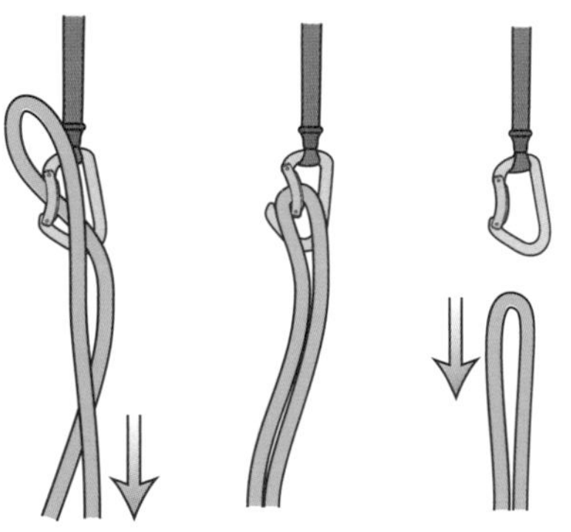

The rope unclipping from a karabiner due to it being initially clipped incorrectly.

Bolts – clipping

A sequence showing a karabiner unclipping from a bolt due to the rope being incorrectly placed in it.

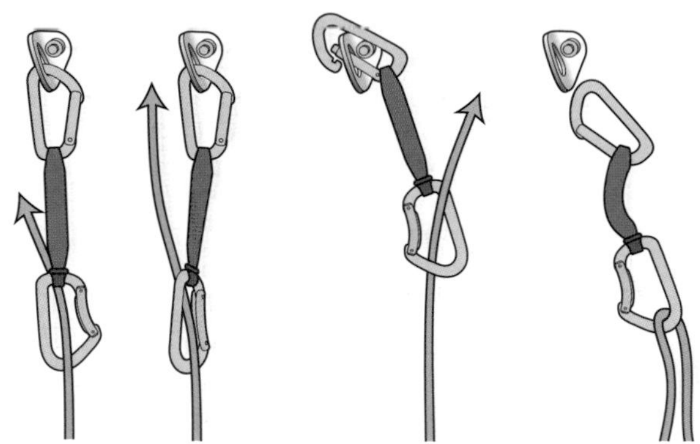

A sequence showing an extender unclipping from a karabiner due to the rope being placed into it incorrectly.

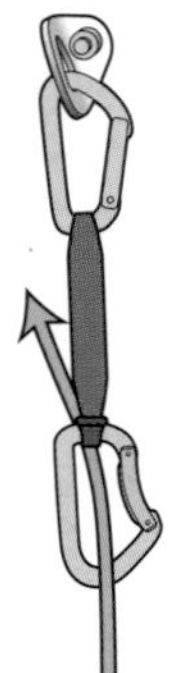

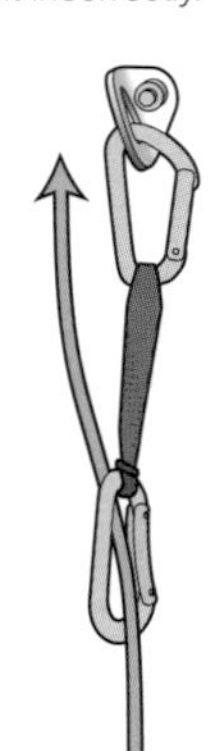

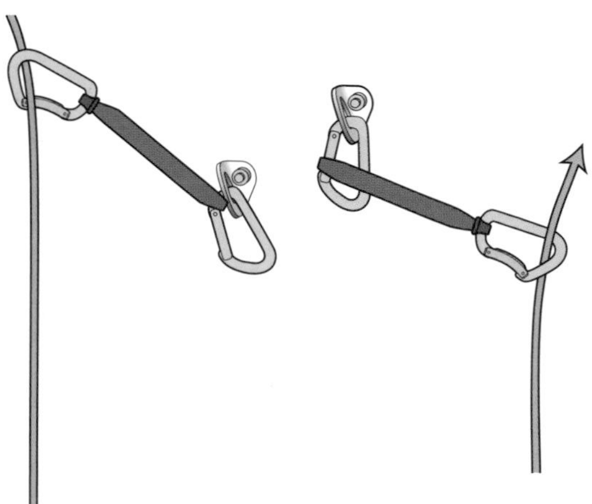

tip

Some bolts present a sharp profile to the clipped-in karabiner, which can cause damage in the event of repeated falls. This could result in the burring of the inside part of the karabiner where the rope sits. For this reason, karabiners that are used for bolted routes are often best marked with tape as such and reserved for that use alone, as they could damage a rope or sling if used in other applications.

Clipping to a bolt

The position from which a climber clips a bolt should also be considered. They not only need to be in a place where they can safely remove a hand to perform the clip, but also in a position where the length of a fall will be minimal should they slip. This is normally best achieved with the waist of the climber being close to the height of the **extender**. Although it may seem safer to be lower than the bolt and reach up to clip it, the large amount of slack rope introduced into the system by pulling it through would mean that a long fall would result, far further than if the climber were higher up the route and closer to the bolt.

Another option is to use **double rope techniques**. These allow the climber to remain close to a bolt, held by one rope, whilst pulling through slack on the second rope to clip the higher bolt. A slip before the higher bolt is clipped will result in the climber only falling the shorter distance, being double the length of the rope between them and the lower bolt.

Damaged bolts

In some situations, damaged bolts can be experienced. If there is any question as to their solidity, they should be ignored and other means of protection sought. If, however, they present a firm anchor to the rock, they could still be used. The two commonest types of damaged bolt are, firstly, where the hanger has been removed but the bolt itself is still well attached. Secondly, where some mechanical means, such as rock fall, has caused the hanger to flatten and thus not allow a karabiner to be clipped in. For both situations, it would be useful to have a selection of **wires** to hand, as they will provide the most convenient method of solving the problem. For the hanger-less bolt, the head of a wire could be pushed down a short distance and the resulting loop of wire placed over the bolt. The head is then pushed up snug and an extender clipped into the other end of the wire as normal. Care should be taken to ensure that the movement of the rope does not cause the wire to loosen and work its way along the bolt, eventually falling off.

A hanger-less bolt with a wire placed over it.

The second problem can be dealt with in a couple of ways. If the gap between hanger and rock is sufficient, a wire with a suitably sized head can be threaded down through the hanger eye, so that it sits on top and cannot pull through. It is then clipped with an extender as normal. Alternatively, if the hanger is badly flattened, the head of the wire is pushed down a way and the resulting wire loop pushed up through the hanger. A spare karabiner is clipped into this, with an extender then going on the other end.

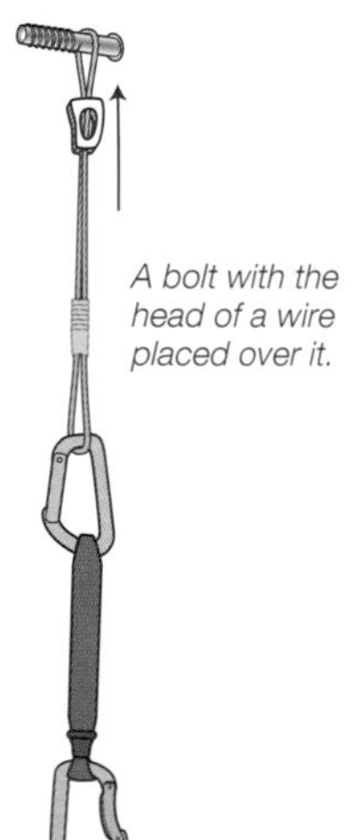
A bolt with the head of a wire placed over it.

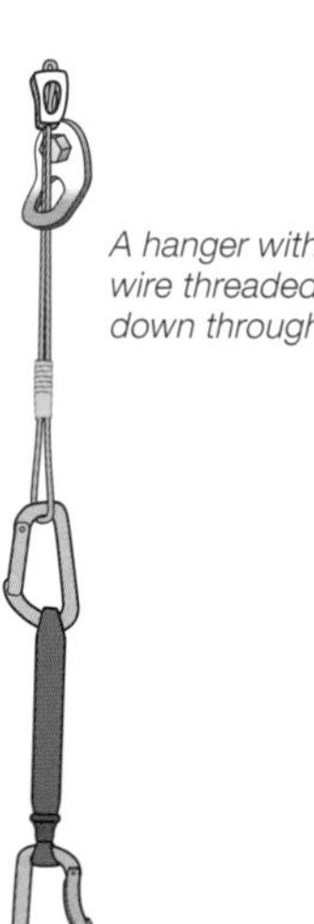
A hanger with a wire threaded down through it.

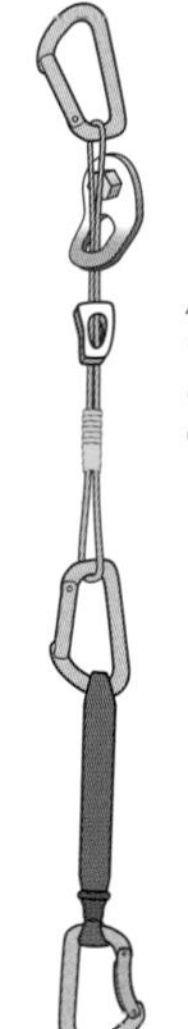
A hanger with a wire loop pushed up and a karabiner clipped in.

Bolted routes – lowering off

See also: abseil loop, belay devices, bottom roping, cowstail, direct belay, equalizing anchors, figure-of-eight knot, lowering, overhand knot on the bight, screwgates, slings.

Great caution should be exercised when **lowering** a partner from the top of a single pitch bolted route, as this procedure causes many accidents. Problems occur mainly due to an incorrect estimation of the length of rope remaining as, if the belayer is not tied on nor the free end of the rope knotted in some way, it can slip through the **belay device** causing the person being lowered to drop. Another cause is in the situation where the climber has had to thread the rope through a ring at the top of the climb, which acts as the lower-off point. If this connection is incorrectly made, the climber could fall, possibly at a point where the rope is unattached.

A good deal of lower-offs are constructed with two bolts being linked by a length of chain, the lowest point of which includes a large ring or snap link through which the rope can be placed. Those which use a snap link or similar device, such as a spiral through which the rope is placed to keep it secure for the lower, present few problems. The climber arrives at the point, places the rope through whatever device is in situ and is lowered off by their belayer. However, chains with rings require a different approach, and two methods for dealing with them are listed below.

Single point lower-off

The first method of lowering will be the most common, the second useful if the climber is concerned about the length of rope being sufficient for them to reach the ground. For both of these techniques, it would be prudent for the climber to have a short sling clipped to their harness in readiness, to use as a cowstail for safety whilst dealing with the chain ring.

METHOD 1

- Once they have arrived at the top of the route, the climber clips themselves into the chain using their cowstail and a screwgate karabiner.
- They pull up a bight of rope and pass it through the ring, tying a **figure-of-eight knot** on to it.

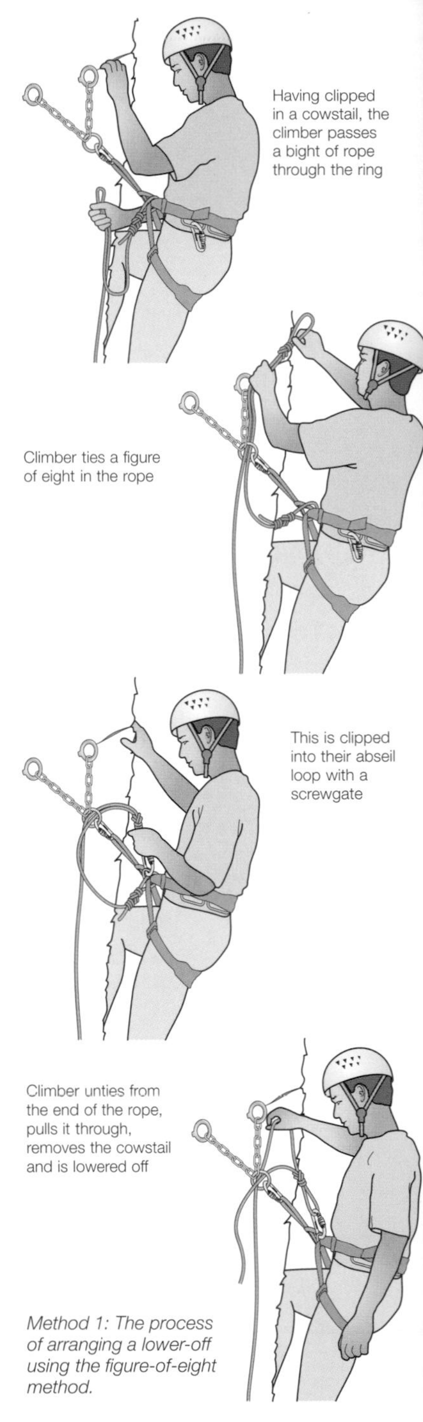

Method 1: The process of arranging a lower-off using the figure-of-eight method.

- This knot is then clipped into their **abseil loop** with a **screwgate** karabiner.
- The climber now unties their original knot, connecting them to the climbing rope.
- The length of rope created by untying is pulled back through the ring. It would be sensible to tuck this section of rope into a suitable point on the harness to stop it hanging down and thereby creating a chance of tripping over it during the descent.
- The climber pulls themselves in tight to the lower-off point and the belayer takes in any slack. The climber then puts their weight back on the climbing rope to check that all is in order. If there were a problem, they are still connected by the cowstail.
- Once they have checked the system, they remove the cowstail and can be lowered to the ground.

METHOD 2

In a situation where the climber opts to retie into the end of the rope, the process is slightly different.

- Once they have arrived at the top of the route, the climber clips themselves into the chain using their cowstail and a screwgate karabiner.
- They pull up a bight of rope from about a metre down and tie a figure of eight or **overhand knot** on the bight in it.
- This loop is clipped on to the lower-off chain and prevents the rope from being dropped during the next phase.
- The climber unties from the end of the rope and passes it through the ring.
- They now retie on to the end. An alternative would be to clip the rope to the abseil loop with a screwgate using a suitably tied figure of eight.
- The first knot, clipped to the chain, is disconnected and untied.
- The climber pulls themselves in tight to the lower-off point and the belayer takes in any slack. The climber then puts their weight back on the climbing rope to check that all is in order. If there is a problem, they are still connected by the cowstail.
- Once they have checked the system, they remove the cowstail and can be lowered to the ground.

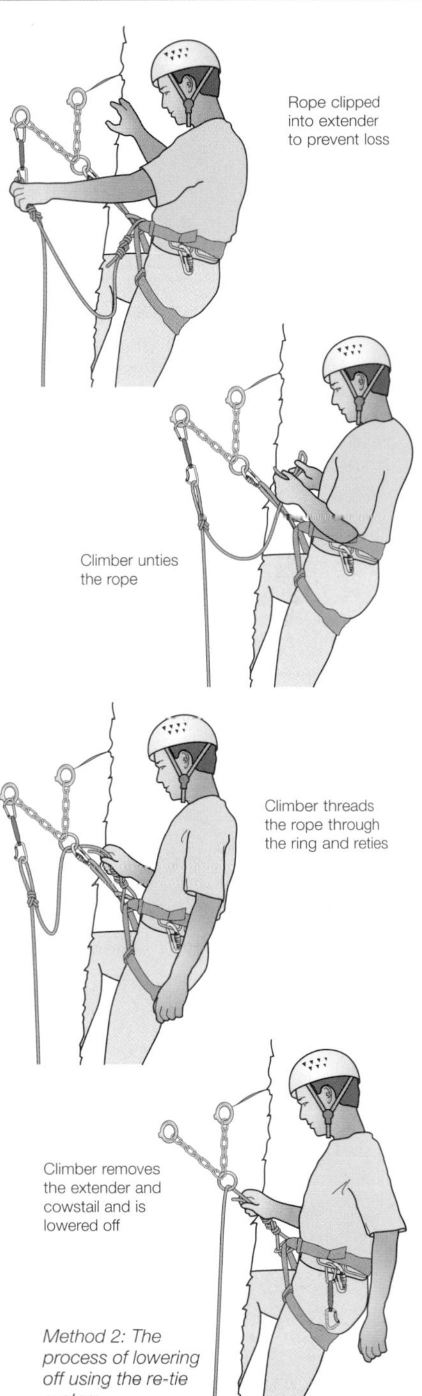

Method 2: The process of lowering off using the re-tie system.

Bolted routes – lowering off

tip

When retrieving extenders during a lower on an overhanging route, the person descending could clip an extender between the harness and the rope running up the route. This will serve to keep them close to the rock during the lower and make reaching each bolt easier.

notes

If the route is to be bottom roped and the top is equipped with two bolts but no chain, a single point needs to be established through which the rope will run. This is best achieved by **equalizing** a **sling**, using screwgates throughout, with the rope running through the single karabiner at the bottom. This will then form a useful attachment point for the last person up to use, so that they can safeguard themselves while they clip in and prepare the lower-off.

Double point lower-off

Some areas are equipped with two bolts at the top but without the linking chain. The sequence for lowering off in this situation is as follows:

METHOD

- A cowstail is clipped into one of the bolts.
- An extender or similar is clipped into the cowstail karabiner.
- The climber pulls up a bight of rope and, using a suitable knot such as a clove hitch, clips it into the karabiner to prevent the rope from being dropped.
- They untie from the climbing rope.
- They thread the rope through both bolts and retie into the harness.
- The climber now removes the back-up bight of rope from the extra cowstail karabiner.
- Once the system has been checked, the cowstail is removed and the climber can be lowered.

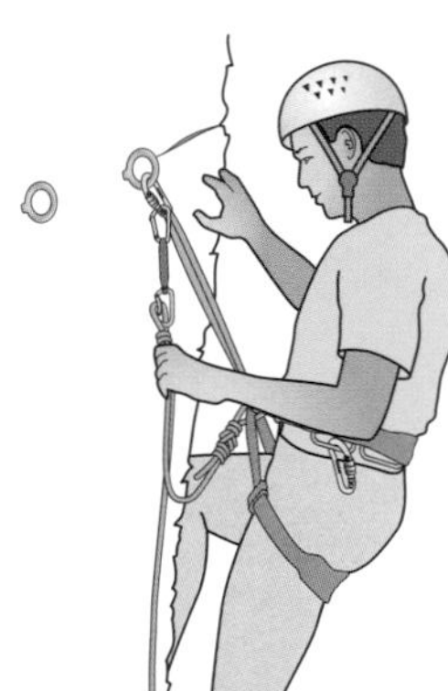

Cowstail clipped into one bolt and rope clipped on to extender to prevent loss

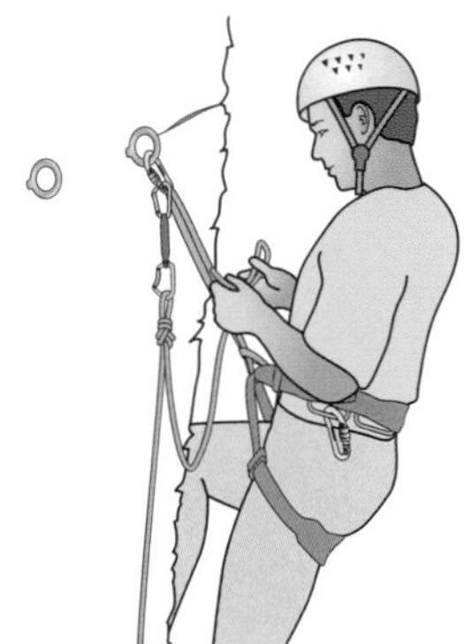

Climber unties from climbing rope

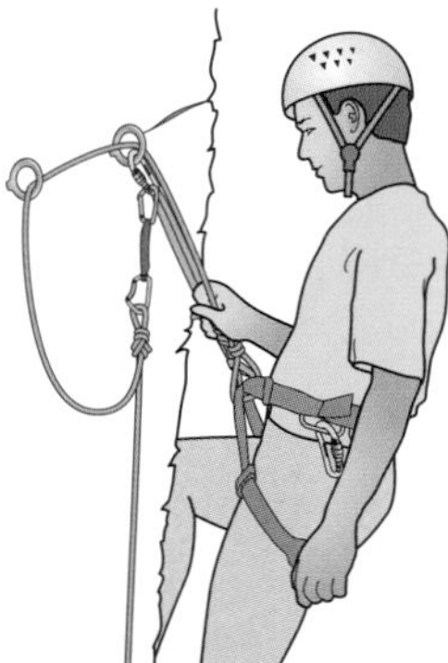

Rope threaded through bolts and tied back to harness

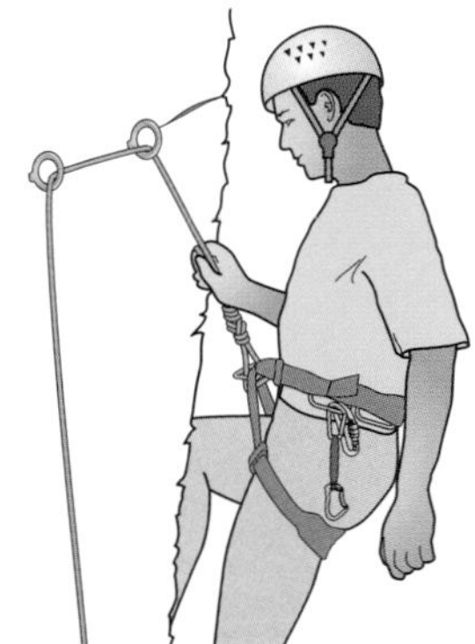

Cowstail and extender holding rope removed and climber descends

The process of lowering off from two unconnected bolts.

notes

It is essential that the dead end of the rope be secured in a fashion that will not allow it to run through a belay device unimpeded. This could be by having the belayer tied to the end in the conventional manner or, more likely, by having an overhand knot tied in it a metre from the end. This will act as a warning to the belayer during the lower that the end is being approached, and will jam in the belay device if control is lost.

Intermediate stance lower-off

Lowering from an intermediate stance can be easily accomplished. The person descending is best lowered from a **direct belay,** although a lower from a belay device on the harness of the belayer would obviously also be possible. However, as many intermediate stances will consist of a chain linked to two bolts, a direct lower is quickest to set up. A number of the processes listed under the 'lowering' entry would be appropriate, in particular the use of an Italian hitch or a belay device with the dead rope being run back to one of the bolts to give the correct angle for braking.

notes

The bent-metal hanger type, usually associated with expansion bolts, must never have the rope threaded through it and be used as a lowering or protection point. The sharp edges and narrow radius of the metal could easily cut the rope if loaded. If lowering off has to occur from this type of hanger, perhaps due to having to descend from a route before reaching the top, a screwgate should be placed in the hanger for the rope to run through. This will also aid later rope retrieval, as the rope will run more easily than if it were placed through the hanger eye.

Left: *The rope running directly through a bolt hanger, which can cause the rope to be cut.* **Right:** *The rope should always be connected with the use of a screwgate or self-locking karabiner.*

Bong

See pitons.

Boot/axe belay

See also; crampons, HMS karabiner, ice axe, Italian hitch, stomper belay, Thompson knot.

A twin skill to the **stomper belay**, the boot/axe belay is a very quick and efficient method of safeguarding the descent of a climber on snow-covered ground. It can also be used efficiently to lower one or even two people over awkward terrain should a speedy descent be necessary. It requires the minimum amount of equipment to set the system in place, simply an **ice axe** and snow of a reasonable density underfoot. The body position of the belayer can also be advantageous, as they will be crouching low to the ground and quite stable in high winds. The main disadvantage with the boot/axe belay is that it is purely designed for descent. Should the person being lowered need to make their way upslope again, the belayer would have to take a hand off the axe, which in turn would compromise the mechanics of the system. It should also be remembered that the belay system is not designed to take a shock load, and for that reason there must never be slack between the belayer and the person being lowered, nor should it be used in a situation where the

Boot/axe belay

notes

Other points to consider would be that the system must only be loaded when the rope is running parallel to the surface of the snow. If it is pulled upwards at a sharp angle, the rope could travel up the shaft of the ice axe and cause excessive leverage that may cause the system to fail. For the comfort of those being lowered without the use of a harness, a waist tie is the best option or, if the descent is to be very steep, would a **Thompson knot** or similar load-bearing system be more appropriate? Finally, it is important that those being lowered have a clear picture as to what is required of them when they have travelled the required distance. If communication will be difficult due to weather or the nature of the terrain, ensure that both the belayer and those descending are in no doubt as to what they should do when the lower ceases. This may include briefings as to cutting a ledge, untying and stepping to the side, or whatever.

person being protected is upslope of the belayer, with the possible consequence of the system being catastrophically loaded in the event of a slip. There is a variety of methods of performing the boot/axe belay, but this is the simplest and, probably for that reason, the most effective.

METHOD

- The system may be set up on either level or sloping ground. If the ground is not flat, a ledge should be cut that can easily accommodate your boot, with the base of it sloping slightly back into the hillside. If **crampons** are being worn, the ledge can be flat, but if crampons are not being worn it will be prudent to fashion a 5cm (2in) lip on the outside edge of the ledge up against which your boot can be braced.
- The system can be worked either left- or right-handed, so if you are a right handed person the right foot would be on the ledge with another smaller ledge having been kicked or cut a metre downslope to accommodate the left foot.
- The axe may now be positioned, with the shaft leaning slightly uphill from vertical aligned just behind the shinbone, with the pick of the axe facing back behind your leg.
- The axe should now be pushed into the snow, with a corkscrewing action sometimes useful in harder ground. The axe head should not go further down than the top of your boot, and once placed the axe should be tight against the boot which in turn should be snug against the lip on the outside of the ledge.
- The rope should be run from a tidy pile, preferably on a ledge cut for the purpose, from behind the belayer. It runs through the legs of the

The boot/axe belay.

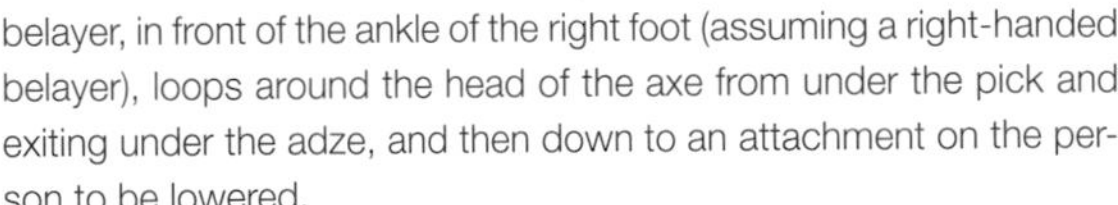

belayer, in front of the ankle of the right foot (assuming a right-handed belayer), loops around the head of the axe from under the pick and exiting under the adze, and then down to an attachment on the person to be lowered.

- The position that the belayer takes up is critical, for once the system is loaded they cannot afford to let go for any reason. A stance is taken that allows them to lean their right hand on to the head of the axe, with the left hand holding on to the rope, positioned right down next to the snow and just behind the right ankle. Holding tight in this position forces the axe downslope on to the boot, which is in turn forced upslope on to the axe, the mechanics of which allow the system to stay in place and support the weight of whoever is being lowered.
- To introduce slack into the system, the left hand is brought forwards slowly so as to decrease the friction around the ankle. Bringing the hand backwards will consequently increase the friction.

This is a remarkably swift and simple method of looking after the well-being of a companion, but a few extra moments during preparation will pay dividends. Running the rope through on to a prepared ledge will help ensure that no kinks or knots are encountered during the lower – remember that you cannot take either hand off the system once it is loaded so to encounter a knot would be disastrous. Also, consideration needs to be given to what is at the other end of the rope. If the belayer is not tied on, then there is a chance that the end of the rope may be allowed to slip through their hands with possibly fatal repercussions. To avoid this, a large knot should be tied at the end of the rope, as well as a smaller one about a metre or so from the end. This will at least give warning of the rope running out and allow communication from the belayer to their partner.

notes

In some situations, it may not be possible to run the rope in the normal manner around the ankle. This could occur, for instance, at altitude if down trousers or high-loft gaiters were being worn, and the softer fabric kept being pulled around the axe by the rope. It is possible to alter the configuration slightly to accommodate this. Once the axe has been pressed home, a sling is arranged around the shaft of the axe right down next to the snow surface, with the ends just beyond the outside edge of the boot. An **HMS** is clipped into this, and an **Italian hitch** used to control descent. It should be noted that this is not an ideal configuration, especially as the hitch will most likely be lying flat on the snow and thus have a chance of jamming, although this problem is rectifiable by making a small scoop in the snow surface at the point the knot touches. Great care should be taken that the correct hand position is maintained in relation to the Italian hitch. This method is still only for descent.

Bottoming out

See also: clove hitch, drive-in ice protection, extender, ice screw, pitons, protection, sling, tat.

This occurs when a piece of **protection**, such as an **ice screw** or **piton**, is longer than the material into which it is being placed. Significant damage can be caused to the equipment, in particular to ice screws whose teeth may be irreparably harmed by an underlying rock layer before anyone realizes what is happening.

Of somewhat more importance is that the strength of the placement will be severely reduced due to the levering effect of clipping the protection with a karabiner through the eye as normal. To reduce this leverage, an **extender**, **short sling** or **tat** can be placed over the protection as a **clove hitch** and slid

notes

Care should be taken to ensure that the sling material is around the smooth section of an ice-screw tube, and not over any protruding thread. A sling placed in this manner will have its strength markedly reduced in the event of a fall.

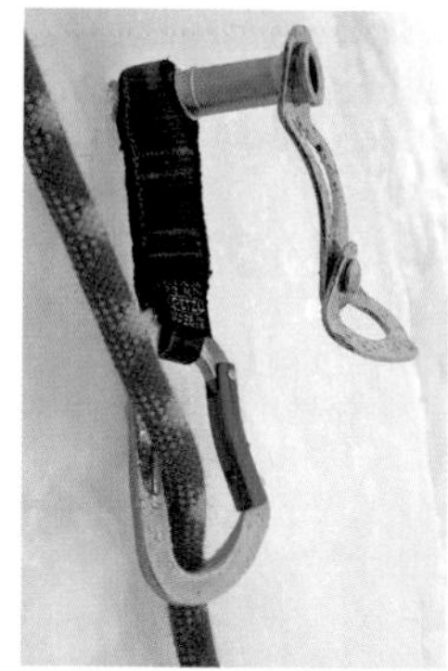

Using an extender to reduce leverage on an ice screw.

along it to rest snugly against the rock or ice, with the karabiner being clipped into this. If an extender is used, one that has the central section sewn back on to itself is very useful, as it will usually provide a good fit to an ice-screw tube. It may be sensible, if the ice is known to be not thick enough at that point, to pre-attach the extender by sliding it up the tube from the teeth end, which will avoid trying to force it over the screw-eye once it has been placed. This would be essential when using screws with long eyes or built-in winding handles, as a closed loop extender would be impossible to fit.

notes

Some ice screws and **drive-ins** come with a floating eye as standard in case bottoming out is encountered. They can be either slid or wound down the shaft until flush with the ice. If the ascent of technical ice falls or thin ice smears is expected, these types of protection are a sensible purchase.

Bottom rope systems

See also: clove hitch, cowstail, group climbing, double figure of eight, Italian hitch, low-stretch rope, overhand knot, pulleys, rope protectors, top rope systems.

A bottom rope system is one where the belayer is positioned at the bottom of the crag, with the rope running up through a karabiner or **pulley** system, then back down to the climber. This is distinct from the **top rope system**, where the belayer is positioned at the top of the crag (see **group climbing** for a comparison of pros and cons between the two methods). There are a number of uses for bottom roping: as a training aid when hard routes can be climbed in safety; when the top of the cliff is unsuitable for climbing up and over due to instability; and very commonly, as a climbing set-up when working with groups of novices.

There are many methods of setting up a bottom rope system, but the one outlined below will probably suit most users. It assumes that two anchors are being used, not too far from the edge, plus a **low-stretch rope** for rigging.

tips

To ensure the smooth running of the rope, if the karabiners through which it is clipped can be clearly seen from the base of the climb, then there is little chance of any problems occurring.

Although heavier, steel karabiners tend to wear more slowly than alloy karabiners, they could be used as the top attachment point through the loop, so that rope wear of the metal is not such a problem.

METHOD 1

➲ The attachment point for the climbing rope will be a **double figure of eight** (hereafter referred to as 'the loop'). If the users are friends out for a day's climbing, then this knot can be tied at around the centre point of the rigging rope, which will allow for adjustment so that it reaches a number of routes from one set-up. If it is being rigged for a group session, it may be sensible to tie the knot a lot closer to one of the ends (best judged after the next step has been completed), as there will then be a long length of rope left at the second anchor should some be needed for emergency reasons.

- An **overhand knot** can be tied a metre or so up from the loop, around both ropes. This can be adjusted once the final position of the system is decided upon, and is useful as it helps to direct the forces efficiently, and reduces rope movement and rubbing on the edge of the cliff top.
- Take one length of the rigging rope, the shorter one if working with groups, back to an anchor point and clip it in with a **clove hitch**.
- The climbing rope can be clipped into the loop with two screwgates. They should be of the same shape, and arranged so that the gates are facing opposite directions and that the screw sleeve closes downwards. This ensures that vibration from the climbing rope during lowers does not unscrew it.

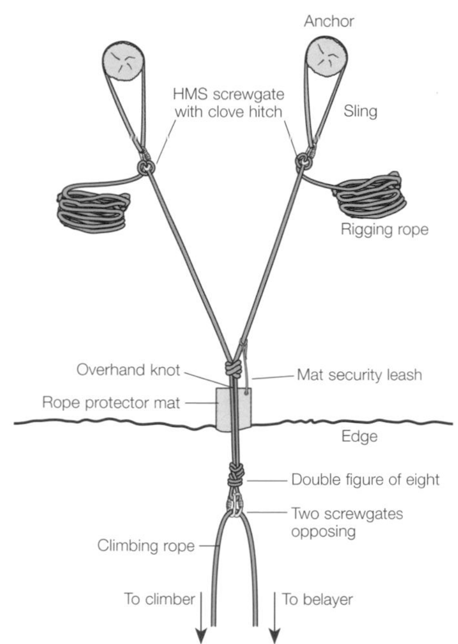

The bottom rope set-up.

- Lower the climbing rope down the cliff so that the weight is on the first anchor.
- Run the other length of the rigging rope back to the second anchor and clip it in, again with a clove hitch. The weight of the rigging rope now makes the adjustment of the system easy, and the clove hitches let fine tuning take place.
- Places where the rope is likely to rub against the rock should have **rope protectors** placed under them, to avoid both damage to the rope and to the rock itself.
- A final check should be made that all screwgates are done up and the rope running in the line that it will take when loaded, and the system is complete.

notes

Consideration should be given to what happens when the climber reaches the top of the route. In most instances they will be lowered back down to the ground, and this is certainly how most group sessions will be organized. However, there may be occasions where the climber wishes to climb over the top, perhaps to rearrange the system on to a different climb. Great care should be taken at this point, as they will end up in a lead situation and a slip could mean that they fall some distance. Thought should also be given to the method of delivering the rope back to the ground, as the safety of the person at the top of the cliff could be compromised should they slip whilst untied. When preparing the rope to be thrown back down, clipping into the rigging rope with a **cowstail** would be a sensible precaution, and one could be ready on the harness if climbing over the top is to happen a number of times.

> **tips**
> If dealing with a group session involving very small children or people of very little weight, it may be a good idea to replace one of the top karabiners with a pulley. When rigging, make the loops of the top knot unequal. Put a karabiner with a medium- to heavy-duty climbing pulley on it on to the shorter of the two loops. Then clip another karabiner to the other loop and on to the climbing rope. This will act as a safety back-up, hanging just below the pulley. There will be a lot of friction lost when using this method, so the judgement of the supervisor should come into play before rigging. If a large person is also in the group, the belayer may experience trouble holding them with such a lack of resistance in the system.

Special considerations

Sometimes, there may be a need to take away some of the loading felt by the person belaying from the ground. In particular, if working with special-needs groups and encouraging them to belay each other, taking away some of the weight borne by the belayer when lowering the climber back to the ground is advantageous. It is possible to arrange the system so that there is an Italian hitch on the karabiner at the top (in this situation, just one karabiner should be used otherwise jamming may occur), and the belayer can then learn to manage the system without the worry of a large loading on them – the hitch will take most of the weight. However, it is quite a judgement call to rig a system where the Italian hitch is out of the reach of the supervisor, and this method can only be recommended for short routes or an indoor climbing facility.

METHOD 2

A second method that helps reduce loading is more practical, and is rigged as follows:

- Set up the top section of the bottom-rope rig as above, except the double figure of eight, when it is tied, is adjusted so that one loop is about 20cm (8in) longer than the other.
- Tie a figure of eight on to one end of the climbing rope, and clip it in to a karabiner on the higher of the two loops.
- Allow a long loop of rope to feed out until it reaches the ground. Then clip the remaining rope into the lower of the two karabiners so that it runs freely. The rope should now run from the figure of eight, down to the ground, back up to the second karabiner, then down to the ground again.
- This has created a system with a mechanical advantage to the belayer. The climber is clipped into the free-running loop and the belayer takes in and pays out with the free end as usual. Because of the method of rigging, the belayer will have to take in more rope than usual as the climber ascends, but the advantage is that the weight of the climber that is held by the belayer, should they fall or when they are lowered off, is dramatically reduced.

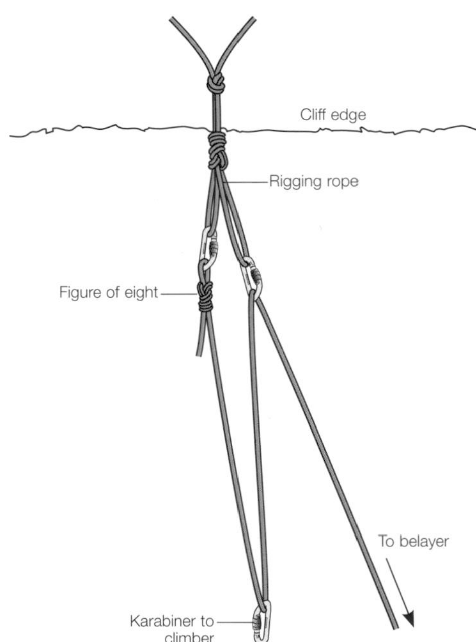

A 3:1 rope set-up.

Bowline

See also: double fisherman's knot, figure-of-eight knot, overhand knot, stopper knot.

Although the popularity of the **figure-of-eight knot** seems to have overtaken that of the bowline, it is still an extremely useful knot in a climber's arsenal. Many will find it to be a superior knot for tying on around the waist when a harness is not used, as it is fast and easy to adjust. As the bowline is also quite easy to untie, it may well also be the preferred method of tying on to a harness when working a hard rock route or when training on an indoor climbing wall where a high number of falls may be expected.

It is absolutely essential that a **stopper knot** is included with the bowline, to stop any chance of the main knot loosening and inverting itself; should this happen, the knot can fail. The stopper knot, either an **overhand** or **fisherman's** will be adequate, should be tied so that it is butted up against the bowline when tightened. It may be found that this stopper knot, tied as it is on the inner circumference of the bowline, gets in the way when subsequently clipping or tying rope and equipment to the tie-in loop, and it is for this reason that many will find the figure of eight to be superior.

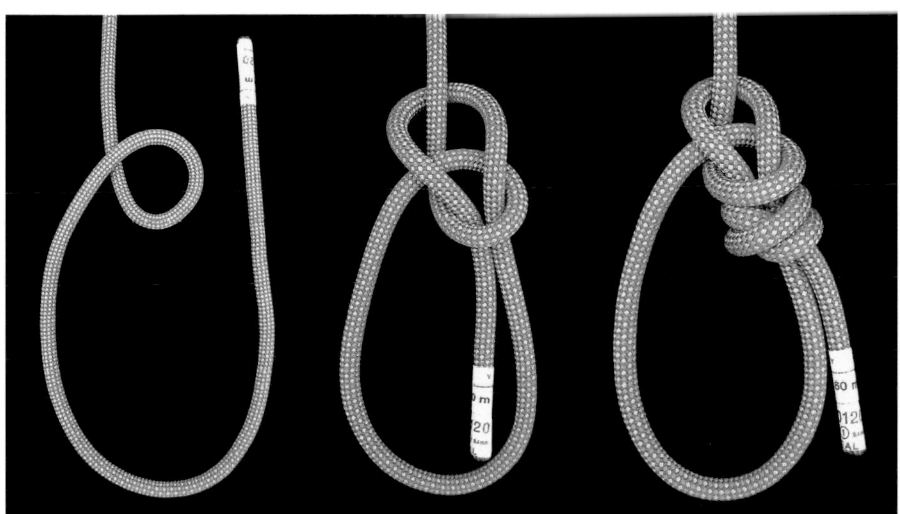

Tying a bowline.

Bucket seat

See also: belaying, buried axe, deadman, deadboy, dead rope, indirect belay, lowering, waist belay.

A bucket seat is a very effective method of securing oneself on snow slopes. Indeed, its very simplicity makes it an effective tool that is often all that is needed to safeguard the **belaying** of a climber up towards you or when protecting or **lowering** a climber down. However, a bucket seat on its own is not suitable for protecting a leader, as the forces exerted on to the belayer when holding a leader fall of any distance may well be sufficient to lift him or her clear of the bucket seat with disastrous consequences. Should the seat be used to protect a lead climber, then it must be linked to a second anchor such as a **buried axe** or **deadman**.

The mechanics of the bucket seat are quite simple. The rope, when loaded and locked off by the belayer, pulls him or her down on to

the front wall of the seat, with most of the load being taken by their thighs. For this reason, the construction of the front section of the seat is the most critical.

Cross-section of a bucket seat.

METHOD

- To make the correct shape, draw a semi-circle in the snow with your ice axe, with the flat front section measuring around a metre across.
- The snow can then be dug out inside the confines of this semi-circle, taking care not to disturb the downslope face more than is necessary. The front wall, the most important part of the construction, should be fashioned so that it is at around 90 degrees to the surface of the snow pack.
- The length of the belayer's thighs determines the depth of the seat. These need to be supported for their entire length once sitting in position so that maximum holding power may be attained. Care should also be taken that there is sufficient room for a rucksack to be worn, as this is advantageous if a **waist belay** is to be used.
- It is worth taking a few more seconds to construct a ledge on the **dead rope** side of the seat, so that the rope stays in one place and does not slide off down the slope.

Buried axe anchor

See also: bucket seat, crevasse rescue, direct belays, reinforced buried axe anchor, slings, T-axe anchor.

This type of anchor system is one of the commonest in use in the mountains, it can be very quick to construct and uses minimal equipment. Correctly prepared, buried axe anchors are very strong and can be used in a variety of situations such as when belaying a leader, as a **direct** anchor, or when organizing an emergency procedure such as a **crevasse rescue**.

notes

It is important to take care on steep ground, to avoid slipping when your axe is not to hand. Clipping in to the sling running from the axe as soon as it is buried is a sensible precaution.

- An area of undisturbed snow should be selected as the site for the anchor. As the strength of the system is in the snow-pack downslope of the axe, disturbing this to any extent with footprints or the like could compromise the strength of the system as a whole.
- Cut across the slope with the pick of the axe at 90 degrees to the fall line or line of loading, making the cut a little longer than the length of the axe shaft. Make a second cut about 15cm (6in) above the first one to the same length.
- Using the adze, remove the snow between the two cuts, ensuring that you do not disturb the downmost internal face – cutting above the upper slot is not a problem but simply uses up more time and energy. The type of snow into which you are cutting will have a bearing on the depth of the slot, but as a rough guideline you will be cutting a slot of around 20cm (8in) deep in very hard snow, and about 40cm (16in) deep in soft snow.

- Time should be taken to ensure that the downslope face of the slot is cut vertically and that it is level along its entire length. The axe shaft will be resting against it and any irregularities need to be smoothed or cut away.
- The attachment to the axe will usually be made with a **sling**, although it is possible to use the rope if a sling is not available. This attachment needs to run below the surface level of the snow, thus a slot needs to be cut at 90 degrees to the axe slot, running downslope towards the stance. The starting point should be at a line about two-thirds along the length of the axe slot. The width of this slot is also important: it should be only just enough to allow the sling or rope to sit in it snugly, any wider and the strength of the snow pack will be affected. The best method for doing this is to run the spike and shaft of the axe down the snow; if the adze is used it will most likely end up giving a slot that is too wide. This slot should run for approximately 1.5m (5ft) below the level of the snow, before emerging at the position to be taken by the belayer. This would likely be a bucket seat if belaying a lead climber, or perhaps a small ledge cut for using a direct belay system.
- The sling or rope should be clove hitched to the shaft of the axe at the centre of its surface area, which would normally be near the head about two thirds of the way up. The clove hitch should now be inverted to stop any chance of it moving along the axe shaft. This is achieved by placing the clove hitch over the axe and then taking one of the lengths running to the anchor and wrapping it once around the axe shaft. Doing this moves the clove hitch to the upslope side of the shaft and ensures that any loading on it will cause it to tighten.
- With the pick vertically downmost, the axe should be placed in the slot and bedded in, ensuring that the point at which the sling or rope is attached corresponds with the vertical slot.
- Run the sling or rope along the vertical slot, ensuring that there has been no debris knocked into it during the process. This would cause the axe to be pulled up at an angle and would stop it from pressing against the bulk of the snow in front of it, dramatically reducing the strength of the anchor.
- A couple of sharp pulls on the sling or rope will ensure that the axe has positioned itself correctly against the downslope face. If a sling is being used, a karabiner can be clipped on to it, and that then used as the attachment point for any system being utilized. If the rope is being run along the slot, the most likely scenario is that it will be attached to your harness already so care should be taken to ensure that it is the exact length required to reach the stance.

tip
In soft snow conditions and once the axe has been placed, snow from upslope can be packed down on top of it to help keep it in position.

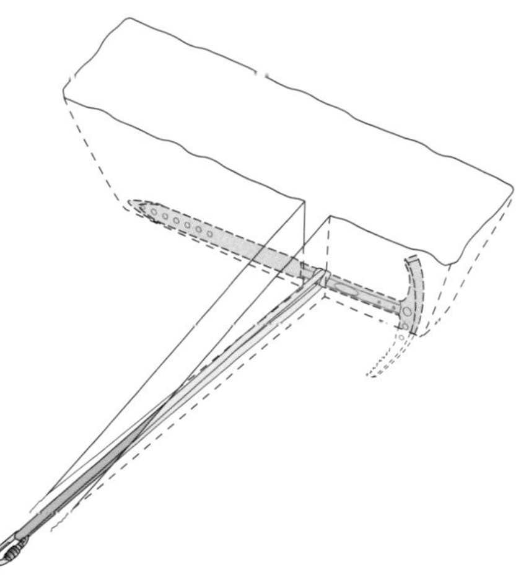

Cross-section of buried axe anchor.

Changing direction on an abseil

See abseil descent – changing direction.

Chest harness

See also: harnesses, Parisian baudrier.

A chest **harness** is of use in a variety of mountaineering circumstances, but is often overlooked for reasons of comfort and style. This is unfortunate, as the benefits of using one in certain situations are great. It is an extremely important tool when connected to a sit-harness to prevent injury.

A chest harness may be utilized in a number of situations. In a group climbing or abseiling session, if a participant is quite young or overweight, and as such has an ill-defined waistline, a chest harness will be important. It will help to cope in the event of them inverting in a fall or when abseiling, as their centre of gravity will be higher than that of an older or slimmer person.

Carrying a load, such as a rucksack, also causes a high centre of gravity. If the person carrying the load has any chance of falling and becoming suspended by the rope, on a technical climb or when crossing a glacier with the risk of falling into a crevasse, they should consider using a chest harness. A full body harness should be considered if continuous load-carrying is to take place in an area where crevasses or other hazards are present.

An improvised chest harness can be fashioned from a sling using the **Parisian baudrier** method. This is of particular use in an emergency, to keep a casualty upright during abseiling, or when requiring a temporary but lightweight chest harness if working at altitude.

Clove hitch

See also: HMS karabiner, slings, snow anchors.

The clove hitch is an extremely useful knot, and one that has its place in all aspects of mountaineering. It is simple to tie, locks readily when loaded and is simple to adjust. It is this adjustability that makes its prime use as a method of attachment to an anchor system, although it can be used in many other situations. A further benefit is that, with a little practice, it can be tied into a karabiner with one hand, a very useful property when arranging an anchor system on steep ground.

As the knot is quite wide, double the width of the climbing rope; it is best clipped into an **HMS karabiner** so that it can sit in its correct orientation when loaded. Using a clove hitch in a 'D'-shaped karabiner could cause it to sit incorrectly, reducing its holding power.

It is important to understand the mechanics of the knot and karabiner combination. The load rope of a clove hitch should be the one closest to the back bar of a karabiner, especially an HMS, so that the load is efficiently transferred along the back bar. In most

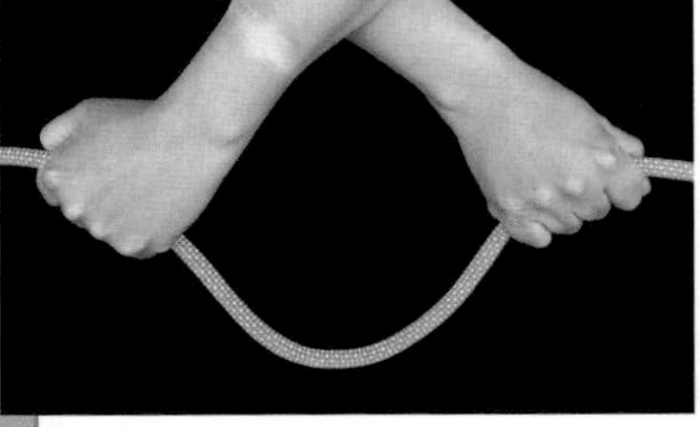

Tying a clove hitch.

Clove hitch on a karabiner.

situations this is not important, as the loading will rarely be sufficient to cause the karabiner to lever open or fail. However, thought should be given to the process of clipping two or more clove hitches into the same karabiner. Even if the load rope of the first one is close to the back bar, the load rope of the second will be some distance away, causing a much greater levering effect on the karabiner. If a third knot is clipped in, the load point would be so close to the gate of the karabiner as to cause concern about possible karabiner failure.

Inverting the clove hitch

In some situations, it is desirable to invert the clove hitch so that it locks off tightly. This is particularly useful when using a sling around a large-diameter object, such as an ice-axe shaft, which is to be used as a **snow anchor**. This is simply achieved by wrapping one side of the sling around the back of the axe so that the hitch rotates on to the opposite side of the shaft.

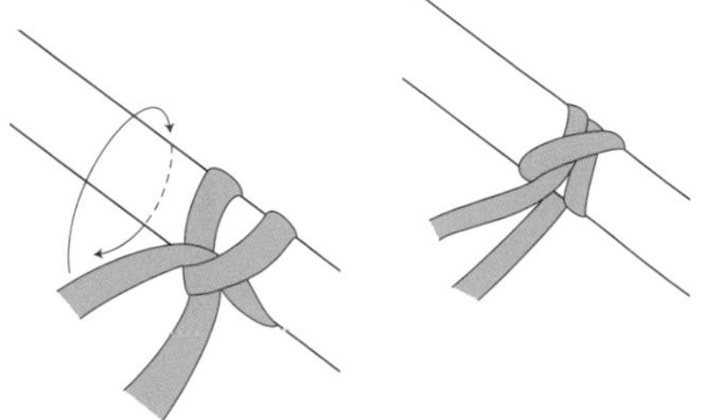
Inverting a clove hitch.

Coiling a rope

See also: overhand knot.

There are many ways to coil a rope. Which technique is chosen depends very much on personal preference, and climbers will usually have their own favourite. The bottom line is that the rope should be capable of being tidied away quickly and efficiently, and more importantly it should be capable of being uncoiled swiftly and without the possibility of knots developing in the process.

Of the three coiling and two carrying methods detailed below, the first is the most likely to cause problems when uncoiling. This is due to the twist that is introduced to allow the rope to sit neatly, as the rope can take on the characteristics of this twist. Should a number of these coils be dropped or, worse still, the entire rope be placed loosely on the ground, there is potential for time-consuming unknotting to have to take place.

METHOD 1 – The mountaineer's coil

- The rope is held in one hand and coils are made by forming a loop of rope with a diameter of around 80cm (32in). The rope should be twisted between thumb and forefinger when the coils are being taken, to ensure that it sits in as smooth a manner as possible. It is this introduction of a twist that can have a detrimental effect on the rope when it is subsequently uncoiled.
- Take coils until about 2m (6½ft) of rope are left.
- The end of the rope that was held to start the coils is turned back on itself to form a bight.
- The long remaining end is wrapped around the top of the coils back on itself, until only a few centimetres are left. It is important that both the loop and the end of the starting bight are not covered by these wraps.
- The tail of the rope is passed through the bight, the end of which is pulled to secure the coils.

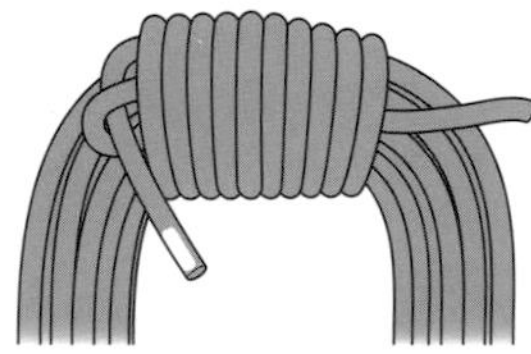
Locking off the rope for mountaineer's coils.

Coiling a rope

When uncoiling the rope, care should be taken to be as methodical as possible and that only one coil is undone each time.

- Release the end from the bight.
- Undo all of the wraps around the coils.
- Unfold the bight end.
- Undo the coils one by one, taking care to have laid the starting end off to one side so that it is not buried.

METHOD 2 – Flaking the rope

The second method, and one that will find favour with the majority of users, is called flaking the rope.

- Find the centre mark of the rope and, with the rope doubled, hold it so that the centre is hanging something less than a metre below your left hand (if you are left-handed, reverse the procedure). You may well find that holding the rope with your palm up will make things easier.
- Using your right hand, now fold the rope back across your left hand and keep repeating the process, alternating the direction from which the rope is laid, until you only have a couple of metres of rope left on the floor.
- Make sure that the flakes that you create are all the same size, and that the rope is being laid across your hand first one way and then the other, so that no actual coils are being created.
- Holding all the flakes in your left hand, wrap a metre or so of the remaining rope snugly a few times around the top of the flakes.
- Pass a loop of rope through the small gap at the top of the flakes, and push this loop down and over the top of the wrap.
- Pulling on the ends will cause this loop to tighten and the process is finished.

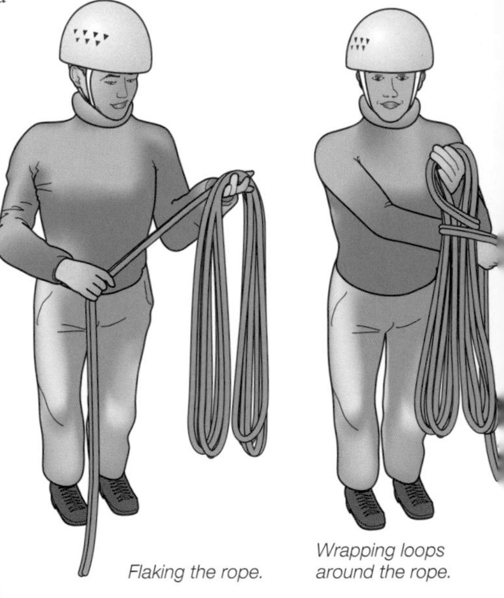

Flaking the rope. *Wrapping loops around the rope.*

Undoing the rope, which should result in no tangles at all, is accomplished as follows:

- Start unwrapping it by taking off the lock-off loop and pulling it back through.
- Unwind the flakes holding the rope together.
- Holding on to one end, lay the rope on the ground and run it through to the other end to make sure that there are no knots – if there are, it will simply be a loop through a loop and easily solved with a quick shake. Ensure that the first end is not lost under the pile of rope.

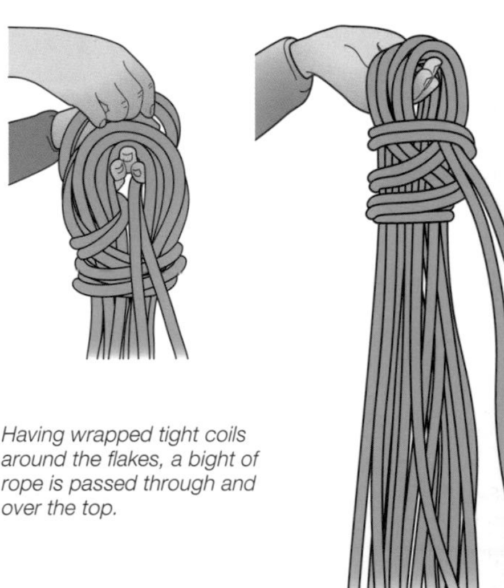

Having wrapped tight coils around the flakes, a bight of rope is passed through and over the top.

METHOD 3 – Snaking the rope

By this means the rope is stored in a manner that does not predispose it to knotting.

- Tie an **overhand knot** on the bight on one end of the rope.
- Taking hold of the rope about 50cm (20in) from the end, pass a loop through the knot.
- Holding the loop, take hold of the rope another 50cm (20in) from the overhand knot and pass this through the first loop.
- Continue in this fashion until all of the rope has been snaked through.
- Secure the final end with a suitable knot.

Releasing the rope when it is needed for use is quite easy.

- Untie the final locking-off knot.
- Pulling on this end will automatically undo the loops.
- Untie the original overhand knot.

A loop is pushed through an overhand knot

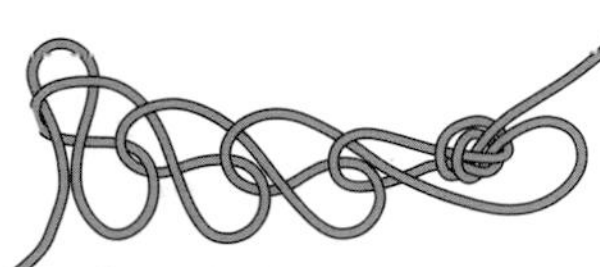

Successive loops are pushed through, then the far end secured

Snaking the rope.

Carrying methods

An alternative method, and particularly useful for single pitch rock climbing on bolts or where the ground is wet or dirty, is to use a commercially available rope bag into which the rope is piled and stored. This is usually a piece of nylon sheet a metre or so square, onto which the rope is simply fed into a pile. The bottom and top ends of the rope are secured on to tabs on the sheet so that they do not get lost, and the whole lot is rolled up and stuffed into an attached mini-rucksack. When needed for use, the rope will not only be tangle-free but will also be on a sheet that will protect it from any dirt and mud on the ground.

Another method is one that is very relevant if a short length of rope is to be carried for emergency use (for instance 30m of 9mm diameter). This rope can be fed into an old stuff sack with one end left protruding. When rope is needed, pulling on the end should result in the tangle-free deployment of as much rope as is required, all packaged in a system that can be conveniently carried in a rucksack.

> **tip**
> Having the centre of the rope marked is extremely useful when coiling the rope. This is often already done by the manufacturer, using either tape or a dye that won't affect the fibres. If there is no marker already in place, it is possible to buy dedicated rope marking ink that is specifically designed to work on ropes without detrimentally affecting them. No other inks or marker pens should be used, and caution should be exerted if wanting to use coloured tape, as the adhesive can sometimes affect the rope.

Coils

See tying off coils.

Cordolette

See also: accessory cord, equalizing anchors, slings.

This is a useful piece of equipment consisting of a length of dedicated rope or **accessory cord** that can be used for, among other things, the construction and **equalizing of anchors**.

Cordolette

Often made from a strong material such as Perlon or Kevlar, a cordolette will typically measure around 6–7m (20–23ft) in length, with a diameter of around 7mm.

It can be used to equalize anchors in much the same way as a 240cm (96in) sling would, but with the advantage that it can be threaded through all manner of awkward places and then tensioned and tied to suit. The extra length also means that anchors that are positioned some distance apart can still be efficiently equalized, sometimes a problem with limited sling length.

The cordolette can also be used for a number of other purposes, such as providing a safety back-up for emergency systems.

Counter-balance abseil

See also: abseil devices, abseil protection, abseil rope – deploying, chest harness, cowstail, escaping the system, French prusik, Italian hitch – locking off, klemheist, Parisian baudrier, screwgate karabiners, unassisted hoist.

A counter-balance abseil is primarily an emergency procedure, used when the most appropriate means of descent is by way of the weight of the person controlling the abseil counter-balancing that of a second person. They descend together with the rope running through a karabiner at the anchor. It's most likely to be used when assistance is needed by a second who has, for instance, sustained an injury, and is a logical progression from **escaping the system**.

For the examples below, it will be assumed that a leader and second are using a single rope on a multi-pitch rock route, that the second has been injured, and that it is not possible to lower them safely and directly to the previous stance.

EXAMPLE 1 – Anchor point within reach

- The system should be escaped. Forward planning may dictate that the safety line used is in the form of a **cowstail**, using the method of a sling tied off into thirds and into which the **abseil device** may be later clipped when needed.
- A **screwgate karabiner** is placed into the load point of the anchor.
- The dead rope coming from the back of the **locked-off Italian hitch** back-up is clipped through this karabiner.
- The rest of the free rope is **deployed** down the crag.
- The leader puts on the abseil device and appropriate **abseil protection**. A position as close as possible to the anchor will help the subsequent steps.
- The back-up Italian hitch can be unlocked and removed and the karabiner it was clipped to retrieved.
- The slack rope should be taken in through the abseil device and protection, with the leader again moving up close to the anchor.
- The leader now needs to lean out on the anchor with all their weight and reach down to release the original **French prusik** holding the weight of the second.
- The weight of the leader is now counterbalancing that of the second. The prusik should be completely removed from the rope, and any spare slings and karabiners used during the escaping the system procedure stripped out and retained.
- The safety rope or cowstail connecting the leader to the system can now be removed.
- The leader can now abseil to the casualty.

It is important to remember that once the French prusik placed during escaping the system is removed, all of the casualty's weight is taken by the abseiler. As such, they should adopt a posture that allows them to lean out from the anchor, safeguarding the second, whilst completing the above procedures.

When abseiling to the second, the leader should strip out any running belays that are passed, as they will not only provide valuable

equipment for subsequent abseils but may also add friction within the system if left, causing problems during the descent.

Once the leader has reached the second, it is important for the two to be connected with a short sling. If they are not, it will be very difficult, even with a conscious and able-bodied casualty, for the two to descend at the same rate. This is due in large to the friction created throughout the system. The connection can either be made with a short sling, enabling the pair to descend side by side or, if the casualty is unable to assist, they should be suspended horizontally across and in front of the leader who can then field them away from the rock and further harm. The provision of a **Parisian baudrier** or some other form of **chest harness** should be considered if the casualty is in a reduced state of consciousness.

Any equipment relevant to the construction of the next anchor system should already have been selected and prepared by the leader, so that minimal time is spent making everyone safe.

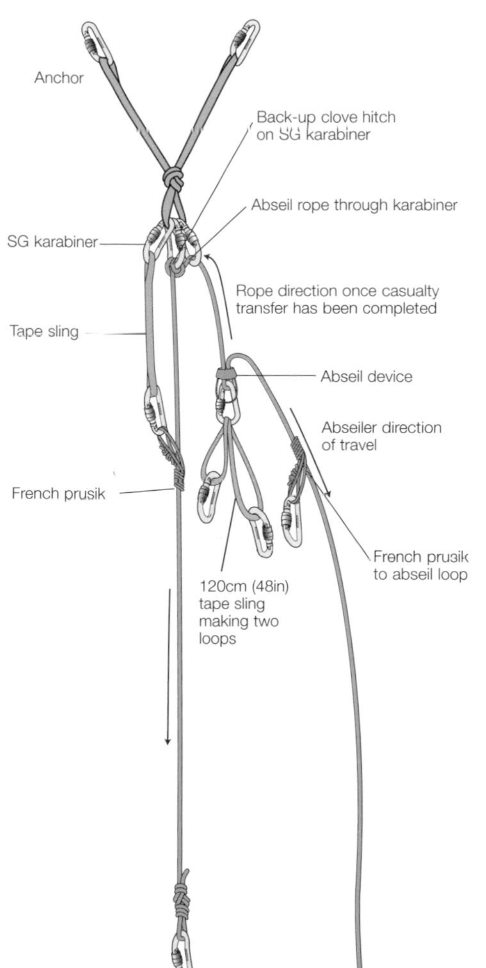

notes

Care must be taken to avoid the rope rubbing and jamming at the point where it runs over the edge from the stance. On rock, sharp edges should be avoided and particular areas of concern such as jagged quartz intrusions could be rounded down by pounding with another rock before the rope is placed in the line of descent. Also, features such as cracks or vegetation could be areas of concern, as the rope could cut in and foul. In snow, some preparation of the edge may have to take place to ensure that the rope does not cut in to the extent that it jams completely. This may entail cutting away soft snow to get down to more consolidated material underneath, or even the abandonment of some equipment, placed at the edge and over which the rope can run.

The distance over which the abseil can take place should be thought through. If a long pitch has been climbed, something over half a rope length, it may prove impossible to have enough rope with which to reach the previous stance. In that case an intermediate stance may have to be constructed on the way down, or even another technique altogether, such as **hoisting** the casualty up to the current ledge, may be more appropriate.

Converting to a counter-balance abseil with the anchor point in reach.

EXAMPLE 2 – Anchor point out of reach

Should the anchor points be out of reach, the procedure only slightly differs to the one mentioned above. When the rope is loaded by the leader as they lean out to remove the original French prusik, there will also be a **klemheist** to retrieve, tied on the sling around the anchor ropes. Also, depending on the anchor set-up, this may be the point at which the rope can be deployed down the crag, as much of it may have been held in place by the klemheist when the system was originally escaped.

Cowstail

See also: abseil device, abseil loop, harness, lark's foot, overhand knot, screwgate karabiner, sling.

One of the most useful pieces of equipment, a cowstail is an extremely quick and safe method for a climber to provide security for themselves at a stance, when abseiling, or if undertaking some emergency procedure.

A cowstail is an attachment to the harness other than the rope, which the climber can clip into a suitable anchor point, leaving them remote from the system and able to perform a variety of tasks.

- The simplest cowstail is formed with a 120cm (48in) **sling**.
- This can be lark's footed around the harness, taking a similar line to the **abseil loop**, linking the leg loops and waist belt section together.
- The sling should be equipped with a **screwgate karabiner**, and can be wrapped around the body of the wearer and clipped into a suitably handy point on the harness, ready to be deployed when needed.
- A knot can be tied at around the halfway point of the sling so as to allow a shorter length to be clipped to the anchor if appropriate.

When abseiling in a multi-pitch situation, it may be a good idea to prepare a cowstail in conjunction with the method used to extend the **abseil device**.

A sling divided into thirds and used as an abseil extender and cowstail.

METHOD

- A 120cm (48in) sling is threaded through the harness as above.
- Approximately a third of the way along an **overhand knot** is tied.
- The karabiner holding the abseil device is clipped into this short loop, which means that there is now two thirds of the sling left.
- A screwgate goes into the end of the sling and the system is ready.

The advantage of this system is that the abseiler can clip into the anchor, make whatever preparations are necessary for the descent such as putting on a back-up, unclip the cowstail from the anchor and descend. Once they have arrived at the next stance they can use the cowstail to clip into the anchor before undoing the abseil device, and so be protected throughout. If no anchor has been rigged, they stay on the security of the abseil rope whilst they carry out the task, then clip themselves on to it and off the abseil rope.

Crag-snatch

See group activities – problem solving.

Crevasse rescue

See also: Alpine clutch, ascending the rope, assisted hoist, belay devices, French prusik, HMS karabines, hoisting, ice screws, Italian hitch – locked off, klemheist, live rope, overhand knot, prusik loops, pulleys, screwgate karabiner, slings, snow stake, tying off coils, unassisted hoist.

Glaciers come in two main forms, 'dry' and 'wet'. These terms are sometimes confusing, as a 'dry' glacier will often have a lot of melt-water on it, and a 'wet' glacier will usually not. However, a 'dry' glacier is one where no snow is present on the surface, generally making them the easiest to navigate through, whereas a 'wet' glacier presents potentially the most dangerous terrain as snow will be present which will be hiding crevasses and route finding will be complicated. A slight hollow in the surface of the snow may indicate the presence of very large holes, and areas that look suspect should be avoided. Even the smallest depressions may be simply the tip of a large cavern that bells out into a huge crevasse. If you need to cross a small depression, and going round it is not an option, always approach it at right angles to lessen the distance across the gap should one exist. Probing with a walking pole or ice axe may well help to uncover any hidden traps.

Falling into a crevasse, with or without a rope, is a most terrifying proposition. Falling far in will normally only happen as the result of stupidity: incorrect footwear, trusting snow bridges late in the day or deciding to not use a rope may all be contributing factors. If a person steps on to an unstable patch of snow, they may well fall partly through to be left supported by their rucksack or armpits, feet waving in the cold void below. The rest of the party should resist the temptation to gather round to help pull them out, as the consequences of this are inevitable. Instead, a rope should be prepared and used as an aid. If the person has trekking poles, these could be used to help spread their weight, pressing down on the centre of the shafts with the poles held horizontally on the surface of the snow.

Using a rope

A far more sensible proposition when crossing suspect terrain is to use a rope to safeguard the party. Should a member fall down a hole, the simplest method of extraction is for as many people as possible to pull on the rope, taking care of their own safety, and the person should eventually be hauled out. If there are only a couple of people in the group and the victim is unable to climb out, then calling for help from other parties in the vicinity is the thing to do, remembering the international distress signal of six long blasts, a minute's pause, then another six.

Preparation of the rope prior to crossing crevassed terrain needs to be thought through and practised. Each person should prepare themselves and the rope in a manner that will allow a number of extraction techniques to be performed if the situation dictates. One method of preparation is as follows:

METHOD

- **Coils** are taken and tied off. It would be sensible for the lead person to tie off at a high point, so that the coils will act as a chest harness should they fall into a crevasse. The following party member/s could be tied off at a low level to stop the chance of being pulled forwards, should the lead person load the rope.
- The distance between people must be carefully calculated. If two people are to travel together, the distance between them should be in the region of 12m. If three people are to travel, this distance is reduced to between 8 and 10m. A 50 or 60m rope is ideal for this type of travel. It is important that there is enough rope at the

disposal of the second or subsequent people so that a loop can be dropped down to the person in the crevasse. This means that if the distance between the first and second person is 10m (33ft), the second person should have at least 20m (66ft) of rope at their disposal.

- If three or more are to be on the same rope, those not at the ends should tie on using a rethreaded **overhand knot** on the bight, keeping the resulting loop end short and clipping this back into the rope tie-in loop with a screwgate karabiner to stop any chance of it unthreading.
- Each person should be carrying a number of items relevant to the terrain that they will be crossing and the number in the party. This will typically be three or four screwgate karabiners, one or two **ice screws** and **slings**, a pair of **prusik loops** and maybe a lightweight **pulley**.
- It would be prudent for each person to have a prusik loop clipped via a short sling to the front point of their harness. This loop should be arranged as a **klemheist** for the front person and a **French prusik** for the remainder, and these knots could be quickly altered from one type to the other with minimal time delay should it become required. The leader's klemheist would be of use should they fall into a crevasse and need to **ascend the rope** to get out, and they will have one prusik attached and ready. The French prusik on the harness of the person left on the surface is immediately to hand so a method of transferring the weight of the victim from them to an anchor system can be swiftly carried out.

Preparing the rope

There are a variety of methods by which the rope may be organized for use as protection on crevassed terrain, and a number of these are given here. One factor that must be remembered, whatever technique is selected as being appropriate, is that the carrying of hand coils should never be encouraged. These simply increase the distance that a victim will fall and makes the resultant shock loading on the person on the surface far greater than if no hand coils were carried.

For two or more climbers, the knotted rope method can provide security through the provision of a number of knots tied at intervals along the length of the rope. The idea is that, should the lead person fall into a crevasse, the knots will cut into the lip and stop them from falling any distance. The length of rope between the front two climbers should be in the region of 20m (66ft) once a series of overhand knots on the bight have been tied. This method works well in some situations, but has the following drawbacks:

- It is time-consuming to tie the knots.
- If a third person is on the rope and will at some stage take over the lead, extra knots will have to be tied when they move forwards.
- As the knots take up extra rope, there will be a lot of weight between the two climbers due to the length used to tie the knots.
- Having knots in the rope may prevent a fallen climber from being able to prusik efficiently out of a crevasse.
- The knots may preclude the use of a hoisting system, as they would not allow the rope to run through a pulley, a French prusik or similar.

It will often be the final point that will decide whether this system is to be used or not.

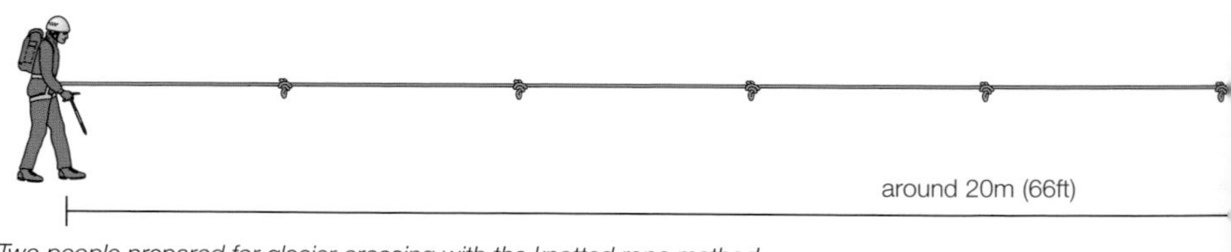

Two people prepared for glacier crossing with the knotted rope method.

However, if a party of three or four inexperienced people are included in a group needing to cross crevassed terrain, the security provided by this system and the ability for the group members remaining on the surface to collectively heave and pull their companion out could make it worth considering.

Extracting climber from crevasse

Should a person at the front of the group be unlucky enough to end up inside a crevasse, by far the quickest method of extraction, should a group pull either not work or not be viable, would be for the victim to ascend the rope. If they are wearing a rucksack, this could be taken off and clipped to the rope in front of them with a karabiner so that is free running. This means that once a little height has been gained the rucksack will not only no longer be a hindrance to the balance of the person ascending, but it will also have the effect of weighting the rope, making the ascent easier.

If the victim is in a situation where to prusik out is not an option, perhaps due to injury or loss of equipment, and those on the surface cannot physically pull them out with the rope, a hoisting system will need to be set up. The initial transfer of weight on to an anchor is a difficult procedure to accomplish if just one person is on the surface. If two or more people are present, one can continue to hold the weight of the victim whilst a second person constructs the anchor. The following demonstrates the procedure for getting out of the system should there be only two people involved in the crossing, one of whom has fallen into a crevasse.

METHOD

- The person on the surface falls backwards when it is realized that their partner ahead of them has fallen, so they are more able to hold their weight. If crampons are worn, their effect of biting into the ice should be considered, and care taken that a leg injury does not occur due to the leverage placed on the person holding the weight.
- If the glacier is of good quality ice, one or two ice screws should be placed at their side and equalized if appropriate. These ice screws *must* be completely sound, as the security of the entire system relies on them. If there is any question as to their holding properties a different system such as a buried axe anchor should be constructed. This will be far more difficult to achieve from a lying position, but it may be decided that the screws will provide sufficient security to hold the victim and they can be used temporarily whilst a more substantial axe anchor is constructed nearby.

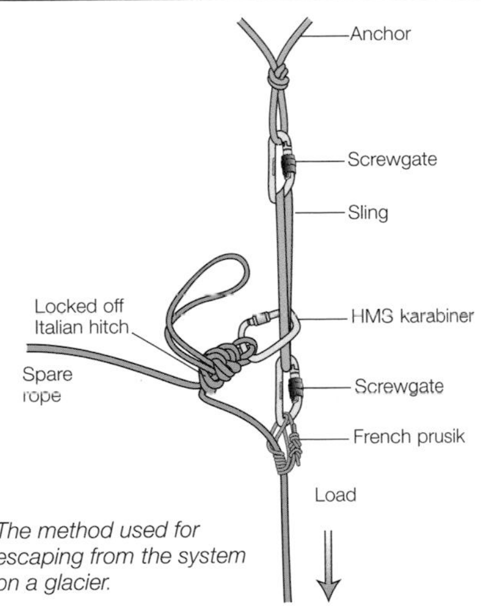

The method used for escaping from the system on a glacier.

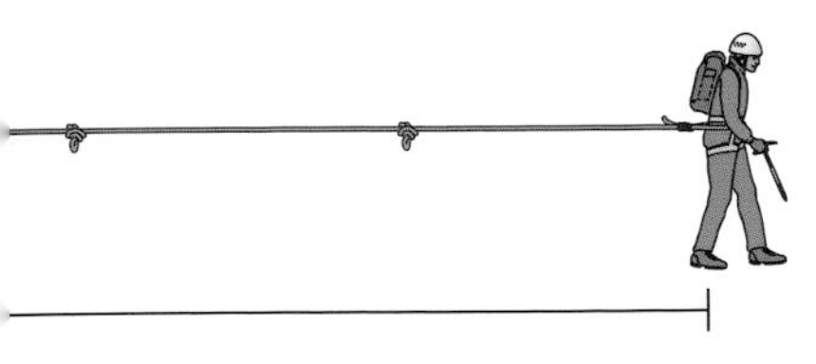

- The French prusik on the front of the harness, along with its sling, is transferred to the anchor.
- The French prusik is pushed as far as possible down the load rope and the weight of the fallen person eased on to it.
- The locking-off knot on the coils can be undone and a little rope pulled through. It is important at this stage that only a small amount of rope is undone in case the French prusik fails.

Crevasse rescue

notes

When a person falls into a crevasse, the rope tends to cut in and take a lot of the strain off those left on the surface. However, the temptation to walk forwards to see what has happened, trusting just the friction of the rope cutting into the crevasse lip, should be avoided and a safe anchor organized before any approach is made.

- An **HMS screwgate** is also clipped into the anchor, and a **locked off Italian hitch** tied into it to act as a back-up in case the prusik slips.
- The rest of the coils can be undone and the person on the surface is free to move around.

Although the person on the surface may be free to move around, they should do so with extreme caution. If the victim fell into the crevasse because it was hidden by snow, there may be other crevasses before it that were stepped over. The rescuer must protect themselves, and the best way for this to be accomplished is for them to clip on to the dead rope coming out of the anchor, perhaps with a **belay device** of some sort, so they are safe as they make their way to the lip of the crevasse so as to assess the next step. They could also prusik along the **live rope** towards the victim.

An overview of the assisted hoisting system in practice.

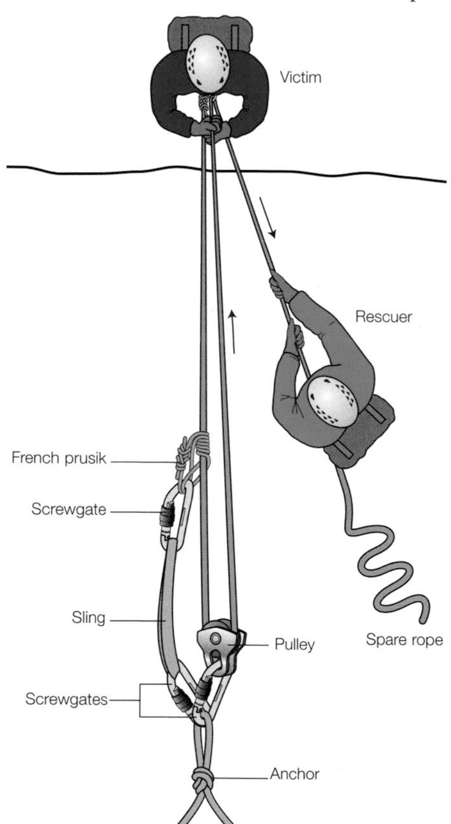

Preparing the lip of the crevasse

Even with a descent of a short distance, a rope will tend to cut into the lip of a crevasse quite deeply and this will have to be rectified before an efficient hoisting system can be put into place. Great care should be exercised if the decision is made to cut away some of the surrounding snow and ice to reveal the rope, as not only will there be a risk of hitting the victim with debris but there is also the fact that a rope under tension will cut extremely easily. Once the lip of the crevasse has been prepared, or even if the rope has not initially cut in at all, some method by which the rope will not be able to dig itself in deeper when hoisting takes place should be constructed. This will be most simply achieved by the insertion of an ice axe under the rope as close to the edge of the crevasse as possible. If this is not practical, perhaps the axe has been used as part of the anchor system, a rucksack, **snow stake** or similar item could be used, ensuring that it cannot be lost into the crevasse by accident.

Hoisting procedures

The assisted hoist: If there is sufficient rope to drop a loop to the victim, then a method such the **assisted hoist** can be used. This will often allow a swift return to the sur-

Opposite: *Route-finding on a complicated Himalayan glacier.*

Crevasse rescue

tips

It is worth spending a moment assessing the best technique for retrieving the victim. It may well be that a lot of time and effort can be saved by simply lowering them to the floor of the crevasse, from where they can walk out. This is one reason why a locked-off Italian hitch is the best means of providing a back-up as it can be released under load.

Crevasse rescue is a complicated series of skills, and as such should be practised before needed. This does not have to be on glaciated terrain, anywhere that allows for a realistic loading to be placed on the rope will do, such as a small crag, snow slope or even a steep grassy bank.

face, as both party members can be pulling at once. It is important for the person at the top to keep an eye on the French prusik knot during the hoist, as its operation may be hampered if it is lying flat on the surface of the ice. The provision of a pulley at the anchor, through which the rope will pass, will do much to reduce friction.

The unassisted hoist: If the assistance of the victim cannot be called upon, possibly due to insufficient rope being available or them being incapacitated in some way, an **unassisted hoist** will need to be set up. This can be accomplished as normal, using a klemheist and a French prusik, or can be made easier by the use of both lightweight and self-locking pulleys, having removed any causes of friction such as an Italian hitch. A variation is shown in the diagram below; this has the effect of increasing the mechanical advantage normally produced by an unassisted hoist.

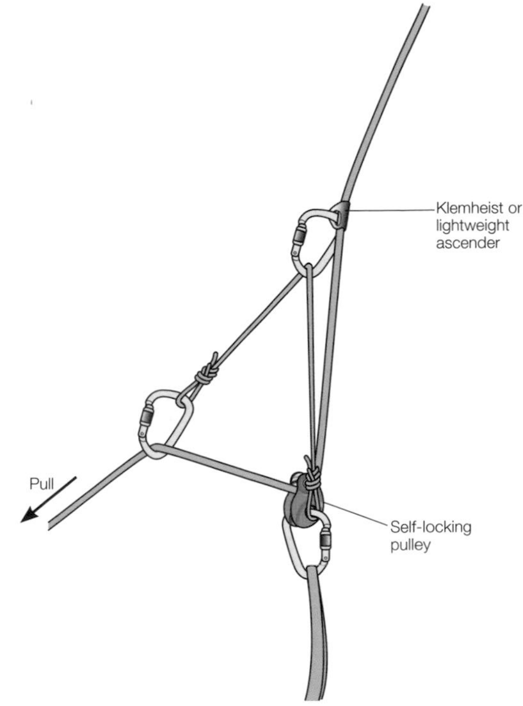

Using an unassisted hoisting system that increases the mechanical advantage of those pulling.

Should the rope to the fallen climber be irretrievably jammed in the lip of the crevasse, as frequently occurs, a very useful hoisting method is as follows.

METHOD

- The system is escaped, and the rope securely fixed to the anchor. This could be with either a clove hitch or a figure of eight.
- A loop of rope is dropped down to the victim. This will be ideally equipped with a pulley and screwgate karabiner, items that the victim may have on them. They clip the screwgate into their abseil loop.
- The top end of the loop is clipped into the anchor in some way that will lock it off when loaded. This could be with a self-locking pulley, or with an Alpine clutch.
- On to the dead rope, coming from the pulley or clutch, goes another screwgate, preferably with a pulley attached. This is connected to the rope running down to the victim with a klemheist.
- Pulling on the end of the rope allows the victim to be raised, with the system needing to be relaxed and the klemheist pushed further down the rope at regular intervals.

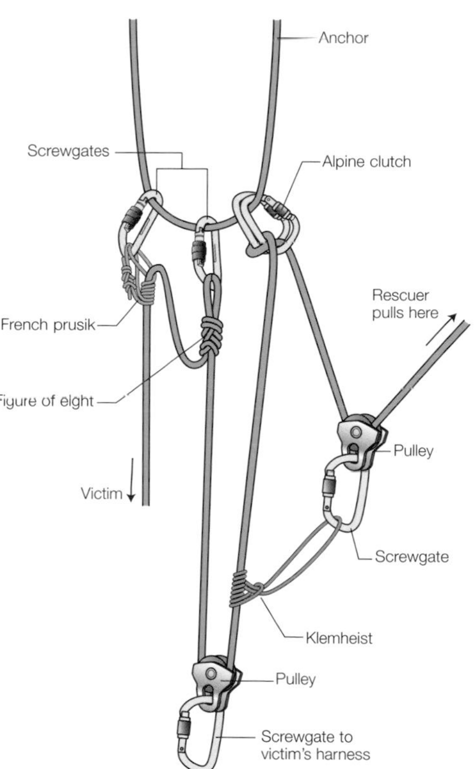

An improved hoisting method, useful if the main rope is jammed in the lip of the crevasse.

tips

If a pulley is not available, using two similar-sized karabiners next to each other will help to lessen the friction at that point, as the rope will now be running over a larger surface area than it would be with just one.

Dead rope

See also: abseil device, belay device, direct belay, Italian hitch, live rope.

The dead rope is the rope on the side of a **belay device, abseil device** or **direct belay** system that is furthest from the person being belayed. It is the section of rope that will be held by the controlling hand and, as it is used to control the friction within the belay system, it must never be released or dropped. It is quite practical to swap hands on the dead rope when taking in or paying out, but the rope must never be completely let free. The term can also be applied to the rope on the unloaded side of a knot.

Deadboy anchor

See also: deadman anchor.

The deadboy anchor is a smaller version of the **deadman**, and can be useful for anchoring in very hard snow. However, it has far less holding power in softer snow than its larger version, and it should not be used where its holding properties are not thought to be 100 per cent. One of the best uses for a deadboy is as part of a tent anchoring system at altitude, where extreme winds may be prevalent, as it gives excellent purchase when compared to normal tent pegs.

Deadman anchor

See also: bucket seat, deadboy anchor, fixed ropes, screwgates.

Although increasingly ignored, a deadman is a very efficient method of anchorage in snow, given the right conditions. Although giving little security in powder snow, it can work well in most other circumstances.

It is a metal plate, either flat or with slightly canted edges on its two vertical sides, and usually with a reinforced striking surface across its top. Most commonly it will have a number of holes drilled through it to help reduce the weight and allow for the snow to re-freeze when it has been placed, making it more secure. It will normally be supplied with about 2m (6ft) of wire attached at the central point, on to which a connection can be made. It can be used for most purposes in snow, such as when belaying, lowering or anchoring **fixed ropes**, and is relevant on ground from level through to moderately steep.

One of the main advantages of carrying a deadman for use in anchor systems over and above that of ice-axe anchors is that you still have your axes with you once the anchor has been constructed, an important consideration on technical ground.

The angle of placement of the deadman is critical, as it requires a 40-degree angle between it and the snow on the upslope side. If it is placed too steeply into the snow it could pull out when loaded, if canted too far back it could pull itself into the snow pack and be influenced by the strength of lower snow layers. To obtain a near as possible perfect placement on the hill, the following method is suggested. However, it should be noted that this process can be altered by a number of variables, not least the fact that on steeper terrain it may be very awkward to check accurately the initial angle as described. A little perseverance and practice initially will give a 'feel' for the correct placement, and experience can later be used to judge how to place the anchor if ideal conditions do not prevail.

METHOD

- The deadman should be placed in a flat area of snow with layers as consistent as possible, so that they cannot influence it when the plate is loaded. The downslope side of the placement should remain undisturbed by foot or axe.
- Place the ice axe into the snow at 90 degrees to the slope. This angle can be checked by using the sides of the deadman as a square.
- The deadman should now be placed across the fall-line, with its pointed base close to the shaft of the axe, but not resting up against it.
- Looking along from the side, bisect the angle between the ice axe and the slope to give 45 degrees. Now tilt the top of the deadman back a few degrees in order to reduce it to 40, and push it into the snow a short way so that it stands on its own.
- The axe can now be used to cut a slot into which the deadman will ultimately sit. Using it as a guide, cut a deep line into the snow with the pick of the axe at exactly the same angle as the plate, off to one side of it. It is important that this slot is cut carefully, as it will become the face down which the deadman is driven and, as such, the guide for the correct angle of placement.
- The snow on the upslope side of this guide slot can now be removed for a few centimetres' width and depth, taking care not to cut into the lower face.
- Using the axe pick, cut a narrow slot running vertically downslope for approximately 2m (6ft), into which the attachment wire will sit. This needs to be at 90 degrees to the horizontal slot, to ensure that the wire loads the plate correctly.
- Holding the deadman flush against the horizontal guide slot, hammer it down into place ensuring that it follows the guide, thus the 40 degree angle, all the way.
- Once the wire attachment point is below the level of the surface of the snow, pulling the wire taught whilst hammering will keep the plate at the correct angle as it is driven in. The depth to which it is buried will depend upon the condition of the snow, but in good stable conditions the striking plate needs to be no further than 5–10cm (2–4in) down.
- It is important that the wire runs directly from the deadman to the belay point. Any snow or ice that has inadvertently been knocked into the vertical slot must be cleaned out with the axe pick, otherwise when the system is loaded the strength of the placement could be compromised.
- Lay the wire along the vertical slot. Use the shaft of the axe or hammer placed through the end loop to give the plate a tug. This will help to seat the deadman into place and

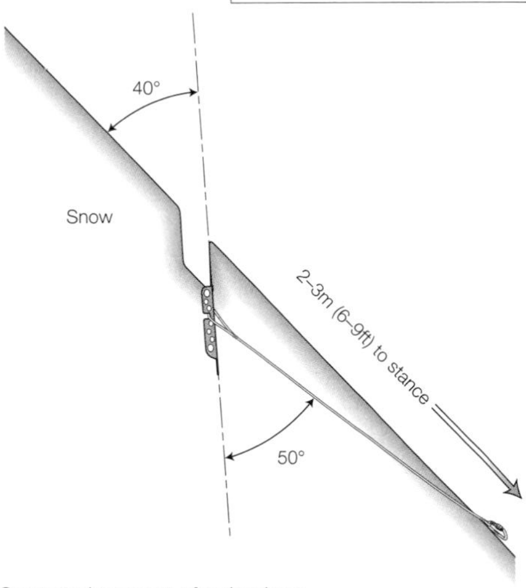

Correct placement of a deadman.

tips

To carry the deadman, wrap the wire around the plate a number of times and then use a screwgate karabiner to secure the end of the wire through one of the lightening holes. This karabiner can then be used to clip the plate on to a suitable part of the rack. As the plate is an awkward shape, the best position in which to carry it may well be clipped into a subsidiary gear loop on a rucksack.

notes

The 40-degree angle mentioned here is a useful guideline as to the working tolerance of the deadman, but will be almost impossible to gauge to the nearest degree when being used on the hill. This angle will be affected by the positioning of the belayer or subsidiary attachment, as there will be variables such as distance, depth of plate placement and depth of **bucket seat** if used.

Deadman anchor

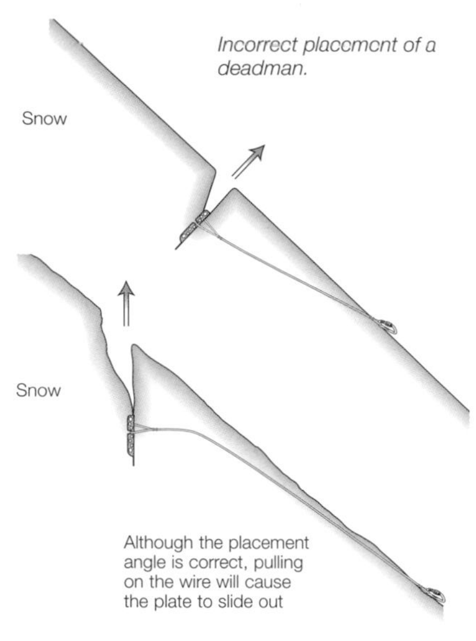

Incorrect placement of a deadman.

help the wire pull straight through its slot.

- ➲ Attachment to the system is most usually done with a **screwgate** karabiner through the wire loop.

Once the plate has been used, it needs to be removed with some care. Over-enthusiastic excavating with an ice axe can damage the plate or, more seriously, the attachment wire. In some snow conditions, pulling upslope on the wire will allow the plate to slide out of its placement slot with ease. In harder snow, or where the holes in the plate have allowed the snow pack to freeze through it, the plate will have to be dug out. Cut down to the striking plate until the depth and shape can be made out, and then proceed with caution when getting closer to the wire.

Denton knot

See also: Thompson knot.

The Denton knot is a technique whereby an emergency harness can be fashioned from a 240cm (96in) sling. The advantage of this over the Thompson knot is that it can be used in ascent as well as descent, whereas the Thompson knot would become dangerously loose if worn when climbing up. The thickness of the sling can also prove to be an advantage, as it will often be more comfortable to wear than a rope harness.

The main problems with the Denton knot are that, in some circumstances, it is possible to end up being suspended upside down, in particular if used when wearing a heavy rucksack. Also, the size of the person wearing it will dictate whether it can be tied at all or not, as the larger the person and the more clothing they wear the more difficult it may be to adjust it correctly. This is not so much a problem with the Thompson knot, which has the advantage of using the available rope and as such can be made reasonably large if required.

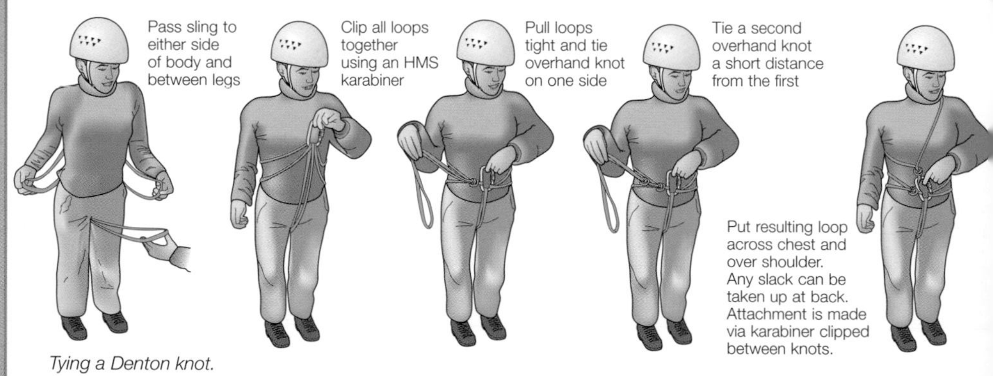

Tying a Denton knot.

Descender

See abseil devices.

Direct belay

See also: direct belays – rock, direct belays – snow and ice, hoisting, indirect belay, moving together, semi-direct belay.

A direct belay is one where any loading placed on a system is transmitted straight through to the anchor, and the belayer is not part of the load-bearing elements. The term direct belay can therefore be applied to a number of situations. It could be as simple as running a rope around a rock with the belayer taking it in hand over hand as a climber ascends, or it might equally be applied to the most complicated of **hoisting** procedures, in which the belayer is not part of the system.

Features of a direct belay

There are a number of advantages of using a direct belay. It can be very easy to set up, in particular if just using rock spikes for protection when **moving together** on moderate ground. Because the belayer is not part of the system they are free to move around as circumstances dictate, even when the system is loaded, as well as being able to escape easily and render assistance if appropriate. Direct belays also allow for a slick changeover at stances should one person be doing all the leading.

A direct belay should normally only be used when a static load would ensue in the event of a fall or in the case of effecting a lower. Should a climber be climbing up and beyond the anchor at which the direct belay has been arranged, it would be most prudent to change from a direct to a semi- or indirect system, as these methods are designed to deal with the forces exerted by a shock-load, such as those caused by holding the weight of a falling climber.

The main disadvantage of the direct belay is that there must be no question whatsoever about the strength and holding properties of the rock, snow or ice into which the belay is arranged. If the system is loaded and the anchor is less than secure, failure could occur which will not only cause the climber to fall, but also have the effect that anyone else attached to the system – the belayer, other climbers – will also be pulled off the stance. Only by practice and experience will it be possible to make the decisions required to judge a particular direct anchor safe. If there is any question as to its integrity, a **semi-direct** or **indirect belay** should be chosen instead.

notes

A braced position should be adopted when using the version where the rope is simply arranged around a rock spike, as it is possible for the belayer to be pulled off balance towards the anchor and lose control of the rope. Being close to the anchor will often alleviate this problem, although this may not always be feasible.

Care should also be taken by the belayer to ensure that their own safety is catered for. In many situations they will most likely feel secure even when not tied to the anchor. However, precautions should be taken if there is any chance of them slipping or being blown off the stance, and they should secure themselves to the anchor.

Although a direct belay rigged on a technical anchor system is an efficient way of bringing up a second, if the route is multi-pitch and the second is to lead through and become the leader for the next pitch, the direct belay may have to be changed. This is due to the different direction of loading the anchors would have to take. A belay device on the harness tie-in point of the belayer, giving a semi-direct belay, would be the most appropriate.

tip

It is important that the end of the rope is secured in some way, especially when lowering, or there is a chance that it could inadvertently be released through the system.

notes

Remember that some rock types, such as granite or gabbro, create a lot of friction, whereas others, such as mica schist or even the trunk of a tree, will not. The friction can be adjusted by wrapping more or less rope around the rock, more for increased friction, less for less. Great care should be taken that the rope will run smoothly. There might be a risk of it creeping up or down the rock a little, and becoming jammed in a crack. This could be very awkward to release, especially under load.

If the belayer is some distance from the anchor, a simple direct belay can be created in the following way: make a loop on the anchor rope, into which an HMS karabiner can be clipped, ready to receive an Italian hitch. To do this, tie an overhand knot on the bight on the rope/s between the belayer and the anchor, an appropriate distance away. The belayer remains attached to the end of the rope, but can untie and escape easily should the need arise while the system is loaded.

Direct belays – rock

See also: direct belays, equalizing anchors, lowering, moving together, SLCDs.

Direct belays on rock are a fundamental part of swift and efficient movement on moderate to technical ground in alpine or high mountain terrain. They are excellent for protecting a second and subsequent climbers, though not for belaying a leader. Climbers lacking the ability to locate efficiently, test and use direct belays when **moving together** are less likely to complete the route than those more practised in the art.

The basic direct belay on rock will be just that: the rope simply placed and managed around a suitable rock spike or boulder. The chosen piece of rock should have its stability beyond question, as failure of the anchor in this, or indeed any other direct belay situation, would be catastrophic. When performing this technique gloves should be worn, as skin is sensitive and will burn through with remarkable ease.

The direct belay can be used for either bringing up a second, for protecting a down-climb or even, in some situations, for **lowering**. The position of the belayer and their hands is important, as it is this that will dictate how the rope runs around the rock. The rope should always be held with two hands and, for lowering, a shuffling motion can be used with neither hand leaving the rope but taking it in turns to grip and pay out alternately. Gripping the rope, as opposed to letting it slide through, is important, as a sliding rope will quickly become out of control.

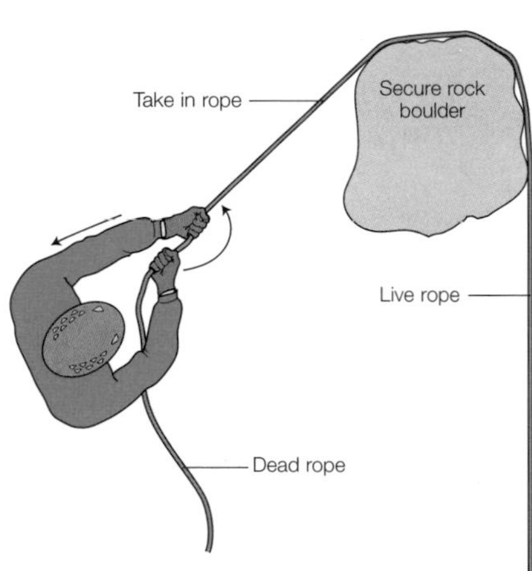

A direct belay on rock.

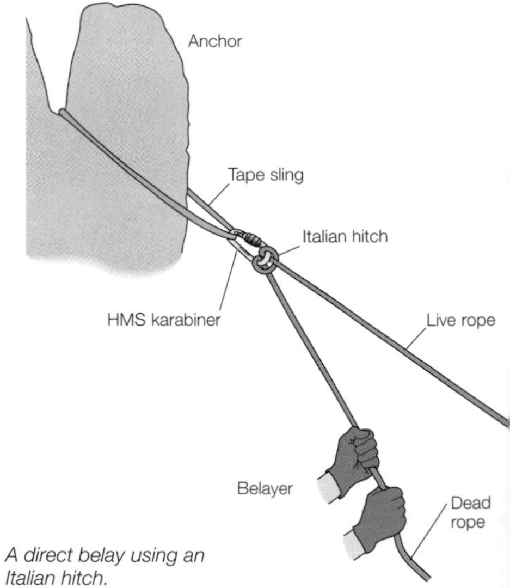

A direct belay using an Italian hitch.

A direct belay on rock is more likely to be used with the aid of protection equipment placed as an anchor. As always, the integrity of these placements needs to be beyond question, and, if there is any concern at all, they should be linked and equalized to avoid the chance of anchor failure.

Direct belays – snow and ice

See also: Abalakov thread, buried axe anchor, cowstail, deadman anchor, direct belays, equalizing anchors, HMS karabiner, Italian hitch, indirect belay, reinforced buried axe, screwgate karabiner, semi-direct belay, snow bollard.

It is possible to arrange sound direct belays in snow and ice, but the strength of the system will always be dependent upon the qualities of the material into which the belay has been constructed. A perfectly equalized and technically correct ice-screw direct belay, which has taken some time to construct, will be worthless if the ice into which it has been arranged is of poor quality.

The simplest direct anchor in snow is the bollard. This is easy to construct and allows a number of methods to be used. It should not, however, be used as a direct belay with the rope running around it, as the friction created will soon cut through and cause failure. The swiftest way to use the bollard once it is constructed is as follows:

METHOD

- Tie a loop in the rope large enough to go around the bollard. This could be at the rope end or somewhere along its length, depending upon the situation.
- Clip an **HMS karabiner** into the loop.
- Tie an **Italian hitch** on to the HMS. The system is now ready for either lowering or protecting a second.
- If the belayer was originally tied on to the end of the rope and they constructed the loop on a bight of rope a little distance from them, they will be automatically anchored once the loop has been placed over the bollard. If the end of the rope has been used to construct the loop, the belayer should also clip into it, using a **cowstail** and screwgate separate to that used for the Italian hitch.

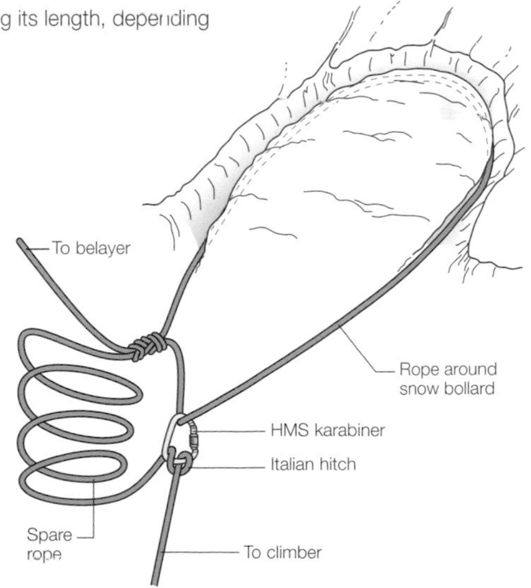

View of direct bollard set-up.

notes

Great care should be taken to ensure that everything is ready and running smoothly prior to using a direct rock belay, particularly in lowering situations. If anything happened that caused a problem, the belayer is unable to escape the system and, unless there are others around to assist, they will be in great difficulty.

The use of **SLCD**s should be avoided when rigging a direct belay. Their propensity to alter their position by 'walking' into a crack when the stem is moved, be it rigid or flexible, makes them unsuitable for use in a system that will have frequent tugs and pulls placed upon it. If they moved from their original position, an SLCD would have altered the **equalization** of the anchors that is so important for the sharing of the load.

Direct belays – snow and ice

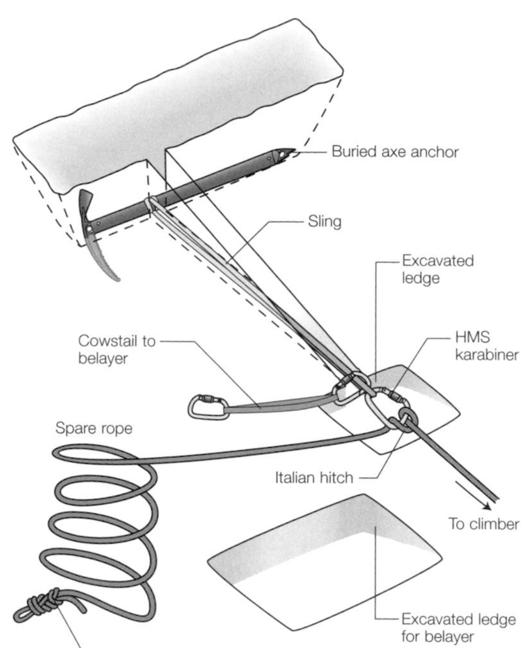

A buried axe anchor with a ledge to accommodate a karabiner.

Buried axe anchors

It is also possible to use a **buried axe**, **reinforced buried axe** or a **deadman** as a direct belay. These should be placed in the normal way, the only difference being that the sling on the axe anchors may need to be longer than if arranging a **semi-direct** or **indirect belay**. The distance down from the placement that the attachment is to be made will very much depend on the quality of the snow pack, but care should be taken not to make the distance too short. A 120cm (48in) sling will often be appropriate, but this may have to be increased to a 240cm (96in) sling in softer conditions.

Once the anchor has been placed, excavate a small ledge at the point where the operating karabiner will sit. This will stop the chance of any part of the system, such as an Italian hitch, from jamming when it is loaded. The belayer can be on their own excavated ledge and attached to the anchor for safety with either the rope or a cowstail to a separate karabiner.

The use of ice screws for a direct anchor should be treated with extreme caution. Ice is more prone to shattering than snow, and its quality can be harder to quantify. At least two screws should be used, and these must be carefully equalized to ensure a constantly shared loading throughout the system. Every effort must be made to make sure that they are not shock-loaded.

An Abalakov thread is a relevant method of rigging a direct belay system, although the time it takes to construct may be a deterrent when more than one thread has to be used.

Directional runners

See also: belay position, opposition placements, running belays.

A directional runner is one that has been placed with the purpose of making the rope take a line that it otherwise might not. This can be seen when placing an upwards-pulling **running belay** at the bottom of a route, where the positioning of the belayer may otherwise cause the runners to be pulled out of place. It could also be used in a situation where the rope may catch itself under a cracked projecting rock and therefore jam – a directional runner will allow the leader to re-direct the rope away from the problem.

Double figure-of-eight knot

See also: abseiling, bottom-rope systems, equalizing anchors, figure-of-eight knot, slings.

This is a useful knot for a number of applications and, although perhaps not particularly helpful for day-to-day rock or ice climbing, finds its place in a number of peripheral skills. One of the properties of the knot is that each loop can be lengthened independently of the other, allowing for a different reach to attachment points. Although this is often accomplished through **equalizing anchors** using slings, it is an option that could be taken if equipment is running low or if weight is at a premium, such as when climbing at altitude.

It is useful when rigging a group **bottom-rope system**, as it can be used as the knot through which the climbing rope suspension karabiners are clipped. Although there would be no problem using a simple **figure-of-eight knot**, many instructors rigging a system that will be intensively used will prefer a knot that means that the entire rigging system is fail-safe up to and over the edge of the crag.

The most useful application for the double figure of eight is as a method of equalizing anchors when rigging a rope system of some type. This may be a single rope down a crag to be used for **abseiling**, as part of a rigging system to direct two anchors to one point or as an excellent and efficient method of using the rope alone to bring two anchors together when rigging **fixed ropes**, for both the main and intermediate points.

If being used as a tool for equalizing sections of a system, the knot should be tied loosely and each of the two loops adjusted to a suitable length before the knot is finally tightened. It is possible to loosen and adjust either of the two loops once they have been clipped into their respective attachment points without having to open the karabiners into which they have been placed.

notes

Great care must be exercised if just clipping into one of the loops of a double figure of eight. In some circumstances, outward pressure on this loop may cause the second one to pull through, causing the knot to fail. If one loop were to be loaded in isolation for some reason, it would be prudent to clip a karabiner through the other, and then clip this back to the rope above the knot to avoid any problems.

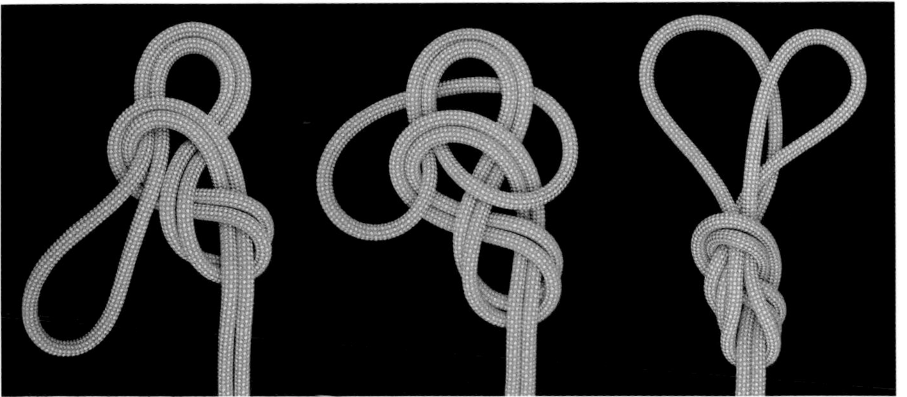

Tying the double figure of eight.

Double fisherman's knot

See also: Abalakov thread, accessory cord.

This knot is used more for the construction of equipment than whilst on the move. However, it can be utilized on the hill to join together two ends of rope to make an improvised sling during retreat, for example, or for joining the ends of an **Abalakov thread** when tied using **accessory cord**. It should not be used to join flat tape.

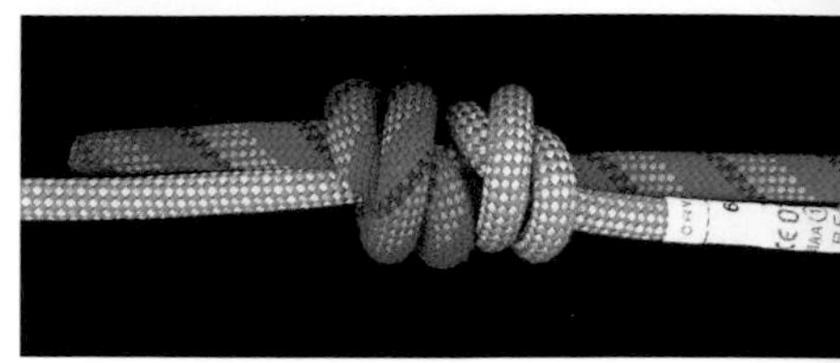

A double fisherman's knot.

Double rope techniques

See also: rope drag, twin rope systems.

Double rope techniques are used in a variety of situations, and are valuable on both short, technical routes as well as longer mountain ascents. They can be useful in reducing **rope drag**, where a single rope will zig-zag across a route and potentially cause problems, and are handy should a long abseil have to be made, as the two ropes can be joined to allow longer distances to be descended. Also, should a rope be damaged by rock fall or a similar incident, the chances are that there will still be a full length of rope left to use for the rest of the route. Once a technique mainly reserved for half-weight ropes, climbers will frequently now use two full weight ropes, as advances have allowed manufacturers to construct extremely strong ropes at a small diameter, which give great strength with little overall weight.

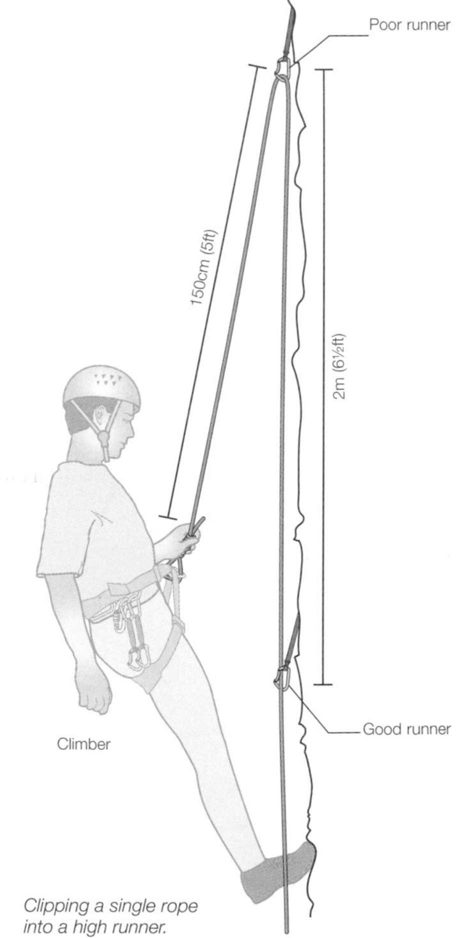

Clipping a single rope into a high runner.

A major plus is the way in which double ropes can be used to safeguard a leader by allowing them to select which rope is clipped into which piece of protection. For instance, let us take a scenario where a leader has a piece of protection at waist level, and has placed a dubious runner at just above head height. If they were using a single rope, they would have no option but to clip into the higher runner. If they then slipped off and the runner pulled out, they would fall the distance of the rope from their harness, up to the higher placement and down to the waist-high runner. If, however, they were using double ropes, one rope could be in the good runner at waist height and the other pulled up and clipped into the higher runner. If the leader now slipped, and the higher protection failed, they would only fall a short distance, being held by the rope through the waist runner.

Double rope techniques also allow for flexibility at a stance. If two anchors are to be taken, one rope could be clipped into each of them, so not requiring a lot of construction. Alternatively, a leader may elect to tie into the anchor system with just one rope, leaving the second rope free for a variety of purposes, such as preparation of the next pitch or for use to solve any problem that may arise.

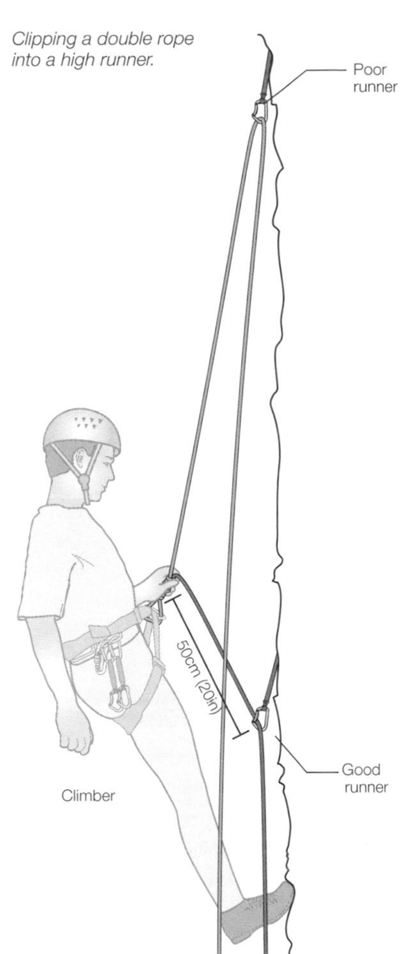

Clipping a double rope into a high runner.

Drive-in ice protection

See also: ice screws.

There are several types of drive-in ice protection, the three main ones being a drive-in screw-release solid section warthog, a drive-in screw-release hollow section snarg, and a hook-in or drive-in leverage release pick-shaped protection.

For most mountaineering situations, the use of the hollow section snarg has been superseded by the modern **ice screw.** These screws are so easy to place as to usually make the pounding in of protection redundant. However, the solid-section warthog still has its place on a winter climber's rack, as it can provide good protection when driven into frozen turf. The mixture of frozen water, mud and vegetation would damage hollow section tubes, but the warthog is sturdy by design. The main consideration during placement is its retrieval, as there needs to be sufficient space all around for its eye to be rotated 360 degrees.

Drive-in ice protection

The third type of protection looks very much like the pick of an ice axe. It has a use as protection on steep terrain where it can be placed into the indent made by an axe pick, thus offering some security, although driving them in deeper with a hammer would often be prudent. It is also useful as protection in iced-up cracks, in frozen turf and can be driven into placements where conventional rock protection would not be able to be placed. Removal is often difficult, and although an up and down levering motion may help, it may need to be cut out of the ice. A number of manufacturers emphasize that these types of protection are only designed to hold bodyweight, as their placement is often too shallow to take the load of a falling climber. However, they are frequently used in situations where leader falls may occur, with the climber placing them taking over the responsibility for their use.

Dynamic rope

See also: abseiling, impact force, lowering.

A dynamic rope is one that will elongate when loaded, such as in the incidence of a climbing fall. This stretching property is fundamental to the safety of modern climbers, as a great deal of force is absorbed by the rope as it elongates, saving injury to the climber and extreme loading on running belay and anchor systems.

They are used extensively in climbing and mountaineering, and should be used on any occasion where the climber has any chance of exerting more force on to the rope than they would do if abseiling or being lowered.

Sea-cliff climbing – serious and committing.

Equalizing anchors

See also: clove hitch, cordolette, direct belays, double figure-of-eight knot, figure-of-eight knot, lowering, multi-pitch changeovers, overhand knot, screwgates, slings, spike anchor, tying on.

The correct function and security of most anchor systems will depend upon all parts of it being loaded equally. This will often not be a problem if the anchor consists of one single point, such as a **spike** or a tree, but if two or more attachment points are being used then a situation needs to be created whereby the placements are sharing the load. Equally importantly is the fact that, should one anchor fail, the remaining anchors are in no way shock-loaded, a situation which could otherwise cause catastrophic failure of the entire anchor system.

One of the quickest methods of equalizing anchors is by **tying on** to them independently. This works well for many situations, in particular single pitch rock climbing, but it does have a disadvantage when used in the context of **multi-pitch** climbing. The problem here is that, if the same person is to lead the entire route, it is quite tricky getting the second and subsequent climbers attached in a manner by which the leader can easily move on. It also makes the use of a **direct belay** system trickier, as well as hampering the execution of some emergency techniques.

The use of **slings** allows a variety of methods of equalization to be accomplished. The minimum length is normally 120cm (48in), although a 240cm (96in) sling will give more leeway should the placements be some distance apart. A **cordolette** could also be used here, and this has the additional advantage that complicated threads can be incorporated into the anchor system.

For the following processes, it is assumed that two anchor points are being used. The first method is usually adopted because it is the quickest, although the anchors cannot be too far apart if a short sling is used.

METHOD 1

- Clip the sling into **screwgates** on the anchors.
- Holding both sides of the sling, pull them down towards the direction in which the load will be taken.
- Create a loop by tying both sides of the sling together with an **overhand knot** on the bight.
- The loop is the attachment point, and can be equipped with one or more karabiners, depending upon the task in hand.

Equalizing anchors using Method 1.

METHOD 2

The second method uses a little less length of sling, and as such is useful if the anchors are a distance apart.

- Tie an overhand knot loosely into the sling.
- Clip the ends of the sling into the two anchors.
- Move the overhand knot along the sling until it is in the direction of loading. Tighten it.
- There are now two independent sling loops. Clip a karabiner into one then the other and use as required.

Equalizing anchors using Method 2.

METHOD 3

The third method also uses less sling, but the clove hitches from which it is constructed make the job somewhat fiddly. The final attachment knot may also tighten to the extent that it is extremely difficult to undo after use if it has been subjected to a loading, such as when **lowering**, and particularly in winter or when wet. This problem is worse if the sling is made from a thin lightweight material. The advantage of this method is the ability to adjust the system once it has been tied.

- Tie a clove hitch in the sling and clip it into the first anchor point.
- Allowing a little slack, tie a second clove hitch and clip it in to the second anchor. This section of slack between the anchors allows for adjustment outwards if need be.
- Tie an overhand knot in the sling to give an attachment point, ensuring that each length back to the anchor is loaded equally.

Equalizing anchors using the clove-hitch method.

Equalizing anchors

METHOD 4 – Using two slings

If the anchor points are some distance apart, or only short slings are available, two slings can be joined together to load the anchors equally.

- Clip the slings into one anchor each.
- Holding them together at the required attachment position, tie an overhand knot.
- The attachment karabiner can now clip into the slings above the knot, or below as shown.

Equalizing anchors using two separate slings tied together.

tip

As mentioned, the knot creating the loop into which karabiners, and thus the loading, is applied, will tighten considerably with weight on it. It may be prudent to tie a **figure-of-eight knot** instead of the overhand knot, or even a figure of nine, which is like the figure of eight but with an extra half turn.

METHOD 5 – Self-equalizing

There is also a method of arranging a sling, clipped into two points, so that it self-equalizes. This method should be treated with caution, as should one anchor fail, the other will be shock loaded as the slack is taken up around the karabiner as it slides forwards. To rig the system, clip a sling into the anchors and cross it over at the centre, clipping a karabiner in at this point. Ensure that the karabiner is clipped through the sling and not just around it, otherwise anchor failure would cause the system to fail completely.

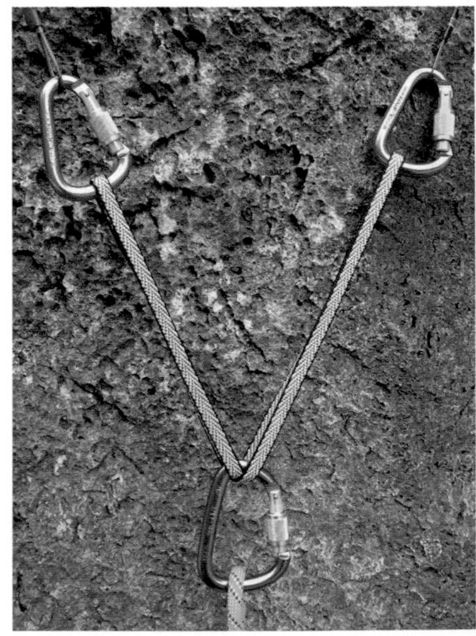

A self-equalizing sling

METHOD 6 – Three anchor points

If there are three or more anchor points needing to be equalized, a long sling can be used in a manner similar to the first method indicated above.

- Clip the sling into each of the three anchor karabiners.
- Get together all of the sections of sling from between the anchors and pull them down equally to one point.
- Tie an overhand knot in all, creating the attachment point.

In some situations, such as during the rigging of **fixed ropes** or when setting up a group activity, as well as in personal day-to-day climbing, the preference may be to use a **double figure of eight**. This has the advantage of being quick to tie and needs no slings, items that may not be immediately to hand.

tip

It is always worth ensuring that the sewn or knotted join of the sling is well out of the way when tying knots. Positioning it along one of the lines of loading as opposed to at the knot or anchor ends will stop it becoming incorporated in a critical part of the system.

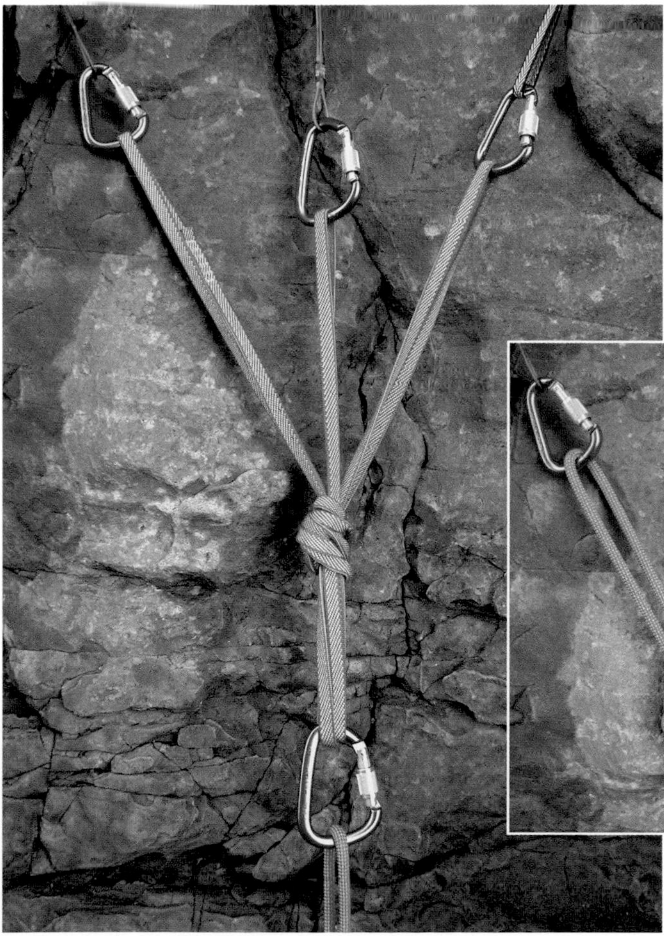

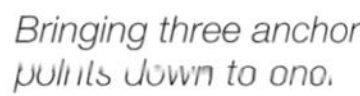

Bringing three anchor points down to one.

An anchor equalized using a double figure-of-eight knot.

Escaping the system

See also: belay device – locking off, bottom rope systems, bucket seat, buried axe anchor, clove hitch, cowstail, crevasse rescue, dead rope, deadman, Denton knot, direct belay, equalizing anchors, French prusik, ground anchors, HMS karabiner, indirect belay, Italian hitch – locking off, klemheist, lark's foot, live rope, overhand knot, prusik knot, reinforced buried axe, screwgates, semi-direct belay, slings, slippery hitch, waist belay.

The ability to escape the system is a skill that is very easily learnt and one that can change a desperate situation into something more manageable. There are many reasons why this may have to be achieved, and if there is thought to be any chance of it having to happen, the measure of taking a **direct belay,** as opposed to **semi** or **indirect,** will allow the task to be carried out swiftly and with ease. As with many emergency procedures, the ability to effectively **lock off a belay device** is central to many of the techniques described here.

The technique for escaping the system when faced with a crevasse rescue scenario is covered under the **crevasse rescue** section.

For the purpose of the first three techniques, we will assume there is a leader belaying a second who has got themselves into difficulty, requiring the leader to make a swift job of escaping the system. To make matters worse, the system is loaded with the weight of the second. The anchor has been **equalized** down to one point of attachment.

The first situation is the least complicated, and assumes that the leader does not need any special equipment to complete the task.

- The belay device is locked off.
- The belayer undoes and steps out of their harness.

Whilst this may seem startlingly simple, it is often overlooked in favour of more complicated and impressive systems. Should the belayer then need a harness to assist their second, they could either borrow one from someone in the area or improvise using a system such as a **Denton knot**.

If the situation or location is more serious, such as on a mountain route where the stepping out of a harness is not an option, the following procedure would be appropriate. This is a technique that relies on the anchor points being within reach for completion.

METHOD 1

- The belay device is locked off.
- A **sling** is attached to the anchor, and adjusted so that the attachment point for a **screwgate** will be just in front of the belay device. This can be achieved by shortening the sling with an **overhand knot** if required.
- A **French prusik** is put on to the **live rope** directly in front of the belay device, with turns sufficient enough to hold the weight of the climber. This is clipped into the sling from the anchor.
- An **HMS karabiner** should also be clipped into the sling. Into this goes an **Italian hitch** which is then **locked off**, using rope taken from a section of the **dead rope** coming from the back of the belay device lock-off knot. This will be used as a back-up for the French prusik.
- The French prusik should be pushed as far as possible down the live rope, so that the system has no slack in it from the prusik through to the sling.
- The belay device can now be unlocked, taking care that the prusik is at no point shock-loaded. If the belayer has been under physical pressure from the weight of their second, it should now be greatly reduced.
- The unlocking of the belay device will have introduced slack into the system, and this should be taken up through the Italian hitch. Care should be taken here as the Italian will have to be unlocked to allow this to take place and then locked off again afterwards.
- The belay device can be removed from the rope. If excessive slack is introduced between the prusik and the Italian hitch due to the device being removed, it should be taken in thorough

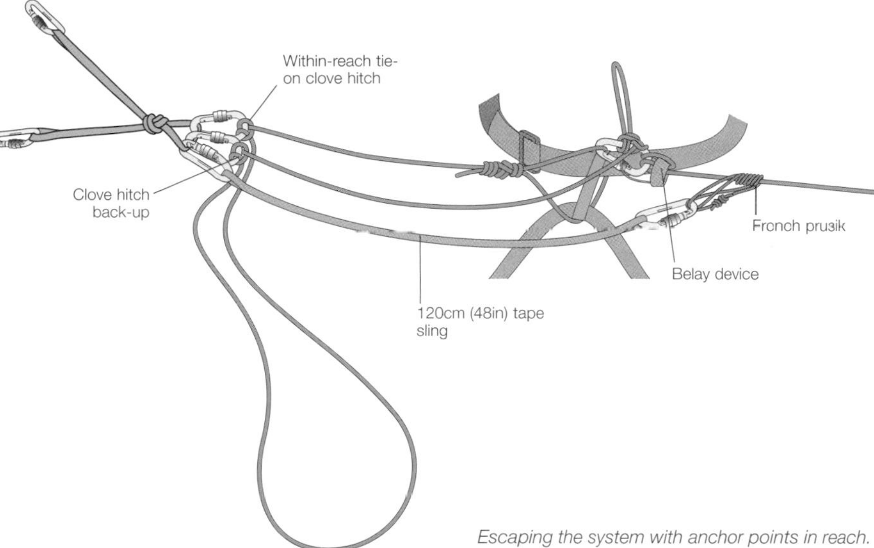

Escaping the system with anchor points in reach.

Italian hitch. Otherwise, a small amount of slack will not matter.

- The belayer is now able to untie from the climbing rope, or do whatever is necessary.

If the anchor point is out of reach, a slightly different process needs to be put into place:

- Lock off the belay device.
- A new anchor point needs to be established, and this is done with the use of a sling. This should be tied around the anchor rope using a **klemheist**, with plenty of turns so that there is no chance that the knot will slip.
- The other end of the sling should be adjusted so that it sits just in front of the belay device.
- The process is continued as for the process above.
- Once the system is escaped, knots should be tied into any slack or loose ends of rope to ensure that the klemheist cannot slide off.

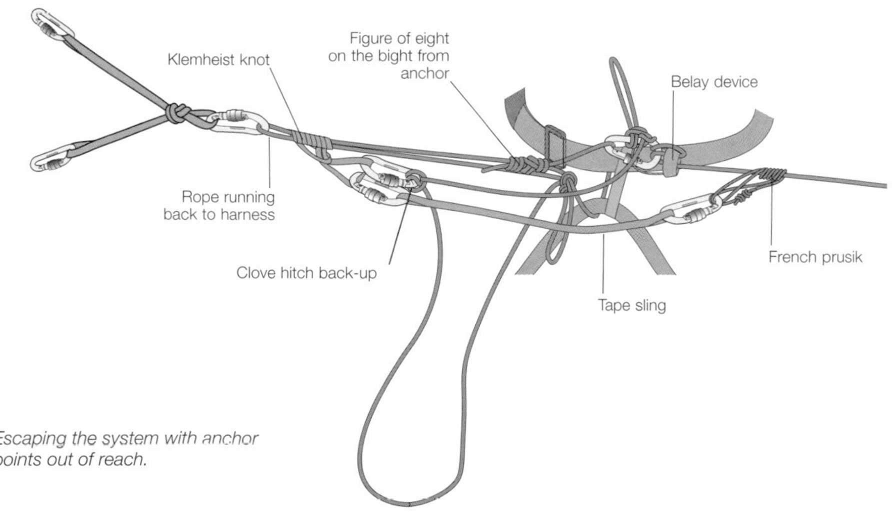

Escaping the system with anchor points out of reach.

Escaping the system

Bottom roping

There is a slight chance that the system may need escaping when running a **bottom roping** session. A method by which this can be swiftly achieved should be practised. For the purpose of these two methods, we will assume that the rope is not loaded and that the climber is refusing to down-climb from a ledge, a situation which might occur when dealing with novices. As such, there may be other people available to help.

METHOD 1

- If other people are available, clip an HMS karabiner into their **abseil loop**.
- A clove hitch from the dead rope is clipped into this.
- If the person assisting is small, as may happen when dealing with children's climbing sessions, clip a second child to them using a sling between their abseil loops so that they act as ballast.
- The belay device can now be taken off the rope.
- It may be best for the new person to sit on the ground, where they are in little danger of falling should the system suddenly be loaded.

notes

In the event of having no other people around, it is important that a solid ground anchor is carefully selected. This can then be clipped into using the appropriate system as above.

If the system is loaded

A second method uses a similar sequence, but is also possible to achieve if the system is loaded to any extent. It should be remembered that this would be extremely unlikely, as if the weight of the climber was on the rope in a single pitch situation they could be lowered to the ground. A drawback of this method is that the belay device will remain attached to the climbing rope and, should one be needed it would have to be borrowed from someone else in the vicinity.

METHOD 2

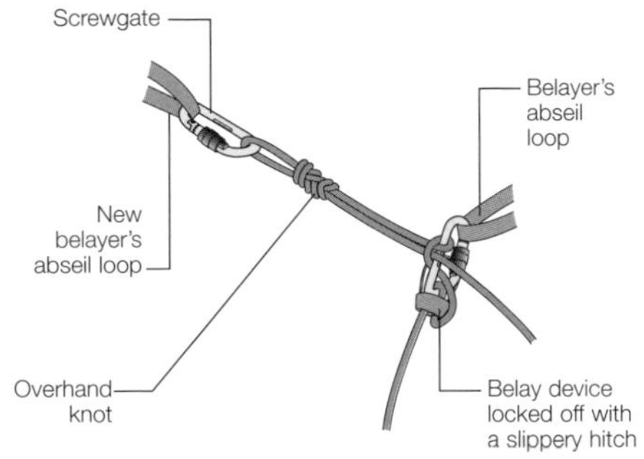

- Start the process of locking off the belay device, as far as tying the **slippery hitch**.
- In the bight of rope created by the slippery hitch, tie an overhand knot on the bight.
- This knot can then be clipped into a helper's abseil loop as above.
- The belayer can then remove the belay device from their harness.

Escaping a loaded system by locking off a belay device.

Escaping a loaded indirect belay

Escaping the system if an indirect belay has been taken and is loaded is extremely difficult. As this type of belay normally means a **waist belay** has been taken, the belayer is part of the anchor and as such will find it very awkward to manoeuvre, not least because their arms are providing the friction and holding power of the system. If the second does not have the rope under load, escape is made that much easier. However, if it is loaded then a lot of effort and not a little patience needs to be exercised by both parties whilst the task is completed. As each situation will be different, huge varieties in the manner that escape is attempted will exist, and no one method can be seen as being perfect.

It should be noted that the use of an

indirect belay system purely using a bucket seat as the anchor under winter or expedition conditions means that there will be no attachment point such as a **buried axe** or **deadman** to which subsequent weight transfer can be made. The digging of an emergency buried axe placement should the need arise might be accomplished with the assistance of a second person, although their presence when most needed would be extremely unlikely.

For the sake of the process below, we will assume that a waist belay has been taken by the leader who is using a **bucket seat** and **reinforced axe** belay at the top of a winter gully climb. The system is loaded, but a percentage of the load is subtracted due to the friction created by the rope cutting into the snow. The karabiner on the sling from the axe anchor is reachable at the back of the bucket seat, and the leader needs to retain their harness so that they can descend to render assistance to their second.

METHOD 3 (from a loaded indirect belay)

- The leader should turn slightly sideways so that they can reach up to the screwgate behind them without too much effort.
- A sling is looped through the karabiner and either both ends are clipped together or the sling is larksfooted around the karabiner. Whichever method is chosen, it is important that the end of the sling finishes at the side-front of the belayer. If the sling is too long, it can be shortened with an overhand knot.
- A screwgate karabiner is clipped into the sling.
- A **prusik knot** is tied around the live rope. The prusik is useful in this situation as it can be tied with one hand. A French prusik or klemheist could also be tied, if the belayer was in a position to use the fingers of their arm holding the dead rope to assist.
- This is clipped into the screwgate on the sling.
- The load is released slightly so that the knot takes up some of the weight, to allow the belayer a little more movement. It is important that they do not undo the waist belay at this point.
- Using a bight of rope coming out of their live-rope side, the belayer should now back up the prusik knot with a locked-off Italian hitch.
- The belayer can now release the weight on to the system and take off the waist belay.

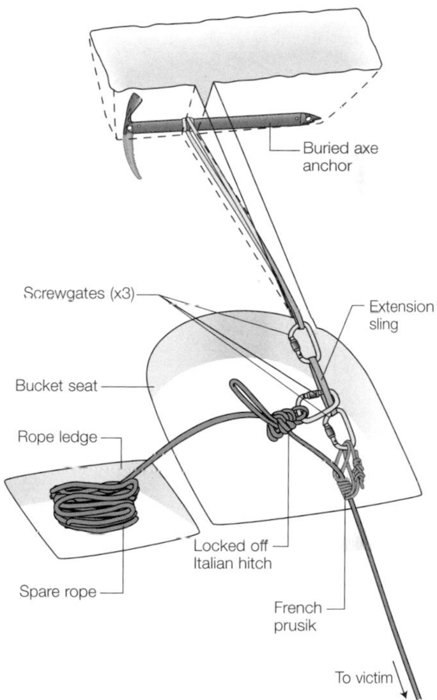

An indirect winter belay system escaped.

Caution

Care should be taken during this process that the anchor has the correct loading maintained on it at all times, and that the angle is not changed with the belayer shifting around at the stance. It should be remembered that the prusik knot will not release under load, and should slack rope be required then an alternative will have to be sought.

If the anchor karabiner is out of reach, extra effort will have to be made to tie a klemheist around the anchor rope, a very difficult task. Somewhat easier would be the process of clipping the prusik to the harness

notes

Sometimes a **clove hitch** may be chosen over the locked-off Italian hitch, as it appears to be quicker and simpler. However, the limitations of using a clove hitch as a back-up, should the prusik knot slip should be thoroughly understood and acknowledged. If the prusik does slip, the clove hitch will certainly stop the rope from running through. However, once it is loaded it will be extremely awkward to undo, making any further use of the system almost impossible.

Great caution should be exercised once the system is escaped. If at any height, personal security becomes paramount, and the precaution of clipping into the anchor with a **cowstail** should be accomplished before the climbing rope is undone from the belayer's harness.

central tie-in loop, backing it up with a karabiner at the same point, and then taking the harness off. This would, of course, mean that the belayer was left without a harness, although one could be fashioned using a Denton knot.

It should be re-emphasized that the process of escaping from an indirect belay is extremely difficult, and situations will exist where it is next to impossible.

Extenders

See also: bolts – clipping, running belays, slings, slings-carrying, snap gate karabiners.

This is the name given to sections of short **sling** used to extend the path of the rope away from **running belays**. The reason for their use is two-fold. Firstly, they allow the rope to run up the route in a better line than it may otherwise have done, avoiding problems with friction and being affected by bulges in the rock or ice. Secondly they help avoid the movement of the rope from dislodging the placement, as it may do if clipped directly to it with a karabiner.

An extender can be of any design and length, but most commonly they will be a small loop of tape of around 15–20cm (6–8in) in length, sewn across the middle so as to form a loop at either end. These loops are then each equipped with a karabiner, one for the rope and the other to be clipped into the protection.

Slings can also be used as extenders, but using shorter lengths is more common. A 60cm (24in) sling works well in bringing runners into line, although carrying them can prove awkward. This can be solved by passing one karabiner through the other and clipping it into the resulting two sections of sling. When it is needed for use, simply unclipping any two sections of the sling will allow it to revert back to its full length with no twists or knots.

Extenders can be purchased ready equipped with a straight gate karabiner at one end and a bent-gate karabiner at the other. It is important that only the straight gate is clipped into the protection, with the bent gate being used for clipping the rope. See the 'snap-gate karabiner' entry for further information.

Opposite: *French rock, bolts and sunshine.*

notes

It should be understood that factors far higher than 2 can be achieved in some climbing-related activities. For instance, Via Ferrata cables that are clipped with karabiners, which are then towed up for security, can give rise to huge fall factors. As an example, if a cable section is 6m long and the attachment to the climber is 1m, should they slip from the top of the section the fall factor would be 6. For this reason, Via Ferrata safety equipment is designed with shock-absorbing properties. This is either by a progressive and controlled ripping of stitching, akin to **shock-absorbing slings**, or by the attachment rope being pulled through a metal plate to achieve a smooth braking effect.

Fall factor

See also: Impact force, shock loading, slings – shock-absorbing, vectors.

The fall factor is the name given to the sum of the equation used to calculate the hardness, or severity of loading, of a fall. The higher the value the more severe the fall. For most climbing conditions, the highest fall factor obtainable is 2, the least is 0. The factor is calculated by dividing the length of the fall by the length of the rope deployed.

There are two versions of the calculation: the Theoretical Fall Factor will give a number based on the simple mathematical equation mentioned above. The Actual Fall Factor is a more complicated equation, which takes into account such variables as the line that the rope takes between runners, and the effect of it rubbing over rock or ice.

The following table demonstrates the Theoretical Fall Factor produced with running belays at two different positions on a lead. The route is multi-pitch.

Length of rope run out from belay	2.5m
Height of running belay	No running belay, force comes directly on to anchor
Length of fall	5m
Fall factor	5m divided by 2.5m = 2

Length of rope run out from belay	5m
Height of running belay	2.5m
Length of fall	5m
Fall factor	5m divided by 5m = 1

It can be seen from the examples above that even though more rope had been run out in the second scenario, the fall factor was half that experienced in the first.

It is important to do as much as is realistic to reduce the fall factor when climbing from a stance on a multi-pitch route. The placement of a running belay immediately upon leaving the stance will go a long way in helping to achieve this.

Figure-of-eight descender

See abseil devices.

Figure-of-eight knot

See also: double figure of eight, group abseiling, group climbing, impact force, overhand knot, screwgates, stopper knot.

This is an extremely useful knot, and can be tied in a number of ways. It is excellent for use when tying on to a harness, and in a different form can be used as a quick, safe and efficient method of tying on to anchors.

The basic figure-of-eight knot has a few uses in modern mountaineering, in particular when tying a loop in the end of the rope for attaching a screwgate, useful if climbing with novices on non-technical ground (it should be said that this method of attachment to the climbing rope is now discouraged in many quarters, as the karabiner adds another, possibly weak and vulnerable, link in the safety chain). It can also be used when securing the first end of the rigging rope when constructing a **group climbing** or **abseiling** system.

Figure-of-eight rewoven

The figure-of-eight rewoven is a very good way to tie on to a harness, and has the added advantage of making a recognizable shape once fully tied. This can be an important consideration if you are instructing or just starting out in climbing. When tying on, the loop created by the rope needs to end up about the same size as the abseil loop on the harness. If there is no abseil loop for a guide, making the rope loop a little less than fist size will be about right.

Once the figure of eight is completed, the end needs to be secured with a **stopper knot,** which can be either an **overhand knot** or a **half double fisherman's knot**. This is to ensure that there is no way that the figure of eight can loosen to any extent. The tail that is left over when the stopper knot is completed should be about 5cm (2in) long.

Basic figure-of-eight knot.

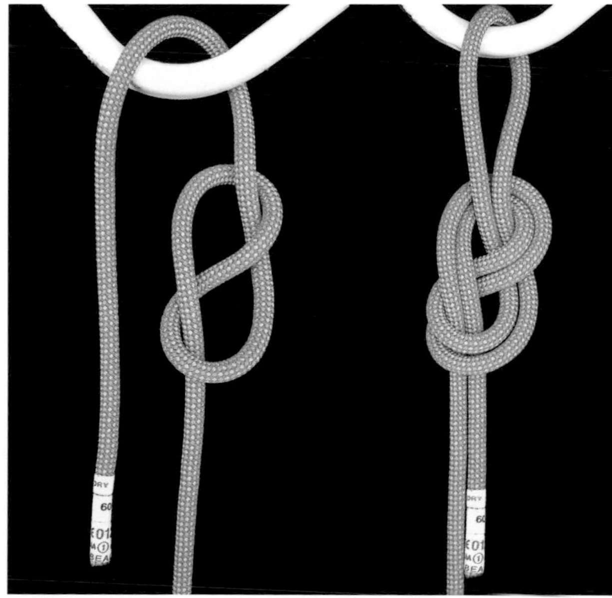

Figure-of-eight rewoven.

notes

There is a method of securing the figure-of-eight rewoven by passing the tail end back through the body of the knot. This method is not described here, as in some circumstances the entire figure of eight can undo and fail. As such, that method of locking off is to be treated with extreme caution, or avoided altogether.

Figure of eight on the bight

The figure of eight on the bight is an excellent knot, ideal for use when constructing belays, and it is relevant for all rock, snow and ice situations. One of the main advantages of this knot, apart from the ease with which it can be tied, is that upon shock loading the knot will tighten within itself, thus preventing a percentage of the force transmitted through holding a fall from reaching the anchor system.

Tying the knot is best started with a bight of around 60 cm (24in) being passed through the tie-in loop of the harness. This means that when the knot is completed the tail that is left over will be around 30cm (12in) in length, important as it ensures that the knot does not loosen and undo. Once the knot is complete, and in order for the knot to be tightened, all four sections of rope – the two from the anchor and the two in the bight – are pulled independently.

Figure of eight on the bight.

Fisherman's knot

See double fisherman's knot.

Fixed rope

Fixed ropes are often the preserve of expeditions to the high mountains, although they can be placed and utilized in almost any climbing situation. Their use may vary from the semi-permanent protection of a short section of technical ground at quite low levels, through to hundreds of metres of rope being fixed and used by expeditions in the Greater Ranges, often with the purpose of safeguarding fee-paying clients who may otherwise have little chance of success on their chosen route. Add on to this the short-term fixing of rope sometimes utilized by capsule-style expeditions, maybe just a few metres in length but providing a swift means of ascent to the previous day's high point, and it can be seen that the fixing of ropes can occur almost anywhere.

Ethical considerations

There are ethical considerations related to the fixing of ropes, and in some quarters an ascent using fixed ropes would be frowned upon and not recognized. The increase in the use of fixed ropes by commercial companies, in order to allow their clients access to the high mountains, is disliked by many traditionalists, in particular where the mountain may well have received its previous ascents alpine-style, that is, with no fixed ropes at all.

Mention should be made of semi-permanent fixed ropes, sometimes provided by local climbers on certain busy routes. These can be of up to 30mm (1in) in diameter, and are designed to be used hand-over-hand on short, awkward sections of ground.

Rope

Fixed ropes can be of any construction, although the semi-permanent ropes used during a long-duration expedition will often tend to be low-stretch ropes, available on reels of a couple of hundred metres or more. The thickness depends on a number of factors. The thinner the rope the lighter it will be, an important consideration at altitude, but also it will be less strong, harder to handle, especially with ascenders and when using thick gloves, and it will be less resistant to abrasion. This final factor is extremely important, as the rope can be completely destroyed in a very short space of time if the action of the wind is of sufficient strength to rub it across rock or ice. Also, the action of a climber using it in either ascent or descent, with the rope again rubbing against wear points, could cause cataclysmic failure. Those choosing to use ropes of around 7mm or less in diameter should take note.

Fixed-rope techniques

See also: abseil devices, Alpine butterfly, ascenders, bowline, cowstail, deadman, double figure of eight, figure of eight, fixed ropes, low-stretch ropes, pitons, snow bollard, snow stakes, stopper knot, wires.

A number of the things to be considered with fixed-rope techniques are outlined here, but often the sheer scale of the task, remembering that ropes may run for hundreds of metres up a mountain, will necessitate many different techniques being employed both for rigging and using them.

In particular on technical ground, where the weight of the climber will be frequently committed to the rope, the type used should be of a **low-stretch** construction. Not only will this avoid loss of height for the climber when it is loaded, it will also lessen the amount of rubbing across wear points due to its limited elongation.

Anchors

Main and intermediate anchors on snow can be constructed from a variety of equipment. **Snow stakes** are frequently used and are excellent for the purpose, but a **deadman** will also be

notes

There is a variety of techniques relevant when using fixed ropes. It should be remembered that the ropes are there for a reason, to bear the weight of falling climbers should a slip occur, not just as a line indicating the route. So they need to be fixed and used in a safe and systematic manner. Unfortunately, and especially in the high mountains, they are sometimes placed with haste, due to the restrictions of working at altitude. Everything should be done by those running or rigging an expedition to ensure that experienced mountaineers place the fixed ropes, and that they are checked at regular intervals for faults such as loose knots, anchors, wear and abrasion.

Fixed-rope techniques

A tied-off snow stake.

very secure. The main difference is that the snow stake can be arranged to hold the fixed rope a little higher than the surface of the snow, helping to avoid it being drifted over, whereas the deadman will be below ground level with a very low attachment point for the rope. If a snow stake is to be used, it is important that the rope will not exert too much leverage on it when in use, as it could pull out of the ground and fail. Another possibility is to use a **snow bollard,** but this should only be constructed where the loading upon it will not be excessive and repetitive, as there is a chance that the rope may pull itself through the layers over time. A sling made from wide tape may help negate this. Ice screws, covered with snow to prevent them from melting out, could also be used in some circumstances.

The diameter of the rope requires careful consideration, and although it would be tempting to choose the thinnest available, thought should be given to both the terrain across which it will be used, and the purpose to which it will be put. Those of a diameter of less than 8mm are not only difficult to handle, but may prove to be dangerous to use in conjunction with some forms of mechanical ascender, some of which cannot tolerate working on such thin ropes. The smaller the diameter of the rope, the more likely it is to be damaged by both use and erosion on the surrounding rock and ice. However, thicker ropes, of around 11mm or so, are far heavier to carry and place, especially at altitude or on technical ground, but are also far more resilient to abrasion and use. Exactly which rope is chosen depends on the terrain to be crossed and the amount of traffic that will be using it. For instance, will it be in place for just a couple of days on steep technical ground, or will it be rigged for use over two or three weeks or more, with many climbers and support staff using it for security in both ascent and descent. Altitude, types of terrain (rock, snow or ice) and techniques to be used all play a part in the final decision.

tip

Although many low-stretch ropes are white, consideration should be given to the terrain across which the rope is to be used. If it is to be rigged on a purely snowy background, give thought to the fact that a white rope that has been partially drifted over is almost impossible to locate, especially at times of poor visibility or at night. In this situation, a coloured rope would stand out better and would help for location at entry and exit points in drifts. For rock rigging, a white rope would normally be locatable under most circumstances.

Anchor distances

The distance that the rope will run depends entirely upon the nature of the ground to be protected, allied with the experience and capability of those who are to use it. Short sections of fixed rope, for instance in place to protect the retreat over a 10m (33ft) steep rock step at altitude, are relatively easy to organize. Longer runs of rope, those often used when siege tactics are employed in the Greater Ranges, take some extra consideration, in particular when deciding the distance between intermediate anchor points. If, for instance, it is decided that a 200m section of steep snowy terrain is to be fixed, it would be extremely sensible to have a series of intermediate anchors along the way, on to which a rope is secured.

Movement of people

To have a number of climbers attached to the rope that was only secured at the top point would be foolhardy in the extreme. Conversely, it would be possible to overdo the number of intermediate anchors to the extent that the time taken for a number of climbers to negotiate each point would cause problems with the speed of ascent, of descent, daylight, weather considerations and the like. In the case of a fixed rope being used on snow for a large number of people, it should be remembered that generally a number of climbers can ascend a section of rope between anchors at once, but only one can abseil. An example would be six climbers making their way up a 100m fixed rope, with intermediate anchors every 25m, on non-technical but otherwise steep snowy ground, using **ascenders** to safeguard their ascent. All six would be able to move close to each other on the way up, with only a short pause at each anchor to allow the changing over of ascender from one section of rope to the next. If we allow 5 minutes per section, with an extra 1 minute for the changeover, this gives around 24 minutes for all six climbers to reach and step away from the top of the fixed rope. In descent however, possibly at the end of a long and tiring day, only one person can abseil off each section of rope at a time, otherwise the person above them on the same section would be locked in place and unable to move due to the descending person's bodyweight. Thus, if we give each climber 4 minutes per section, including changeover time at intermediate anchors, it would take 36 minutes for all six to descend safely to the bottom. This obviously has ramifications for the number of climbers that are allowed to go up during a day, as it may not be mathematically possible for them all to descend safely before either bad weather or darkness overtakes them. This of course assumes that they will be travelling as a unit, and if this is not the case then the problem would be less. However, as expedition climbing, and that with clients in particular, often relies on large numbers of people traversing the same terrain at the same time, it is a major consideration for any leader to take on board.

Knots

A number of knots are suitable when fixing ropes. For the main and intermediate anchors a **figure-of-eight knot** is quite adequate, ensuring that the one placed on the main top anchor is well tightened and includes a **stopper knot** to prevent any chance of it becoming loosened, sometimes a problem with low-stretch rope. Although an **Alpine butterfly** may seem like a good knot to use for the intermediate anchors, a little thought will show that they will only be loaded in a downwards direction for most of the time and so it may be a little excessive. A falling climber will load both anchors

notes

The amount of rope allowed between anchor points needs to be considered. If abseiling is to be undertaken, as will often be the case, there should be sufficient play in the rope to allow the person descending to put their **abseil device** into the system and control it. However, if too much slack rope is allowed, it may use up rope length that would better have been saved to allow for a longer section to be fixed. Not having the rope attached at the bottom end of an abseil section would be advantageous, as it would prevent the build-up of twists within the rope, which could cause abseil devices to jam.

tips

If separate lengths of rope are to be used, as opposed to a single long run from a reel of 200m or more, then the joints between the ropes will be best fashioned to coincide with intermediate anchors. This dispenses with the problem of having to negotiate knots during movement up or down sections.

Fixed-rope techniques

tip

A very useful knot for the top anchor, appropriate when two points are being used for security such as when rigging anchor points on rock, is the **double figure of eight**. This has the advantage that the two loops can be adjusted independently of each other, allowing for both anchor points to be loaded equally.

associated with that particular rope section, but will end up below both of the anchors, allowing any knot to retain its correct dynamics. One advantage of the Alpine butterfly, however, is that it is relatively easy to undo once it has been loaded, a property that it shares with the **bowline**.

Wear and tear

Huge amounts of damage can be caused to fixed ropes by abrasion, both by the effects of climbers constantly loading and unloading the system (even with low-stretch ropes) and by the action of the elements, in particular the wind moving sections of the rope back and forth across sharp or abrasive objects, such as rock outcrops in the middle of snow fields. Keeping the distance between anchor points reasonably short in trouble areas will go some way to alleviate the problem, but all users of the system must be aware of any potential trouble that could arise. Careful route planning is the best method of ensuring that wear points are kept to a minimum, and it may be prudent to route rope lines a little further around obstructions in order to stay well clear of the hazard.

Fixed ropes on rock routes are less easy to protect from abrasion, and constant observation of the state of the rope is important. The way in which ropes are directed out from main anchor points should be considered, and it may be found that a little cunning re-routing of the rope can lessen the problem. For instance, if the main anchor point has been arranged at a convenient location on the rock but next to a slight bulge, there could be a chance of abrasion occurring. However, if a nearby section of rock included a placement into which, for

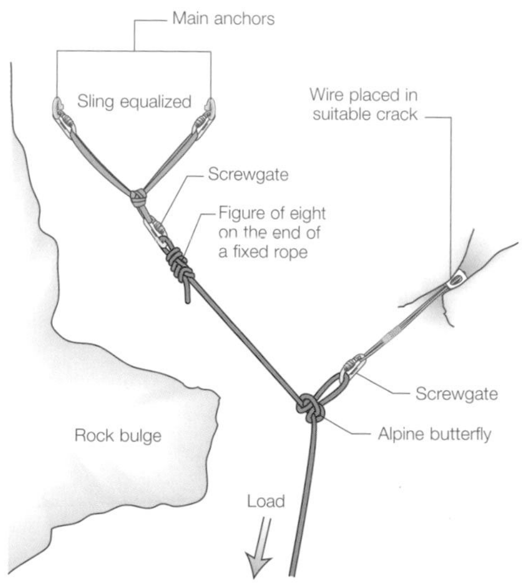

A wire providing the means of keeping a fixed rope away from a rock bulge.

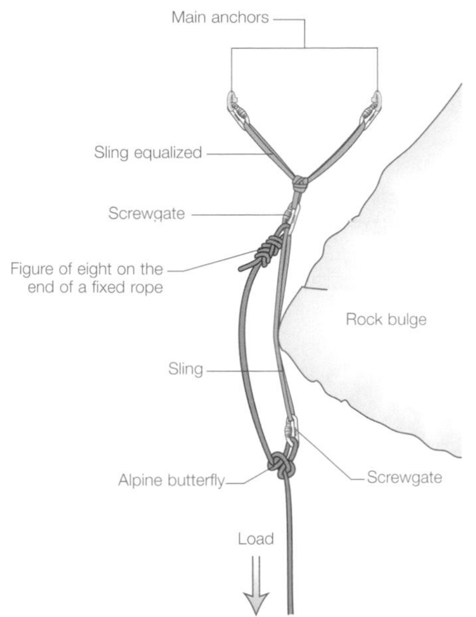

A sling providing back-up security against abrasion on rock anchor.

example, a **wire** could be located, then the rope could lead from the main anchor, across to the wire and then down into the first section of rope. This wire would then act as a directional runner, with the majority of the security being provided by the two-point main anchor. **Pitons** are useful in this situation, as when well placed they are able to withstand loading in a variety of directions.

In extreme cases, and in areas where abrasion is very likely to occur even given all of the preventative measures taken, it may be as well to double up sections of the system to provide back-up in case of failure. For instance, if the rope at an anchor point will be rubbing across a section of rock, and there is no way that it can be re-routed, a sling could be used to help safeguard it. A sling of a length longer than is needed to pass the problem is required, and one end is clipped into the anchor. The second end is clipped into an Alpine butterfly tied in the fixed rope at an appropriate distance past the obstruction. Should extreme chafing occur and the sling snap with the weight of a climber on it, there is then the back-up of the rope to prevent the whole system from falling apart.

Passing anchors

The transition from one section of rope to another is one that should be undertaken with extreme care, especially on descent where tiredness and the lateness of the hour can often result in a lapse of concentration. For most examples of ascent and descent on both rock and snow, a **cowstail** with karabiner

notes

If the fixed rope is taking all of a climber's weight, such as when using ascenders for both hands and feet, resting can take place by simply sitting back in the harness. However, the ascent can often be more tiring for a climber when their weight is not fully committed to the system, such as when using a mechanical ascender on snowy terrain. This is because their leg muscles are often taking most, if not the entire, load, and the angle of the terrain underfoot makes the calves tire out quickly. For this reason, it would be thoughtful if those rigging the rope in the first place were able to construct a ledge at each changeover point including the bottom and top, cut where the removal of the snow will not compromise the strength of the anchor. This will also go some way to providing extra safety for the person ascending or descending, as they can get their feet flat on to a ledge and so be more stable whilst occupied in the changeover procedure. Although seldom possible on steep rocky terrain, a similar provision of an appropriate ledge through sensible route planning would make the transition to the subsequent section of rope an easier task.

attached is essential in order to provide security. If using an ascender for ascent on snow, the cowstail should be clipped on to the rope and trailed up behind the climber. When they reach an intermediate anchor, the cowstail is taken off the first section of rope and clipped into the next, resting above the anchor point. The ascender can now be removed and also placed above the anchor, and the ascent continued. In this manner, the climber will be safeguarded throughout the manoeuvre. If they remove the ascender first without clipping the cowstail above the anchor and then slip, they will fall the length of the previous section of rope, not only shock-loading anchors but also possibly injuring other climbers.

When descending, using an abseil device of an appropriate type, the cowstail method is still used. This time, the cowstail karabiner is left above the intermediate anchor until the abseil device is securely placed on the rope below. The cowstail is then removed, clipped on to the appropriate section of the rope and the descent continued.

The ends of the fixed rope need to be readily identifiable, particularly the top section for descent. This is not too much of a problem on rocky terrain, as there may well be particular features that can be used to aid location. The process is far more difficult in snowy terrain, and consideration should be given to how easy location can be achieved. The piling up of snow into a pyramid is one solution, although if the weather is windy this may not last too long and be deemed not worth the effort. Marker wands, often coloured bamboo poles bought locally for the purpose, are probably the most practical solution, and the top end of a fixed rope, essential for use in descent, should be identified by more than one pole, in case it is blown or knocked over. The use of oxygen cylinders as markers on higher peaks can also be advantageous, as they are frequently brightly coloured. The top of a fixed rope is also an ideal place to make a bottle-dump, as it would be a natural stopping point for anyone load-carrying to that height.

tip

When using ascenders or descenders on rock, the cowstail may well be best clipped into the anchor to which the rope is attached for security whilst changing on to different sections of fixed rope. This ensures that the climber is kept tight into the system, often desirable on this type of terrain.

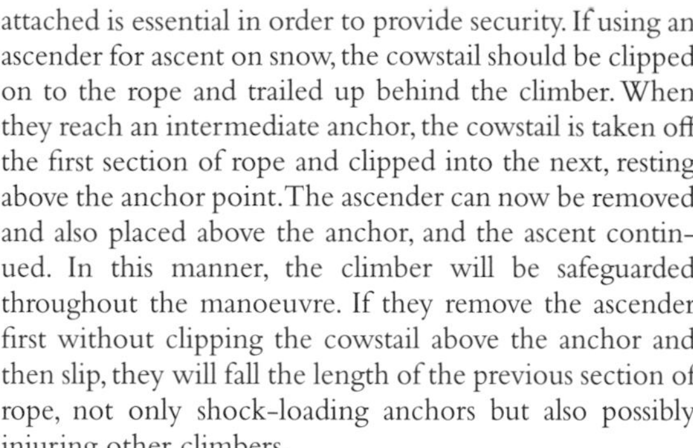

Abseiling in Chamonix.

Fixed-rope techniques

Foot brake

See boot/axe belay.

Free abseil

See also: abseiling, abseil position, abseil protection, anchor, ascender, cowstail, hoisting, klemheist, pendulum, prusik loop, sling.

A free abseil is one where the person descending has no contact with the rock or ice for the majority of the descent. Often used as an exciting end to a day's activity with a novice abseiling group, a free abseil in a multi-pitch rock or mountaineering situation poses a number of problems. The most important of these is the method by which the abseiler manages to secure themselves to an intermediate ledge or stance, which may be some considerable horizontal distance away.

If the ledge that is to be attained is of a reasonable size, and the distance that the person ends up hanging from it is not too great, self-initiating a **pendulum** will usually solve the problem. However, care should be taken that injury cannot occur, either if the ledge is not reached or that a failed attempt will result in the abseiler swinging out of control and hitting another part of the rock or ice.

It would be prudent to be prepared with a cowstail, ready to clip into any existing bolts, chain or **anchor** system. If the ledge formed part of the route of ascent, forethought may well have been applied and a loose **sling** left clipped into the anchor, with an end trailing in a convenient position ready to be caught and clipped during the descent.

Trail rope

If the line of abseil is to be some way out from the intermediate stance that has to be gained, and is down the route of ascent, the second could have rigged a trail rope when climbing up, down which they could abseil, using it to guide them in. This would be particularly appropriate, for instance, where the final section of a multi-pitch route means negotiating a particularly overhanging roof. The process for rigging and completing this for two or more people is as follows:

METHOD

- Before the final person leaves the stance to climb up, they attach a trail rope to the anchor, tying the other end on to their harness as normal.
- As they climb, they tow the rope up behind them. If it has been prepared neatly on the ledge there should be no chance of it tangling. It could be clipped into a few of the first runners to lessen the chance of its own weight pulling it off the ledge, but this should only be done where the team is happy that they will be able to unclip the trail rope from the runners during the descent with no problem.
- Once the climb is finished, the last person up abseils using the climbing rope, prepared and protected in the usual manner. The trail rope has either been tied off to the top anchor point, or is still attached to them, depending on the situation outlined below.
- Stopping at a point level with or just below the ledge (or running belay if it has to be unclipped), they use either a **klemheist** on a **prusik loop**, an **ascender** or similar means to progress along the trail rope to the ledge. If the distance is great, they will have to release themselves a little lower at intervals on the abseil rope to ensure that they are making progress in a slightly upwards direction and not trying to pull themselves down towards the stance with increasing difficulty.
- Once they are at the stance, subsequent people can descend. If the trail rope was tied to the top anchor by the first abseiler, the final person removes it and ties it to their harness.

  1 If they have tied on to the trail rope they can abseil and then be pulled or **hoisted** across by their partner using the trail rope.

  2 If the first person down took the trail rope back

with them, once they reached the ledge they should have loosely tied off the ends of the abseil rope to the anchor, allowing just enough slack for subsequent people to abseil under control. This should be sufficient to guide them down to almost the right spot, and, once again, it would be prudent to have a cowstail ready to ensure quick and secure clipping into the anchor.

Safeguarding the rope ends

The ends of the abseil rope, in any free abseil situation, should be knotted, unless there is no question that the ends of the rope reach the ground. This is often best done by tying a single overhand knot into each rope, about a metre from the end, which allows the ropes to untwist independently. If there is a chance that the abseil could end up with the person descending hanging in space at the end of the rope, a method by which a foot-loop is created may be an option. This is made by tying an overhand knot in both ropes, pulling a little slack on to one side and then tying a second overhand knot a metre further up. The slack side allows a foot to be placed in the abseil rope at the top of the final knot, giving the ability to take some of the weight off the harness.

French prusik

See also: clove hitch, Italian hitch, klemheist, prusik loop.

The French prusik is a most useful knot, and is deployed in a wide variety of both everyday and emergency systems. Its main advantage over a number of other knots tied using a **prusik loop**, such as the **klemheist**, is that it can be released whilst under load, an essential property with some hoisting and lowering systems.

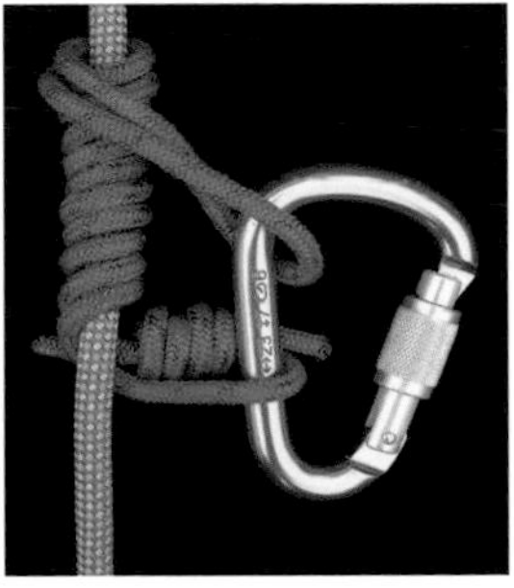

The French prusik knot.

When the French prusik is being used as part of an emergency system, it is important that it is backed up by another method, such as a **clove hitch** or tied-off **Italian hitch**, into a separate karabiner. There is a chance that the load rope could creep through the coils of the French prusik, and if it were not backed up there could be a catastrophic failure of the system.

Full body harness

See harnesses.

notes

The method of creating a foot loop in the abseil rope by tying them together should not be used if an Italian hitch is the method of descent. This would result in a high degree of twisting and tangling in the rope, possibly preventing the abseiler from even getting to the end. In this situation, tying a separate knot in each end of the rope would be sufficient.

In a group abseiling situation, if a person with an ill-defined waistline is abseiling, thought should be given to furnishing them with a chest or full body harness. This is due to the possibility of them inverting when negotiating the final section of rock before the abseil becomes free, as many people will have the tendency to lift their feet too high, possibly causing them to swing upside down should they have a high centre of gravity.

tip

When wrapping the prusik loop around the rope, ensure that the knot tied when forming the loop is excluded from any of the coils, otherwise the prusik will not grip the rope efficiently.

Glacier travel

See crevasse rescue.

Grades

The following series of tables gives a comparison of grades, both summer and winter, for a selection of countries worldwide. These are for guidance only, as there is some leeway in their interpretation, particularly on the harder routes. Home-nation mountaineering associations will be able to advise on graded lists not included here, and to clarify any local anomalies and discrepancies.

Rock-climbing grades

(see table opposite)

The UK system is two-tiered, with a letter prefix and number suffix. This system allows the climber to find out details about the severity and seriousness of a climb, taking into account factors such as protection and how sustained the route is, as well as informing them of the grade of the hardest technical move or sequence. For the purposes of the table, UK technical move grades are given in bold. Thus, on a VS climb you would expect the technical standard to be at 4c. However, it could vary up or down by a couple of places, with VS5a giving a well protected but hard route, and VS4b denoting an easier route but with fewer runners than usually expected. Longer climbs will often have an overall seriousness grade but several technical grades, showing the difficulty of moves on individual pitches, for instance a five pitch climb may be graded at VS 4b, 4c, 4c, 5a, 4b.

Bouldering grades

'V' grade	Font grade
V0-	3
V0	4
V0+	4+
V1	5
V2	5+
V3	6a, 6a+
V4	6b,6b+
V5	6c, 6c+
V6	7a
V7	7a+
V8	7b
V8+	7b+
V9	7c
V10	7c+
V11	8a
V12	8a+
V13	8b
V14	8b+
V15	8c

Aid climbing grades

Grade	Description
A0	Equipment is already in place and used with ease.
A1	Relevant equipment is easy to place, and will provide some security in the event of a fall. Progress is often made simply by pulling on the placement.
A2	Awkward placing of some aid equipment. Some placements may be of questionable strength.
A3	Difficult aid climbing, taking time to place equipment. Poor placements likely, resulting in some gear being stripped out in the event of a fall.
A4	Very difficult placement of gear, which will usually only hold bodyweight. The consequences of a fall are severe.
A5	Extreme aiding, with placements only just holding bodyweight and little chance of realistic protection along the pitch. A fall may result in the gear on the entire pitch stripping out.

UK SERIOUSNESS	UK TECHNICAL	FRENCH/ SPORT	RUSSIA	NORWAY	USA	UIAA	SOUTH AFRICA	POLAND	AUSTRALIA
Moderate			II	1	5.1, 5.2	I, II			4, 5
Difficult	**3a**	2	III+	1, 2	5.3, 5.4	II		I	5, 6
Very Difficult	3a, **3b**	2	IV–	1, 2	5.4	II+		I	6, 7, 8
Hard Very Difficult	3b, **3c**	2+	IV	2, 3	5.4, 5.5	III–		II	8, 9
Mild Severe	3c, **4a**	3	IV, IV+	3	5.5, 5.6	III		II, III	9, 10, 11
Severe	**4a**, 4b	3+	IV+	3, 4–	5.6	III+, IV–	13	IV	11, 12
Hard Severe	4a, **4b**, 4c	3+, 4	IV+	4	5.7	IV–	14	V–	12, 13
Mild Very Severe	**4b**, 4c	4	V–	4	5.7	IV, IV+	14, 15	V–, V	13, 14
Very Severe	4b, **4c**, 5a	4, 4+	V–	4+	5.7, 5.8	IV+	15, 16	V	14, 15
Hard Very Severe	**5a**, 5b	5, 5+	V	5–	5.9	V–, V, V+	17, 18	V+	15, 16, 17
E1	5a, **5b**, 5c	5+, 6a	V	5, 5+	5.10a, 5.10b	VI–, VI	19	VI	17, 18, 19
E2	5b, **5c**, 6a	6a+, 6b	V+	6–, 6	5.10c. 5.10d	VI+, VII–	20, 21	VI+	19, 20, 21
E3	5c, **6a**, 6b	6b, 6b+	V+	6+, 7–	5.10d, 5.11a	VII–, VII	22, 23	VI.1+	21, 22
E4	**6b**, 6c	6c, 6c+, 7a	VI–	7	5.11b, 5.11c, 5.11d	VII+, VIII–	24, 25	V .2	22, 23
E5	6b, **6c**	7a, 7a+, 7b	VI	7+	5.11d, 5.12a, 5.12b	VIII, VIII+	26, 27	VI.3	23, 24, 25
E6	6c, 7a	7b+, 7c, 7c+	VI+	8–, 8	5.12c, 5.12d, 5.13a	IX–, IX	27, 28	VI 3+, VI.4	25, 26, 27
E7	6c, 7a, 7b	8a, 8a+	VI+	8+, 9–	5.13b, 5.13c	IX–, X	29, 30, 31	VI.5, VI.5+	27, 28, 29, 30
E8	6c, 7a, 7b	8b, 8b+	VII	9	5.13d, 5.14a	X, X+	32, 33	VI.6, VI.6+	29, 30, 31
E9	7a, 7b, 8a	8c, 8c+		9+	5.14a, 5.14b	XI–, XI	33, 34	VI.7	31, 32
E10	7b, 8a	9a			5.14c, 5.14d	X1+, XII			32, 33

Grades

The table on p. 106 displays the generally accepted categories for aid climbing, but variations do exist. The addition of a + sign may be used to denote variations between grades, a popular format in the USA. The letter 'C' may occasionally be used in place of 'A' to represent a 'clean' ascent, where no intrusive marking or damaging of the rock will occur, such as when using SLCDs instead of pitons.

European Alpine grades

The ED grade is open-ended, and categorized as ED1, ED2 etc, to cope with the rise in climbing standards and equipment. Some guidebooks may use the ABO grade at the very top end, standing for 'Abominablement difficile', reserved for routes of the most extreme difficulty and seriousness.

Grade	Description
F (Facile – easy)	A straightforward climb, maybe with a simple glacier approach. The route if snow and ice, will be consistently of an easy angle. Any rock climbing will be low-grade scrambling.
PD (Peu difficile – not very hard)	Possibly comprising an awkward glacier approach or retreat, routes with tricky scrambling or snow and ice slopes of 35–45 degrees. The length of the route and the altitude may be more than that encountered at F.
AD (Assez difficile – fairly hard)	Snow and ice slopes of up to 55 degrees, with short sections of grade III rock possible.
D (Difficile – hard)	Snow and ice slopes up to 70 degrees and rock climbing in the region of IV and V.
TD (Très difficile – very hard)	Serious routes, with snow and ice of up to 80 degrees, rock in the region of V to VI, possibly including aid moves. The objective danger may be high.
ED (Extrêmement difficile – extremely hard)	Very hard and serious routes, displaying 90-degree snow and ice, rock of grade VI to VII, aid pitches and high objective danger.

Alaska grades

The Alaska system is cumulative, where a grade, for instance AK3, will include all the elements of those coming before it, in this case AK1 and AK2. It takes into account overall seriousness, including factors such as avalanche hazards, cornicing, the poor weather often found in the region, altitude and extreme cold. Thus, a route with few technical sections may in fact get a high grade if the team has to move fast whilst making constant snow-structure evaluations and needing to cope with cornice hazards.

Grade	Description
AK1	No technical difficulties, with simple glacier crossings.
AK2	No major technical difficulties, but may include narrow ridges, altitude and accompanying weather-related problems.
AK3	Big routes with steep ground requiring technical climbing and possibly the passage of corniced ridges.
AK4	Difficult, sustained climbing.
AK5	Difficult, involved sustained technical climbing and bivouacking.
AK6	Very hard, with long distances over technical ground and little option for retreat.

North American and European Ice Climbing grades

This two-part system consists of Roman numerals giving the seriousness of the route (encompassing the length of approach, objective danger and duration of the climb), and numbers to denote the technical difficulty (graded for the hardest pitch). These two scales are shown in separate tables below. The first table gives the prefix to a grade, denoting the type of climbing that is being described.

Grade	Description
WI	Water ice.
AI	Alpine ice, often formed from a metamorphosed snow base.
M	Mixed ground, indicating that both rock and ice are encountered.

Seriousness

Grade	Description
I	A route only taking a couple of hours, with non-technical climbing and an easy descent.
II	A route with an easy approach and climbing of moderate technical standard. Time for completion in the region of three to four hours. Easy descent, often by abseil.
III	A route taking half a day, involving a longer approach, more intricate descent and low-altitude multi-pitch climbing. There may be a rock fall or avalanche hazard.
IV	A climb at altitude or in a remote area, taking most of the day to complete. Multi-pitch in nature, objective hazards may be high and descents complicated.
V	A route that takes at least a day to complete, often only attainable by a fast and competent party. Objective dangers are likely to be high and the climb long and technical, often at altitude. Descents may involve multiple abseils.
VI	Taking over a day to complete, this grade contains climbs of a high technical severity in alpine-like settings with sustained technical difficulties and serious rock fall, avalanche, crevasse and extreme weather possibilities. Only the most technically competent, and physically fit parties are likely to succeed.
VII	The hardest and most serious of climbs, involving great personal risk and the need for high technical, physical and mental competence. Only attainable by the few.

Technical difficulty

Grade	Description
1	Water ice of up to 50 degrees or a long snow slope requiring basic skills.
2	Water ice, including sections of up to 70 degrees, including good protection and belay opportunities.
3	Sustained water ice climbing at between 70 and 80 degrees, possibly with short steeper sections followed by a rest. Protection is still good.
4	Sustained climbing on 75- to 85-degree ice, or vertical sections of around 25m (82ft) with periodic rests. Protection is reasonable.
5	Sustained multi-pitch ice climbing on vertical terrain, giving little or no chance of rest. Generally good or reasonable quality ice.
6	Serious multi-pitch routes with sustained difficulties over long distances on vertical ground. Protection can be hard to place due to the ice being poor in places. Mixed ground may be encountered.
7	Poor quality, thin, vertical, or overhanging ice smears, with poor or purely psychological protection. Very technical climbing needed to produce upward movement, including sections of extreme mixed ground. High possibility of ice failure on icicles or chandeliers.
8	The most extreme ice routes possible, involving all the above factors and more.

The scale is often left open-ended for mixed routes.

The above system is designed to be consistent across the different terrain and surfaces. For instance, WI6 should be the same difficulty as M6, which will be the same as AI6. On routes with a large variation of terrain, various prefixes and suffixes may be used, for instance M5, AI3. Also, routes that may display a tendency to fall down, such as fragile chandelier ice, can be given an X rating,

and those that have a particularly committing run-out can be labelled with an R. This then allows a lot of information to be given about any route, although the result may look like a scientific calculation: VI/AI3, WI5, RX.

In some areas, where the climbing is in a non-remote setting such as a roadside icefall, just the technical grading may be applied, as there would be no serious commitment such as a long approach or avalanche hazard.

Russian Alpine grades

These use a system different to that laid out in the rock climbing grade comparison table, and has parallels with the UIAA system which is noted here using Roman numerals.

Grade	Description
1B	Roped climbing of a low technical nature.
2A	Several pitches of moderate roped climbing.
2B	Multi-pitch routes at around UIAA II+ and III standard.
3A	Up to two pitches of grade III climbs, making up a section of a multi-pitch route.
3B	A long route, typically taking a day to complete, which includes up to two pitches of III+ or IV climbing.
4A	IV+ climbing on a multi-pitch route that will take a day to complete.
4B	A route with a number of pitches at IV+ and up to V+.
5A	Grade V climbing routes that may take one, two or three days to climb.
5B	Routes of 48 hours length encompassing ground at grade VI+ level.
6A	Long routes taking two or more days to complete, with sustained sections at grade VI or VII
6B	Extremely long, sustained and difficult routes, with climbing at VII and VIII or harder.

Mixed grades

These are often used to categorize dry-tooling climbs, where ice may or may not be encountered.

Grade	Description
M1–M3	Low-angled, easy routes with little technical skill required.
M4	Ground up to vertical, requiring technique to progress.
M5	Sustained vertical dry tooling.
M6	Ground that may be overhanging for some of its length, necessitating good technique.
M7	Difficult, overhanging ground, involving hard climbing of up to 10 metres in length.
M8	Ground presenting overhangs verging on the horizontal, requiring powerful and technical tool technique. May include crux longer than those encountered on M7 ground.
M9	Sustained vertical or overhanging ground with difficult tool placements, also ground with roofs of 4–6 months.
M10	Horizontal ground of 10 metres or more, or 30 metres of overhanging ground providing no opportunity for rests during a series of extremely powerful moves.
M11	Extreme climbing of 40 or 50 metres on overhanging ground or across 15 metres of roof.
M12	Extreme climbing, encompassing all within the M11 grade and more, as well as questionable placements.

Scottish winter grades

This is a two-tier system, where the Roman numerals denote the seriousness and difficulty of the climb and the number denotes the technical grade of the hardest section of the route. The two tables below list the features of each element.

Seriousness

Grade	Description
I	Easy ridges and snow gullies of around 45 degrees. Cornices may be present.
II	Routes with short sections of difficult ground, either ice pitches or rock steps, followed by good resting areas. Ridge climbs would equate to easy summer scrambles.
III	Routes that give a more sustained outing than at grade II, with mixed routes equating to around 'Moderate' summer standard.
IV	Completion of a route involves the climbing of long sections of steep ice of up to 70 degrees, or shorter sections of vertical ground. Mixed routes, of 'Difficult' or 'Severe' summer standard will need good axe technique, including technical torquing, to overcome them.
V	Sustained routes with ice of 70 degrees or more for long distances as well as vertical ground. Mixed routes will be very hard, up to around summer 'Very Severe' standard.
VI	Ice pitches will be vertical for quite some distance, and the ice often of dubious quality. Mixed routes will be technical summer 'Very Severe' in standard.
VII	Extremely hard routes, offering technical moves on overhanging sections or very thin ground and mixed routes of a very highly technical nature.
VIII	Harder than grade VII, very few climbers will attempt this grade and fewer will succeed.

Difficulty

Grade	Description
1	Easy angled snow and ice with no technical difficulty.
2	Steeper ground than that found at grade I but generally with excellent quality ice and good protection.
3	Ice of up to 60 degrees, but still giving good opportunity for sound runners and belays.
4	Ice of up to 70 degrees, still of good quality.
5	80 degree ice, with less chance of resting than before. Ice quality may not be particularly good and protection tricky to place.
6	90 degree ice, giving tiring technical climbing and with protection being difficult to place securely.
7	Very steep, sustained and poor-quality ice, with protection opportunities few and far between.
8	Extreme climbing, at the very highest standard.

This system allows the description of a route to be reasonably precise, given the constraints of the winter environment. Grades such as VI5 or VI6 work in a similar fashion to summer UK grades, where some flexibility is attainable within the system to describe the routes that may have the same seriousness but offer separate degrees of difficulty.

Ground anchors

See also: ABC, dynamic rope, impact force, slings.

Ground anchors are designed to be used on single pitch climbs, to secure the belayer and save them from an upward and inwards pull in the event of them having to hold a fall. On multi-pitch climbs, the belayer will normally be anchored as a matter of course, but if an intermediate stance is on a particularly large ledge and an anchor system has not been constructed, it may be sensible to consider doing so here as well.

Tests have shown that the movement of the belayer for 1m before the ground anchor takes the load is optimum for reduction in the **impact forces** that a fall will create. However, in most situations the belayer will secure themselves somewhat more tightly on to the anchor, and in this case it is important that the **dynamic** properties of the rope are allowed to come into effect if a fall should occur. The use of **slings** as the only means of connection is to be discouraged, as they are generally of a non-dynamic nature and as such transmit a huge proportion of the force of a falling climber through to the anchor.

The considerations for ground anchors are as follows:

METHOD

- Is one needed? At either end of the scale, climbs with a large amount of running belays or ones with minimal and poor runners may make the use of ground anchors redundant. On a climb with many runners, especially if the belayer is of a heavier weight than the climber, the team may be happy using just the mass of the belayer to keep the team safe. On a route with minimal and poor runners, the fact that the belayer is not secured may indeed make the route safer for the leader, as the lifting of the belayer when tension comes on to the belay device will do much to reduce the loading on critical placements.
- Other than the cases above, there may well be a requirement for the belayer to be secured. Ideally a rope from behind, considering the **ABC** of climbing, would be of most benefit, and a convenient boulder, tree root, bolt or linked ice screws would make a suitable attachment point.
- If there are no attachment points behind the belayer, one may be arranged low down at the foot of the climb, with the anchor rope coming up to the belayer. Although not directly in line, this will do much to stop them being lifted up in the event of a fall.
- If neither behind nor low down in front is practicable, the next preferable would be a point at around head height. In the event of the leader falling, the belayer can sit their weight back on to the system and use their entire bodyweight to their advantage.
- The security of the belayer should be considered if the ground underfoot is not even. It is not unheard of for a belayer to slip at the foot of a climb and pull their leader off. For this reason, an anchor at the height mentioned above would be a sensible precaution against accidents.

Group abseiling

See also: abseil device, dynamic rope, figure-of-eight knot, HMS karabiners, Italian hitch – locking off, low-stretch rope, overhand knot, slings, stopper knot.

Group abseiling is one of the commonest activities involving rope work. Unlike **group climbing,** which is normally only practised on cliffs or artificial climbing structures, abseiling can take place on all of these, as well as from bridges, buildings, cranes, in fact from almost anywhere that an anchor can be found and people safely transported to the top. For the comfort of the abseiler, it is worth rigging the system with as high an anchor point as possible, so that when they lean back ready to take their first steps they are already supported by the ropes. Constructing a system that has been rigged parallel with the ground and expecting a novice, or even experienced abseiler to lean back on it could cause problems, as controlled balance when leaving the stance can be difficult to achieve.

For the purposes of the following, it will be assumed that the system will be set up on a cliff, using three anchor points. Two **low-stretch** rigging ropes will be used, along with a **dynamic** one for the safety rope. A number of **slings** and **HMS karabiners** will also be required, along with an abseil device, possibly a figure-of-eight descender.

METHOD – Basic rigging

- Select the anchors and equip them with screwgate karabiners.
- Using one of the rigging ropes, tie a **figure of eight** on the end and clip it into the first anchor.
- Trail the rope towards the edge of the cliff, then back to the second anchor and clip it in. Repeat the process for the third anchor, laying the second trailed loop on top of the first. Once the third anchor is clipped bring the rest of the rope forwards to the loops as well, creating a third loop and laying the spare rope off to one side.
- The rope will now be tied together with an **overhand knot** to create the central point from which the abseil and safety ropes are controlled. Holding the three loops together, pull one of them out to make it longer than the others by 20–30cm (8–12in). Tie the loops together, pulling the various strands tight once completed.
- The position of this central point is important, as it must be close enough to the edge of the crag for the operator to be able to reach it should the need arise, but far enough away from the edge so that the person abseiling can lean back and fully load the system before being too close to the edge. As a guide, the central loop will probably work best when situated approximately 2m (6ft) back from the edge, once the knot has been tied, but every situation and rig will be different.

This is the basic rigging of the central point completed. The next part will be to rig the abseil rope.

tips

If a figure-of-eight descender is being used, the abseil rope could be pushed upwards and lock itself off with a lark's foot at the top of it. This may occur if the device is dragged down over an edge. However, if the rope is threaded on to the figure of eight by first pushing the loop down through the big hole and then up over the smaller one, this will usually get rid of the problem.

notes

Low-stretch rigging ropes are an important part of the set-up of an abseil system. Although dynamic ropes could be used, they present a number of problems. Firstly, they tend to stretch by design, which means that a nervous abseiler has to commit all of their weight to the system before the stretch is negated, which may do little for their confidence. Secondly, the stretch will cause parts of the system to rub on the rock and may damage the rope. Thirdly, the rubbing of the rope on the rock may well cause undesirable erosion. This final point is important, and the provision of rope protectors or small sections of carpet over which the rope can run will help.

Group abseiling

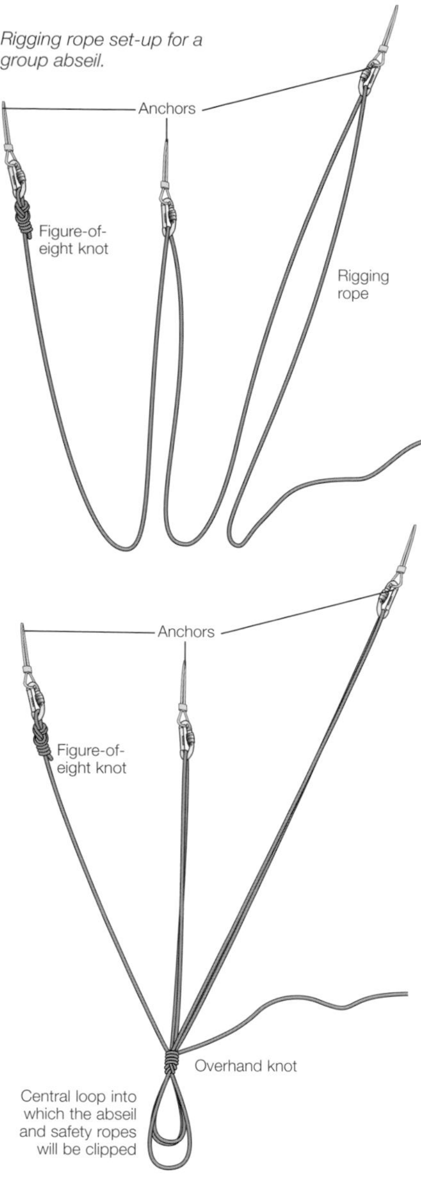

Rigging rope set-up for a group abseil.

notes

There should be a check before the abseiler descends that there are no loose bits of hair, clothing or helmet straps that could be caught in the abseil device.

One length of rope

It should have been decided by now whether to use either one or two lengths of rope for the participants to abseil on. Most times it will be a single thickness, but if there are a lot of larger group members or the friction needs to be increased due to the type of abseil device that is being used, two lengths would be better. The following assumes one rope will be used.

METHOD – Rigging the abseil rope

- Using the second low-stretch rope, hang the end over the edge of the cliff until it is about a metre above the ground. This will be the correct length, as it will stretch slightly when used. To have too much rope on the ground will cause problems, as kinks can occur that may jam the system up, or at the very least make the removal of the abseil device difficult for a novice to achieve.
- Keeping the rope in that position (lightly trapping it under a foot will help), clip it into the two shorter loops on the central point with an HMS karabiner, using an **Italian hitch**. Ensure that the HMS is clipped into the system with the gate opening uppermost and the wide end with the Italian on. Now tie off the Italian hitch, making sure that at least 30cm (12in) of loop is left over once it is done.
- The spare abseil rope should be neatly flaked into a pile close to the rig.

Once the abseil rope has been set up, the next step is the safety rope for the abseiler. This is best done with a dynamic rope, as it has better knotting abilities than a rigging rope and handles a lot better.

METHOD – Setting up the safety rope

- Uncoil the dynamic rope close to, but out of the way of, the rig. The bottom end of the rope can be clipped into one of the anchor points if there is any chance that its own weight will cause it to run away over the edge of the cliff.
- The top end of the rope needs to have a figure of eight tied into it, ensuring that the tail, once the stopper knot has been tied, is very short and thus has little chance of catching in the abseil device.

This should then be equipped with a screwgate karabiner.

- This section of rope now needs to be clipped on to the central point with an HMS karabiner and an Italian hitch on the longer of the loops. The reason for this is, should the system be loaded and the abseil and safety karabiners be side by side, they would be very likely to jam together and make further working of the system very difficult. By extending the Italian hitch it can now operate independently and, if loaded, will not jam up against anything.

Safety of the supervisor

The safety of the supervisor also needs to be considered. Although it is being placed third in the list here, there should be a constant evaluation of the safety of anyone involved in rigging the system, and if it is felt that their safety may be compromised at any point they must secure themselves before continuing. There are a number of choices. The two most common are:

- A cowstail. The use of a cowstail is a very efficient way of running the session, as it can be promptly unclipped if the need arises. It can be left on the harness to be used as a personal safety when rigging and de-rigging, and can be adjusted with an overhand knot in order to give the correct length for the supervisor to be near the edge but still safe. The best attachment on the rig will be into one of the loops of the central point, which will then give the security of all three anchors. If the solidity of the anchors is beyond question, it could be clipped on to one of the ropes running from the anchor to the central point. The advantage of this is that it allows the supervisor to move away from the edge whilst still being protected, as the karabiner will slide up the rigging rope as far as it is allowed.
- The back end of the rigging rope used on the anchors can also be used as the safety for the supervisor. Where the unused section comes out of the back of the overhand knot that created the central loop, a clove hitch can be tied which is clipped into an HMS karabiner on their abseil loop. This means that they are secured by all three anchors, are able to adjust the length of the safety to suit, and have the ability to walk a similar distance behind the rig if need be.

tips

A very common cause of problems with abseiling sessions is that, even despite proper preparation, wispy strands of hair can get caught in the abseil device. This will not usually cause it to jam, but will cause great pain to the abseiler who will generally refuse to descend further. Having a number of cheap hair bands clipped on to the back of the supervisor's harness, ready to be handed out if necessary, is a good way to avoid this problem arising.

notes

Group safety has to be paramount, and great care should be taken with group management at the top of the cliff. The temptation for group members to rush forward to the edge in order to watch their friend abseiling should be discouraged, and a forward limit line set up.

notes

To help reduce the chance of anything catching in the abseil device, it makes sense to extend it away from the body. This can be achieved by attaching a 60cm (24in) sling between the harness and the abseil device. If a figure-of-eight device is being used, the sling can be threaded through the smaller eye before being connected to the harness, which has the positive effect of removing a karabiner from the system. This method also gives the abseiler a focal point for placing their non-controlling hand, which can now grasp the extension sling instead of the abseil rope itself.

Group activities – problem solving

See also: abseil protection, belay device – locking off, bottom rope systems, counter-balance abseil, dead rope, escaping the system, French prusik, HMS karabiner, Italian hitch, live rope, screwgates – jammed, top rope systems, Y-hang.

Group activities are often areas where problems occur. This is very often due to a lack of preparation or briefing given by the person running the session. Many potential problems can be avoided at the early stages by proper planning and by informing the participants exactly what is required of them. The nature of the route to be climbed or abseiled will also have a bearing on possible problems occurring, for to have nervous novices presented with a ledge half way up a route that is causing them problems will often entail them refusing to leave its security, giving the instructor no option but to resort to a technical solution.

A number of problems are covered under their own headings and reference should be made to the relevant sections including **escaping the system**, **screwgates – jammed**, **Y-hang** and **abseil protection**. However, there are a few procedures that are peculiar to group sessions.

Problem 1

For the first scenario, a novice climber is stuck on a ledge on a short single-pitch route and is refusing to be lowered, despite the best coaxing efforts of the instructor and his companions. However, he has indicated that he would be willing to climb to the top. This would mean, though, that he would be in a lead situation, something to be avoided at all costs when dealing with novices. The instructor is belaying.

METHOD

- The instructor needs to escape the system.
- Having briefed those left on the ground as to what is to follow, they make their way to the top of the crag and regain eye contact with the stranded person.
- Selecting an anchor, the instructor clips in an HMS karabiner and puts an **Italian hitch** on to it. The rope used could either be a spare, an end of the rigging rope or one borrowed temporarily from a nearby group.
- The end of this rope has a figure of eight tied in it and a screwgate karabiner clipped on.
- The end of the rope is passed down to the stuck climber, who clips it on to their **abseil loop**.
- The belayer on the ground at the bottom of the climb can now undo the belay device and take it off the rope if necessary.
- The climber can now continue over the top, belayed from above by the Italian hitch.

notes

Great care should be taken by the instructor to ensure that the correct part of the harness has been clipped, and if there is any question at all then they must abseil to the climber to check. It would be all too easy for a nervous novice to fail to clip the karabiner to the correct point.

Problem 2

Should it not be possible for the climber to climb up (relevant for either bottom or top rope session), or perhaps if they are an abseiler who has taken to a ledge and refuses to move, then the instructor may need to go down to them and perform a 'crag-snatch'. It should be said that this manoeuvre is not without its problems, not least the time taken to achieve it as well as the psychological effect on the marooned person. However, with prior practice it can be performed with reasonable slickness. For the following scenario, it is assumed that a climber has taken to a ledge

and refuses to move. The belayer has already escaped the system and is at the top of the route.

METHOD

- ➲ A spare rope is dropped down the route. This could be part of the rigging rope, a spare rope or one borrowed from another party.
- ➲ The instructor descends to the stranded person using the Y-hang set up.
- ➲ The instructor attaches them to the Y-hang sling, connecting it to their abseil loop.
- ➲ The original climbing rope can be released. This can either be done by untying the knot at the climber's harness, or having the people on the ground undo the belay system.
- ➲ The instructor then positions the climber next to them, with their weight committed to the abseil rope, and descends.

tip

When abseiling to a person, always stop a little above the intended point. This allows for slow adjustment of height, as it is far easier to inch down an abseil rope than it is to go too far and have to inch back up.

notes

It should be stressed that this technique is very difficult to perform on all but the easiest of climbs, although it is ideally suited to a slab-type route. Also, if the person stranded is a lot smaller than the instructor, as may be the case when working with children, the technique would be uncomfortable and possibly dangerous for them. This is because they would be expected to counter-balance the instructor should the latter slip whilst making their way up, potentially pulling the smaller person up and off their perch.

Problem 3

If the problem occurs on an easy climb, such as on a slab, it may be possible for the instructor to go up to the person from below to help them down. Although this could be done by soloing, the safety of the instructor is paramount so a simple system can be set up.

METHOD

- ➲ The belay device is locked off, either conventionally or by clipping the **dead rope** to another party member.
- ➲ A **French prusik** is placed on the **live rope** directly above the belay device, with its securing karabiner being clipped in to the karabiner connecting the device to the instructor.
- ➲ The belay device is unlocked.
- ➲ The instructor makes their way up the route, pulling the slack though the belay device as they go. Should they need to stop, the French prusik will ride a short distance up the rope and grip it. Care should be taken to not introduce excessive slack into the climbing rope.
- ➲ When they arrive at the stranded climber, they connect them to their abseil loop with a short sling, allowing both to abseil to the ground in a manner similar to that for a **counter-balance abseil**.

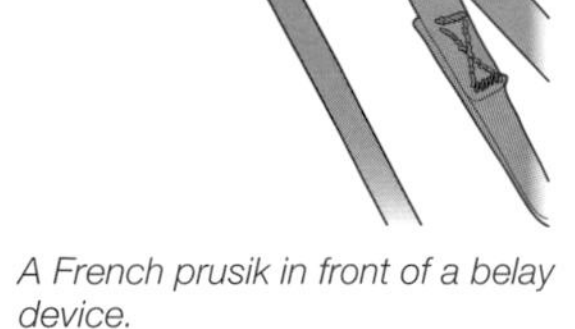

A French prusik in front of a belay device.

tip

As with any use of the French prusik, care should be taken to ensure that it does not start to run otherwise it could burn through or strip the climbing rope. It would be a good idea to have someone on the ground holding on to the dead end of the climbing rope as the ascent progresses, so that they can back up the instructor in the event of a slip. Pulling down on the dead rope will cause the belay device to lock off.

Group climbing

See also: bottom roping, top roping.

There are two general methods to choose from when working with a group. These are **'top roping'** and **'bottom roping'**. The main difference between them is the positioning of the belayer. Exactly as the name implies, for top roping the belayer is at the top of the climb, and for bottom roping they are at the bottom. The reasons for choosing either of the methods when deciding how to run a session are many and varied, depending upon factors such as group ability, type of crag, number of participants in the group, and objectives for the day. Opposite is a comparative table, listing a number of the pros and cons of both top and bottom roping. The final decision should be made not just on the ease with which any given system can be set up and controlled, but by the aspirations of the group members themselves.

Limestone climbing at Cala Magraner, Mallorca.

TOP ROPING		BOTTOM ROPING	
Pros	**Cons**	**Pros**	**Cons**
Quick to rig.	Usually difficult for the belayer to see all of the moves on the climb, so unable to offer advice.	Given the group members' ability to belay, the surpervisor can move around freely and manage more than one rope at a time.	The rigging of the system can be time-consuming.
Allows the climber to complete the route and gain a feeling of achievement.	Communication needs to be clear and effective, otherwise confusion can be caused.	A number of participants can be occupied with various tasks at one time.	The supervisor is away from his or her group whilst rigging the system.
Good for those seeking a progression and who wish to learn to climb for themselves.	A novice climber may feel that they have failed if they do not reach the top of the cliff.	Those seeking a progression can learn to belay with a variety of techniques.	Participants do not get to complete a climb from bottom to top.
If nervous the climber is approaching the belayer who can offer encouragement, and as such they receive a psychological boost.	Group management at the top of the cliff requires close attention, may be difficult when belaying.	Group management is eased by the supervisor being with his or her group all the time.	Bottom roping in isolation may lead participants to think that it is the way to climb.
Can allow those seeking a progression to belay each other under supervision.	Often only one person is occupied at any one time.	The supervisor can see all of the moves and offer encouragement and verbal assistance when necessary.	Care must be taken that the route chosen is not needed by other climbers.
	Group management becomes an issue, as some members will be at the top of the crag whilst others remain below.	Concerns over cliff-top group safety are not an issue.	If nervous, participants may be more anxious when some distance above the ground, away from other people.
	Difficult to check the method by which the climber is attached to the rope.	There is less of a feeling of failure should the climber not achieve the top.	Climber may refuse to be lowered back to the ground.
	Top roping can accelerate environmental damage, both at the cliff top and on descent paths.	Environmental damage to the top of the cliff and descent routes is minimized.	
	The descent of the group needs to be managed.	The attachment of the climber to the rope can be checked easily.	

HMS karabiner

See also: belay devices, double rope techniques, Italian hitch.

An HMS karabiner can be recognized by its wide shape, and as such it is sometimes referred to as a 'pear-shape' karabiner. Its design, which does away with the sharp angles at both ends of the back bar that are characteristic of 'D'-shape karabiners, allows it to be used effectively in systems that require the use of an **Italian hitch** friction knot. The hitch is able to slip easily through the wide end of the karabiner without hindrance from the tighter angle of the D-shape, which may cause the knot to jam.

An HMS karabiner is also very good for use with a **belay device**, as it allows for a smooth taking-in and paying-out action, especially when using **doubled ropes**.

Although often larger in physical size than D-shape karabiners, an HMS will most often have a lower strength rating as the load is applied to the body of the karabiner some distance from the back bar.

Hangers

See bolts.

Hanging hoist

notes

It is obviously important to have the rescue method prepared before hoisting the victim, as they could not be held suspended for a long period of time. However, it will be possible to hold someone long enough to clip them into a second rope or on to a Y-hang. Their own rope end needs to be dispensed with in some manner and this would most likely be achieved by untying it. Cutting through their rope with a knife is also an answer, being aware as to how easily rope under tension cuts and cutting away from the rescuer's own rope. Any initial attachment to the victim must be through their abseil loop, as the rope tie-in loop will cease to exist at the end of the procedure.

See also: abseil loop, klemheist, screwgate, Y-hang.

The hanging hoist is a technique that allows a person suspended on the end of a rope to be removed from it, either on to another rope or, more likely, on to a **Y-hang** or similar abseil system.

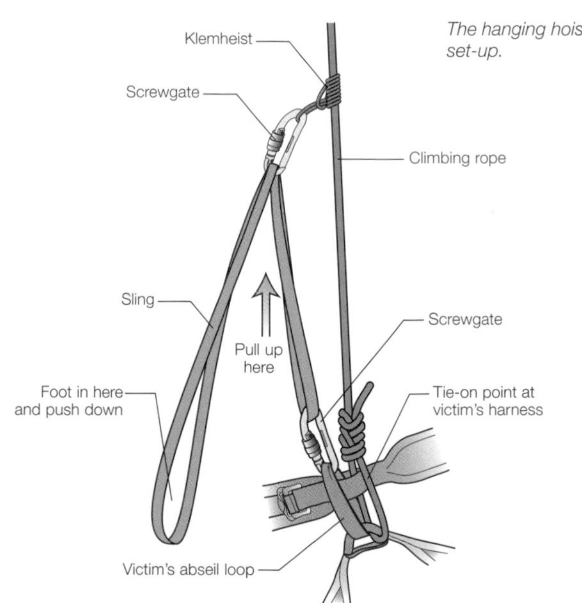

The hanging hoist set-up.

METHOD

- The rescuer abseils in an appropriate manner to the stuck climber. They should stop approximately a metre above them, as to descend too far would render the system useless.
- A **klemheist** is placed on the climber's rope, along with a **screwgate** karabiner.
- A 120cm (48in) or other suitable length sling is clipped into the climber's **abseil loop**, and run up through the screwgate on the klemheist.
- The foot of the rescuer is placed in the sling. Pushing down with the foot whilst at the same time pulling up on the climber's harness will allow their weight to be taken off the end of the climbing rope.

Harnesses

A good harness is fundamental in providing comfort and safety to a climber in the event of a fall. It should be chosen with a specific task in mind, and climbers who spend time out in summer, winter and Greater Ranges may well have a harness for each particular discipline.

Modern harnesses can be categorized into two main types: a sit-harness and a full-body harness. The latter has fallen out of favour in recent years, with the feeling that its extra weight and bulk makes it not worth persevering with. This is an unfortunate trend, as a full body harness is excellent at providing support

FEATURE	FUNCTION
Adjustable or fixed-size leg loops	Adjustable leg loops are useful when the harness has to be put on over many layers of clothing, or when wearing crampons.
Abseil loop at front	For all but a few very specific uses, a sewn abseil loop at the front of the harness is essential. It is the fundamental attachment point for many procedures, from personal abseiling through to complicated rescue techniques.
Padding throughout	Padding may be required for harnesses used for some higher-grade rock routes, or for rock climbs that will take some considerable time to complete and where hanging belays will be taken. Padding is often seen as a hindrance for expedition climbing, as it is bulky, gets in the way and could have a tendency to freeze up.
Single or double buckle on waist belt	Harnesses that have adjustable leg loops may well also come with two buckles on the waist belt. These allow a lot of flexibility when fitting the harness over bulky clothing, and let the user accurately adjust the position of the centre point to suit their requirements.
Drop-seat, adjustable/detachable leg loops	This is a useful function for an expedition harness, as it allows for calls of nature to take place whilst remaining tied in.
Provision of equipment loops	Usually personal choice, the provision of equipment loops will often decide which harness is being purchased. Some designs allow the wearer to add their own loops as the situation dictates, although most have a fixed system.
Rear sewn belay loop	Often provided on harnesses in the past, this feature is often now thought to be redundant. If a load is applied to the rear belay loop, with the weight also applied to the front loop, the effect will be to squeeze in the ribs of the belayer.

should the climber end up hanging free whilst wearing a rucksack. If a sit-harness is worn, there is a risk that the climber will invert, possibly exacerbating any injuries sustained, and certainly making the task of self-righting and rescue more arduous. A full-body harness should also be considered when climbing with children under 12 years. The centre of gravity of a child is higher than that of an adult, so the possibility of them inverting during even a simple fall is high.

Sit-harnesses are by far the most popular type, and they are available in a variety of sizes, colours, designs and functions. There are a number of features to look out for when purchasing one and some of these are outlined in the table on p. 121.

Full-body harnesses

Full-body harnesses are often used where a fall could result in the climber hanging free, with the chance of them subsequently flipping upside down. This could happen in crevassed terrain, or where a load is being carried on technical ground. Full-body harnesses, although slightly heavier than a normal sit-harness, provide excellent protection in these situations.

Hauling

See also: assisted hoist, dead rope, figure of eight knot, HMS karabiners, hip hoist, live rope, pulleys, stirrup hoist, unassisted hoist.

Hauling is a method of bringing up a load to a ledge or similar place, using the strength of those already there and a variety of mechanical techniques. It is most commonly used on long multi-pitch routes for hauling sacks containing essentials such as water and overnight kit, as these would be too heavy to carry on the back for any period of time. Hauling can also be used to bring up a climber who is hanging free. This system has a parallel with **assisted** and **unassisted hoists**, which are covered elsewhere. Hauling is, however, in a different classification as it is usually a technique that is planned with equipment such as **pulleys** being carried for the purpose.

Basic hoist

The basic hoist can be exactly that: the load being pulled up either hand over hand or by being tied to the end of a rope which runs through a karabiner above the head of the climber, they then pull on the rope and the load ascends. Although simple, this will only

A Petzl Mini Traxion being used to prevent rope slippage when hauling, in conjunction with a variant of the Yosemite hoist technique.

work for the very lightest of loads and as such is probably best avoided. Hauling a load like this is extremely tiring and if the climber let go of the rope the load would simply drop to the bottom again, possibly stripping the anchor with it.

Using a pulley

An improvement is to use a pulley with a built-in camming system. This means that as the load is pulled up the pulley eases the task, and if a rest is needed the cam will bite on to the rope and prevent it from falling. Doing this hand over hand is awkward at the best of times, so to combat this a variation known as the Yosemite hoist can be utilized. The system is set up as above, but instead of the climber using their hands to haul the load, an ascender is placed on the dead rope, with a short sling attached. The climber's foot goes into this and they can then use their bodyweight to help raise the load. Obviously an improvement to just pulling up hand over hand, this still means that a load of any weight is tiring and difficult to lift. In fact, the mathematical formula demonstrates that, if the weight to be hauled is 80kg (176 pounds) then the pull that has to be exerted to lift it is 112kg (247 pounds).

Improving mechanical advantage

To get past this problem, a system in which the person hauling has a mechanical advantage can be set up. The use of pulleys will greatly ease the hauling procedure, and it is very helpful if these are available to the team.

METHOD

- Clip a pulley with built-in cam into the anchor. The haul rope goes through this.
- Clip a lightweight pulley, preferably swing-cheek, on to the **dead rope**.
- Using a karabiner from the small pulley, clip this on to some kind of active or passive ascending device placed upside down on to the **live rope**.
- Pulling up on the dead rope now allows the load to be lifted.
- Once the ascender has reached the main camming pulley the load rope can be slackened, the ascender moved back down the rope and then the process repeated.

The mechanical advantage of this system allows a load to be effectively reduced by over 50 per cent. This means that an 80kg (176 pounds) load feels like one of only 36kg (79 pounds) to the person lifting it.

A hauling system using pulleys and cams to lift a load.

A lightweight hauling system set up using two Tibloc ascenders.

Using lightweight ascenders

If weight is at a premium the above may not be practicable, as pulleys and ascenders will probably not be carried. In this case a very similar system can be set up using small passive ascenders. This will not give as good a mechanical advantage as using pulleys, because some friction will be created due to the rope running across karabiners. However, this slight loss of efficiency will be made up by the lightness of the system. It should be noted that the karabiner on the anchor holding the upper ascender should be an **HMS**. This is because, depending on the type of ascender being used, it might have to swivel through the karabiner in order to grip the rope when a load is applied to it.

Heavy loads

To deal with the heaviest of loads, extra mechanical advantage over and above that already gained is desirable. In this situation, an extra rope clamp and pulley are needed. Set up the original pulley system as above. The dead rope can now be hauled using a secondary system employing the other end of the rope in one of two manners. This is dependent upon whether it is more convenient for the hauler to pull the load from below or from above. If pulling upwards is favoured:

METHOD

- The end of the haul rope is clipped into the anchor using a **figure-of-eight knot** or similar.
- A rope clamp, such as an ascender, is clipped on to the dead rope of the original system, orientated to take an upward pull.
- A karabiner is clipped to the clamp, and this is in turn connected to a pulley, which is placed on to the rope coming from the anchor.
- Pulling upwards on the new rope will allow the load to be lifted easily.

If pulling down is favoured:

- An ascender or similar clamp is placed on to the dead rope of the original system, arranged to take an upward pull.
- This is connected via a karabiner to a figure-of-eight knot in the end of the haul rope.
- The haul rope is taken up to the anchor and through a pulley.
- Pulling down on this rope now initiates the hauling.

notes

The extra rope used for the final two variations will most likely be that of the other end of the haul rope. However, this need not be the case, as the end may have been used as part of the anchor system. In this case, any rope can be utilized, most likely a section of the climbing rope.

Hoisting with a high mechanical advantage. The load is lifted by pulling up on the rope.

Hoisting with a high mechanical advantage. The load is lifted by pulling down on the rope.

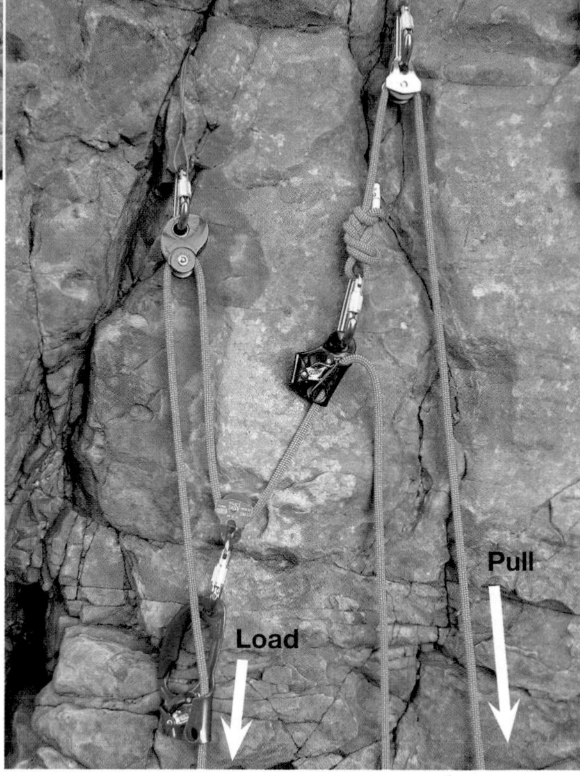

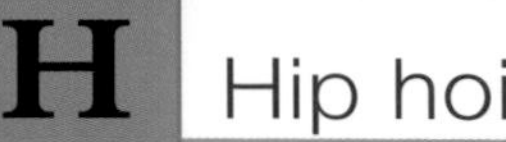

Hip hoist

See also: abseil loop, Alpine clutch, ascenders, dead rope, escaping the system, live rope, self-locking belay devices.

This technique is useful on a stance with a high anchor point, where the belayer can get themselves in a line between the anchor and a fallen climber. It is a method of raising a climber, using the leg muscles of the belayer. Efficient under many circumstances, it can be hard work for a lightweight belayer trying to hoist a heavier second.

METHOD

- The belayer gets themselves safely in a position from where they can operate the hoist. This may well initially necessitate **escaping the system**.
- The rope needs to be connected to the anchor in a manner that will allow it to be easily taken through and then automatically locked off. An over-riding factor will be that if slack has to be introduced into the system, a method using a **self-locking belay device** or **Alpine clutch** may not be appropriate, as they cannot be released under load. However, in most cases they will be the best options. For this sequence, we will assume that an Alpine clutch has been chosen.
- The belayer must connect a means of gripping the rope between their abseil loop and the **live rope** to their second. This would most likely be achieved using a klemheist or French prusik, but an ascender would also be appropriate if available.
- The belayer bends their knees and slides the knot or ascender down the live rope.
- As they stand up straight, they also pull on the **dead rope** coming down to them from the anchor.
- Once upright, and with the load taken by the Alpine clutch, they slide the knot or ascender back down the rope, bend their knees and repeat the process.

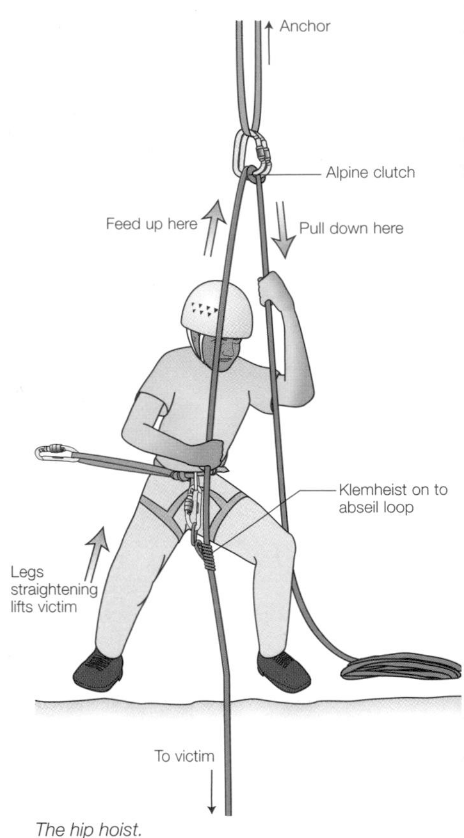

The hip hoist.

Hoisting

See assisted hoist, hip hoist, unassisted hoist and hauling.

Opposite: *Good use of double rope technique to reduce rope drag on a tricky diagonal line.*

Ice-axe retrieval

See also: accessory cord, lark's foot, overhand knot, slings, snow bollard, tat.

It may be necessary to retrieve an ice axe that has been used as an anchor for an abseil. To have to do this in the first place will probably mean that all other possibilities for an abseil anchor have been considered and then dismissed as being either impractical or unsafe. For instance, using a snow mushroom should be considered before that of a retrievable axe abseil, but the snow into which it needs to be dug may be of insufficient width, such as in a narrow gully.

tips

To ensure that the correct side of the rope is pulled during retrieval, clipping a free-running karabiner on to the relevant side will provide a reminder once the next stance has been reached.

METHOD

- Select a suitable section of snow and push the axe into it vertically to make a hole of axe shaft width.
- It is very useful if a second ice tool is available, such as a hammer, as it helps the mechanics of the retrieval work smoothly. It is possible to perform the technique with just one tool, but the chances of the axe jamming during retrieval are dramatically increased. Assuming that a hammer is available, it should be attached to the axe by the hole in the head. This can be easily done with a sling, most likely with a **lark's foot** arrangement.
  - A piece of **tat** or **sling,** 120 or 240cm (48in or 96in) long, is attached to the hole by the spike at the bottom of the ice axe, and the axe is pushed back into the vertical hole made in the snow. Take care that the cord or sling is not damaged during this process and made unfit for future use. The axe head can, for the moment, be left protruding a little from the level of the snow.
  - The hammer or second ice tool is placed horizontally, pick flat on the snow, butted up against the axe. This second tool will allow the cord or sling connected to the bottom of the axe to be pulled without it cutting into the snow and jamming.
  - The centre point of the rope to be used for the abseil is placed around the head of the axe. A small **overhand knot** on the bight is tied on the rope close to the axe head, and a karabiner is used to connect it to the sling from the axe.
- The head of the axe can now be pushed down further to the surface of the snow, ensuring that it doesn't go so far as to grip the rope and prevent it being pulled around the shaft.
- Both the abseil rope and the cord or sling connected to the bottom of the axe are run over the top of the horizontal second tool, and the rope deployed.
- Retrieval is accomplished by a strong and sustained pull on the relevant side of the abseil rope. This pull should not stop until the tools have been recovered, as to do so may result in them jamming in the snow on the ground above.

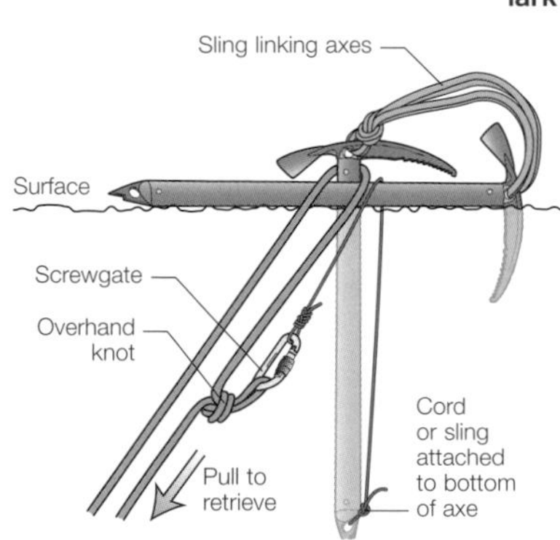

The set-up for an axe retrieval.

notes

If there are two ropes being joined together to facilitate the abseil, ensure that both the connecting overhand knot and the rope join are on the same side of the axe system.

Care on retrieval

Extreme care must be exercised when the ropes are pulled for retrieval, as two ice tools will be accelerating towards the bottom of the rope. It is important to keep everyone out of the way and for the person tasked with the retrieval to keep a careful eye on the direction of the ice tools' descent.

Ice bollard

See also: abseil rope retrieval, sling, snow bollard.

The ice bollard is an effective but somewhat time-consuming method of arranging an anchor, either for belaying a climber up or, more likely, for a lower or abseil descent. The latter cases are more likely because of the time that the anchor takes to construct, and it would only be in exceptional circumstances that a leader would opt to use one. However, in descent, although time is most likely at a premium, there may be issues with the amount of equipment available, and the bollard requires no gear to be left behind.

Shape

It is, as the name suggests, a bollard or mushroom shape similar in design to the **snow mushroom,** and is chipped out of the available ice. It will only be as strong as the material from which it is made, so care should be taken to choose a suitable location that not only offers ice of a suitable quality, for instance that does not shatter when struck, but that is also of a sufficient depth for the bollard to have holding power when constructed. For it to be slightly pronounced, such as at a bulge, would be advantageous as it would make the excavation a little easier, but examination should be made to ensure that the bulging is not due to the ice sitting over a boulder which would mean the ice at that point would be of a lesser depth.

Size

Ice bollards will generally be around 30–40cm (12–16in) in diameter, with a depth of around 10cm (4in). This will, of course, vary given different ice conditions, but the width would never normally be much less than 30cm (12in) as there would be too high a chance of fractures within the ice pack meeting and causing the bollard to fail.

METHOD

- Select a suitable area of ice and scrape out an outline of the area to be cut in a horseshoe shape. The lower ends must not meet, otherwise the strength of the bollard will be compromised.
- Use the pick of the axe to cut carefully around the shape. It is important that the inner section of the bollard is disturbed as little as possible.
- Using a combination of axe pick and adze, cut out the bollard to the desired shape and depth.
- The bollard should be mushroomed slightly, particularly at the top, to prevent a rope or **sling** from slipping off.
- The bollard is ready to use. If it is for an abseil, the rope can be placed directly around it as subsequent **retrieval** should be straightforward. If it is to be used for a lower or belay, a sling could be placed around it and a stance taken up some distance below.

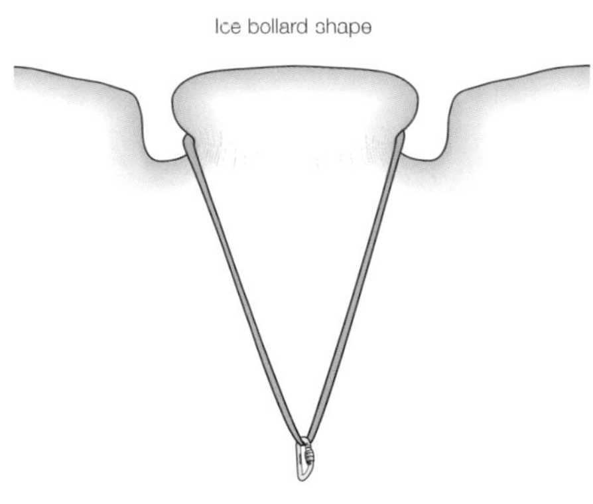

An ice bollard.

Ice screws

See also: bottoming out, equalizing anchors.

Ice screws used to be very awkward to place, requiring a hole to be tapped into the ice and then one hand to hold and turn the screw whilst the other wielded a hammer which tapped on the top until the teeth bit. It would normally then take a cranking motion with the hammer or axe pick through the eye of the screw to get it to wind all of the way in.

Modern screws are very different, and money is well spent on choosing a good design with a large bore, prominent thread and well profiled cutting teeth, four being the optimum.

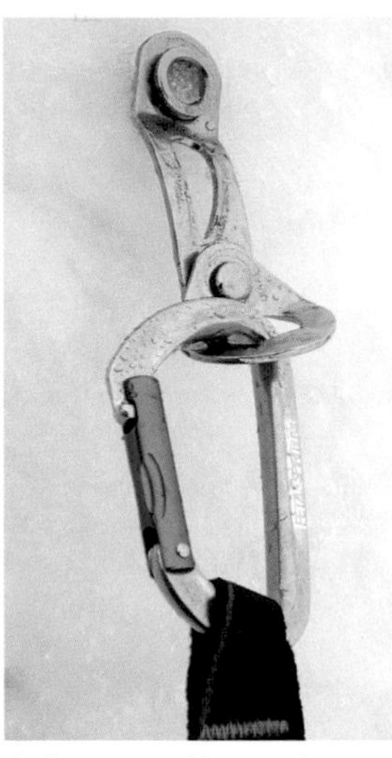

An ice screw with a rotating hanger eye. This means that the screw can be clipped to the rope during placement and retrieval with no fear of dropping it.

Placement

The placement of an ice screw will only ever be as good as the ice into which it is made. If any opaqueness or 'dinner plating' appears (the shattering of surface ice, often falling away in large 'plates') as the screw is wound in, the screw should be removed and the rotten ice removed with the axe, the surface cut down to an area flat enough to allow the hanger of the screw to rotate, and the placement continued.

The screw needs to be placed at 90 degrees to the surface of the ice. Most placements into good ice using modern screws should be relatively simple. Holding the screw between hip and chest level, rotate the cutting teeth back and forwards for about half a turn, three or four times to roughen the surface and so aid the teeth biting. Then turn the screw in the correct direction until it is fully home, ensuring that the hanger is on the downslope side in the direction of loading. The screw should have extruded a solid column of ice from its core as it was wound in, but if this core exhibits signs of melting or significant air pockets, the screw should be removed and another area sought.

notes

Ice screws should always be used in pairs when constructing a main belay, as the effect of shock-loading a single screw may be enough for the placement to fail. To avoid the chance of 'dinner plating' occurring, the screws should be placed a metre apart diagonally and then either brought to one point using an **equalizing** method or tied into carefully using the rope, adjusted so that each screw takes half the load.

If the screw has not been fully screwed home before it bottoms out, it needs to be tied off in some fashion to reduce leverage. See the entry under **bottoming out** for specific advice.

After removal

On removal of the screw, it is important that the core of ice that is most likely remaining inside the screw is removed. This

tip

Care should be taken when carrying ice screws that they do not puncture expensive clothing or equipment and that they themselves do not become damaged. Many are supplied with rubber teeth caps, and these are best left in place until the screw is needed for use. However, these are awkward to remove and store on a route. A good remedy is a purpose-designed ice-screw holder, which keeps the equipment secure and out of harm's way until needed, but allows size selection to be easy.

can be done by either gently warming the tube a little by placing it in a pocket for a short while, or by using a tool such as a multihook and prodding it out. If the core is not removed and it freezes into place, the screw will be unusable. Gentle tapping on the head of the screw may help to ease the core out, but care should be taken to not hit the thread as this may damage it irretrievably and render the screw unfit for future use.

Maintenance

Ice screws need a certain amount of maintenance after use, and they should be dried out and not just stowed in a rucksack. An application of lubricant, if they are not to be used for some period of time, would be well worth doing, as it will not only prevent corrosion but will also help the screw to preserve its ice-core clearing capability. They also need to be kept sharp, and regular checks should be made to ensure that the cutting teeth do not become blunt or burred. If sharpening is needed, this should only be carried out using a hand file and not a mechanical grinder. Any filing should be carried out in a manner that will ensure that the geometry of the cutting edges is maintained, as to change the shape of the cutting teeth will dramatically alter the performance of the screw.

tip

Although many modern screws are highly polished not only to ease placement but also to reflect the heat of the sun, some solar absorption may occur and weaken the placement. This is particularly noticeable when top or bottom roping an icefall. To avoid this problem, once the screw has been placed, a few centimetres of snow or ice can be packed over the top, helping to dissipate the heat of the sun.

Ice-screw retrieval

See also: Abalakov thread, accessory cord, ice screws, overhand knot, prusik loop.

Although other methods of organizing an abseil anchor may be both more appropriate and safer, such as an **Abalakov thread**, snow bollard or rock anchors, in some extreme circumstances it may be decided upon to abseil using a single ice screw. If so, its retrieval may be desirable if gear is at a premium and everything must be done to keep equipment losses to a minimum. However, the pros and cons of committing weight to a single screw should be thoroughly considered, and if there is any chance of anchor failure a more secure method should be sought.

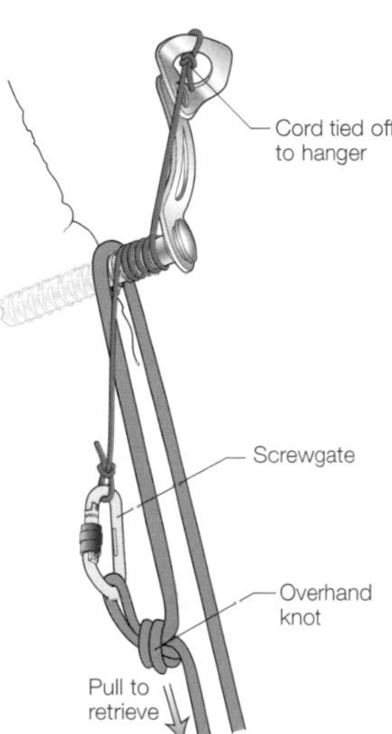

The set-up for a retrievable ice-screw system.

METHOD

- The screw is placed into a relevant section of ice, with the amount of turns that it took to place it being remembered. The hanger of the screw should end up a little above the surface of the ice, as the rope used for the abseil will fit between it and the surface, and it should end up pointing uphill, 180 degrees to the direction of the abseil.
- A length of **accessory cord** or an untied **prusik loop** is fastened on to the eye of the screw.
- This cord is then wrapped around the top of the screw in the opposite direction to the teeth. In other words, if the screw was placed in

notes

The retrieving of an ice screw should be carefully considered. If the ice is of a quality that allows safe descent using just one screw and equipment is at a premium, an Abalakov thread may well be a better and safer alternative.

notes

If there are two ropes being joined together to facilitate the abseil, ensure that both the connecting overhand knot and the rope join are on the same side of the ice screw.

tip

To ensure that the correct side of the rope is pulled during retrieval, clipping a free-running karabiner on to the relevant side will provide a reminder once the next stance has been reached.

a clockwise direction, the cord should be wound round it anti-clockwise. The amount of wraps should be a couple more than the turns that secured the screw in the first place.

- The abseil rope is positioned over the screw with the centre of the rope at the top. It should sit snugly between the screw's hanger and the ice with no gap, to ensure that it does not exert any leverage.
- A small **overhand knot** on the bight is tied on to one side of the abseil rope, close to the ice screw.
- The cord is clipped into this using a screwgate karabiner.
- Once the abseil is completed, pulling with constant force will cause the ice screw to be unscrewed from its placement, and it will be pulled down with the rope.

It should go without saying that great care should be taken when executing the final pull, as there is a danger of injury if the screw is pulled down at speed towards the climber.

Ice threads

See also: Abalakov thread.

An ice thread is the term given to the use of natural ice as a running belay or anchor point. The thread may be constructed, such as in the case of an **Abalakov thread**, or natural, such as when using a large icicle. The strength of the thread will only ever be as strong as the ice from which it is constructed, and great caution should be exercised before attaching any system to a naturally occurring ice anchor. Icicles, in particular, may be structurally poor, and the part that joins on to the lower surface may have meagre adhesion. Indeed, it may not be touching at all, and simply have a layer of snow masking the gap. Excavation will be able to give a result, although if the use of the thread is critical, care should be taken to ensure that it is not disturbed more than is necessary.

The quality of the ice can be hard to judge, although ice that has spent some time building up will often be more stable than ice that has formed as the result of a snap freeze. Clues can be gained whilst climbing, as the constant shattering of ice under axe and crampons will give warning of brittle conditions.

In extreme cases it may be possible to climb through a hole in the ice, thus threading the leader and trailing rope at the same time. Some routes require this as part of the exit pitch, but again great care must be taken with the quality of the ice, and to be sure that the icefall itself is securely anchored into place.

Impact force

See also: belay devices, clove hitch, direct belay, dynamic rope, fall factors, figure-of-eight knot, indirect belay, kiloNewtons, semi-direct belay.

The impact force is the loading taken by any given part of the protection system, such as a running belay, in the event of a fall. To have a low-impact force on a running belay is desirable, as this will go some way towards helping the gear stay in place and lessen the shock-loading on the climber. The lessening of the impact force is essential in places where marginal runners have been placed, such as in dubious rock, or in the case of ice protection. Two variations of the term 'impact force' will be discussed here: that given to dynamic ropes when being tested to international standards, and that created in a practical situation when a climber falls from a route on to a running belay.

International standards

Dynamic ropes will have an impact force rating when tested to international standards. The lower the rope's rating the more able it is to absorb energy. For instance, a rope rated with a 10 kiloNewton (kN) impact force will have approximately 30 per cent more loading effect on the top runner in the event of a fall than a rope with an impact force rating of 7kN. This is calculated with the belayer using a belay device in a dynamic manner, but if an auto-locking device is used this differential rises to around 35 per cent.

The following table shows the comparison of impact forces created by a fall of 8m with a fall factor of 1.4.

Given rope impact force	Force on runner in kN
Using dynamic belay device: 7.2kN 12kN	Using dynamic belay device: 5.6kN 8.25kN
Using auto-locking belay device: 7.2kN 12kN	Using auto-locking belay device: 8.85kN 14.35kN

It can be seen that there is considerable variation between the use of certain ropes with given impact-force ratings, allied with the type of belay method selected. The difference between the use of a dynamic belay device with a 7.2kN rated rope, compared to an auto-locking device with a 12kN rated rope is over 250 per cent, a major factor when considering equipment and techniques for specific routes.

Factors that can influence impact force

- **The elasticity of the rope.** If one rope 'stretches' more than another, this will absorb energy.
- **The line that the rope takes up the route.** A straighter line will allow the rope to absorb more energy than if it were zig-zagging between runners.
- **The type of belay device used.** A 'slick' belay device will allow a little rope slippage and gradual slowing of the falling climber. A 'grabbing' belay device will cause more loading to be exerted on the system.
- **The type of belay system used.** An **indirect belay** will give a lot of rope slippage and reduce the force the most, with a **direct belay** being the least dynamic. The **semi-direct** belay will be the most common and can help to absorb energy, given the belay device used (see above) and factors such as the weight of the belayer, whether they are tied down etc (see below).
- **Knots.** A **figure-of-eight knot**, either used to tie on to the harness or as part of the anchor system, will tighten throughout, absorbing energy. Knots such as the **clove hitch** are static, and will not act as efficient absorbers.
- **The type of harness used.** Some harnesses with extensive padding will absorb energy more efficiently than ultra-lightweight designs.
- **The belayer.** A heavy belayer may go some way to increasing the impact force as, even if they are not anchored at the bottom of the route, they may not be moved upwards enough to absorb energy. A lightweight belayer, conversely, may allow the impact force to be far reduced by being lifted up when loaded, but care should obviously be taken that they will not be injured themselves in this event.
- **The climber.** A heavy climber, falling on to a direct belay, will produce a far higher impact force than a light climber falling on to an indirect belay system.
- **The movement of the belayer.** If the belayer is tightly attached to the ground, their body weight cannot provide the inertia that would be desirable for reducing forces applied to the system.
- **The use of energy-absorbing devices on the running belays may significantly reduce impact force.** In particular, slings designed to fail-safe at a certain loading, manufactured in a series of folds and with the aim of the stitching failing in a certain sequence when a large load is applied, are very often used on ice routes where the runners are of a questionable quality.

Effect of belay method on impact force

It is important to consider the difference in impact force created by belaying in both a direct manner, for instance from bolts on the intermediate stance of a multi-pitch route, and from a semi-direct belay at the harness. The rope used for the following calculations has been manufactured to take a load of 7kN.

	Direct belay	Semi-direct belay
Rope out	4m	4m
Last runner	1m	1m
Length of fall	6m	6m
Fall factor	1.5 (6 ÷ 4)	1.5 (6 ÷ 4)
Loading at runner	11kN	9kN
Loading at belayer	4kN	3.5kN
Loading on falling climber	7kN	5.5kN

It can thus be seen that the process of belaying in a semi-direct manner reduces the impact force by 18 per cent over the direct belay method. This is because of the inertia created by the load coming on to the belayer, and their subsequent slight movement upwards.

The weight difference between climbers can dramatically alter the effect of impact force. The use of ground anchors is to be encouraged in most situations, as to do so will help prevent injury to the belayer, but there should be consideration in providing sufficient slack in the system so that the weight of the belayer may be moved slightly to help lessen the effect of the impact force on the system. Research has demonstrated that the ability for a belayer to move freely upwards for approximately 1m will give optimum loading reduction, but with the proviso that this extra movement will not cause the falling climber to hit the ground. The use of dynamic rope for the anchoring section of the belay system will also go a long way towards alleviating any problems.

The relationship between impact force and the weight of climber and belayer are examined in the following calculation. For these purposes, we will assume that the belayer is not anchored at the bottom of the route.

	Belayer heavier than climber	Climber heavier than belayer
Belayer's weight	80kg (176 pounds)	50kg (110 pounds)
Climber's weight	50kg (110 pounds)	80kg (176 pounds)
Rope run out	8.5m	8.5m
Falling point	3m above last runner	3m above last runner
Basic mathematical fall length	6m	6m
Fall factor	0.7 (6 ÷ 8.5)	0.7 (6 ÷ 8.5)
Loading at runner	5.5kN	6kN
Loading at belayer	2kN	2kN
Loading at falling climber	3.5kN	4kN
Lift on belayer	1m	2m
Total descent by climber (inc belayer lift and rope elongation)	8m	8.5m

It will be noticed that in example two, the original height gained by the climber of 8.5m is the same as the total fall height, so the climber will hit the ground.

Rope drag

Another factor that affects the impact force on any given part of the system is the route that the rope takes as it makes its way up through a number of runners. If the rope is allowed to run in a straight line, the energy-absorbing properties of the rope will be efficiently used along its entire length, from the belay device through to the falling climber. If, however, the rope has to take a zig-zagging line up the route with the runners being out of line, the ability of the full length of the rope to absorb energy is much reduced, so more impact force is placed on the critical sections, such as the top runner. For this reason, if a route is expected to have running belays to either side and not to be in a straight line, a sensible precaution is to use a double rope technique, which would allow each rope to run straight, and so be able to absorb more of the energy created by a falling leader.

Indirect belay

See also: indirect belays, semi-direct belays, waist belay.

An indirect belay is one where the anchors take little of the load. Most often, this is accomplished with a **waist belay** or body belay. The advantage of this method is that the belayer absorbs a significant proportion of the loading. Anchor placements that are less than perfect, such as most ice and snow anchors, will therefore not have the full force of a fall placed on them. This force would obviously be a lot greater should a **semi-direct** or **direct belay** be chosen, and thought should go into the appropriateness of the belay technique at the outset.

Italian hitch

See also: abseiling, abseiling with a harness, belay methods, clove hitch, dead rope, direct belays, French prusik, Italian hitch – locking off, live rope.

The Italian hitch, also known as the Munter hitch, is a very useful knot, with a place in belaying, **abseiling** and backing up technical systems. It is tied in a similar fashion to the **clove hitch**, so care must be taken that one has not been tied in error where the other was needed.

Maximum braking

When being used as a friction hitch, maximum braking is achieved when the live and dead ropes are parallel. For this reason, the hitch should normally be placed behind or upslope of the belayer. An advantage here is that a second, upon reaching the stance, can continue a little way behind the belayer and still be protected, an advantage when working with novices or when utilizing a direct belay on steep technical ground. A further advantage is that it can be easily locked off, even when under load, and as such lends itself still further to belaying novice seconds.

Uses

The Italian hitch has uses as an abseil method, although it will tend to cause the ropes to twist if used over a long distance where the rope is unable to hang free and unravel.

It is excellent for use when backing up an emergency procedure that uses a French prusik as part of the system. Should the prusik knot slip the Italian hitch can be untied and so alleviate any jamming that might otherwise occur had a different knot, such as a clove hitch, been used.

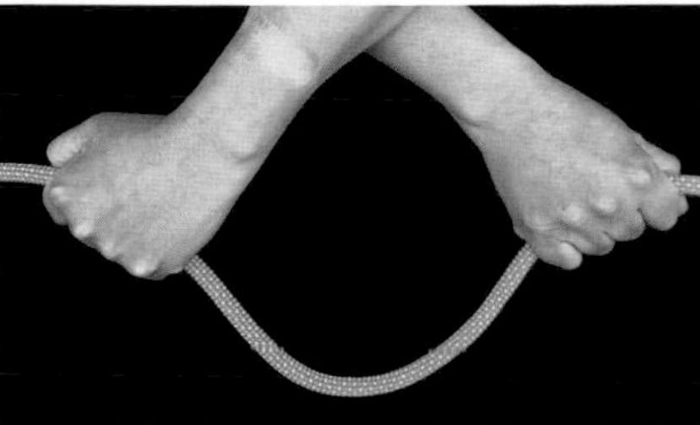

Tying an Italian hitch.

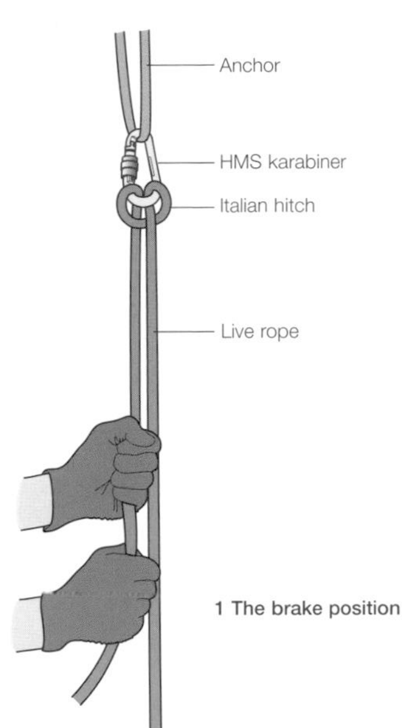

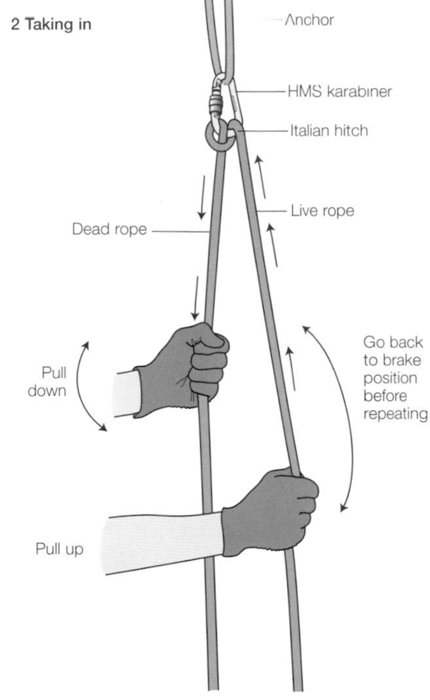

Using an Italian hitch as a direct belay.

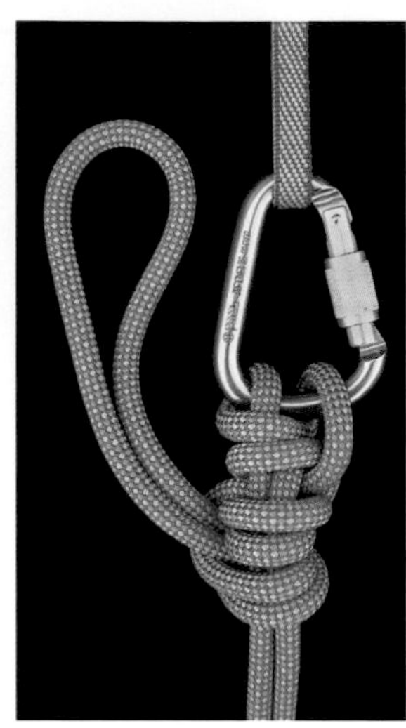

A locked-off Italian hitch.

Italian hitch – locking off

See also: abseil rope, direct belay, group abseiling, HMS karabiner, Italian hitch, releasable abseil, safety rope, slippery hitch.

Locking off an **Italian hitch** is an extremely useful and simple skill to master. This can be done with the system either loaded or unloaded. If the former is ever likely to be the case, prior practice is essential to ensure that no slippage of the rope takes place whilst the locking off is carried out. It is important that the Italian hitch is always clipped into an **HMS karabiner**, otherwise the system could jam if the knot inverts.

Locking off the hitch is central to the **releasable abseil** system, recommended for use when running **group abseiling** sessions. It means that, should a problem occur and the abseiler become jammed on the **abseil rope**, it can be released from the top whilst under load, with the weight of the abseiler being taken by the system **safety rope**.

When using a **direct belay** to bring up a second on a multi-pitch route, the ability to lock off the hitch is also very useful. Should the same climber be leading all of the pitches, once the second has arrived at the stance they can be locked off on the anchor and the leader can continue climbing.

Usually starting with the Italian hitch orientated on to the paying-out side of the karabiner, the locking-off procedure consists of starting with a **slippery hitch** with approximately 60cm (24in) of bight being used. This should be pulled up tight to the karabiner and then secured with two half hitches that are pulled up snug to the slippery hitch. There should be a loop of rope left over of approximately 30cm (12in) in length, to ensure that the knot has no chance of unravelling.

Jammer

See ascenders.

Jumaring

See also: ascending the rope, fixed-rope techniques.

Jumaring is the name given to the ascent of a fixed rope using ascenders. It is so called after the original Jumar rope ascender, and is now a generic term used for convenience. Many modern ascenders have superseded the Jumar, and the technique of jumaring is covered under other headings.

Karabiner brake

See also: abseil devices, abseil rope, abseiling, Italian hitch, screwgate karabiners, wires.

The karabiner brake is a method of controlling descent during an **abseil**, using the friction provided by the wrapping of the **abseil rope** through a series of karabiners. Although this technique is normally overlooked in favour of the use of a conventional **abseil device** or **Italian hitch**, the main advantage that it offers is the ability to add friction to the system by the addition of more karabiners, as may be necessary when dealing with an emergency situation.

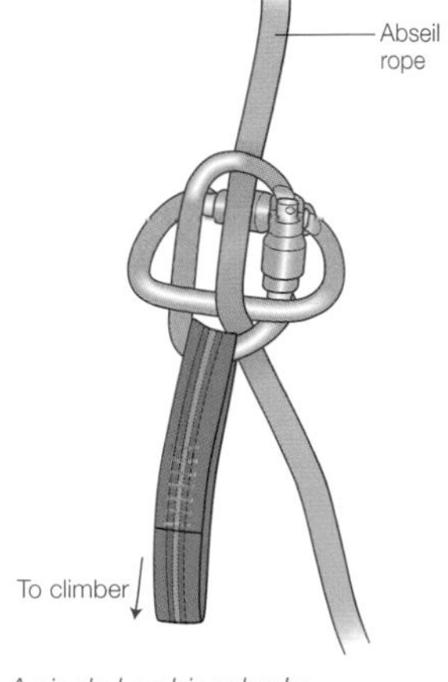

A single karabiner brake.

Using screwgates

If **screwgate karabiners** are to be used, care should be taken so that the locking sleeve, if touched by the abseil rope during the descent, will be locked tighter and not unscrewed. One pair of karabiners is unlikely to provide enough friction for the safe descent of an adult, and so two or more sets of karabiner brakes can be linked together. This can be achieved with the use of a **wire**, with its head having been pushed down a little towards the swaging. One brake is clipped into the eye of the wire, the other into the loop above its head. Karabiners can also be used to link the brakes together, and if so it should be ensured that they are sitting at the tightest curve of the brake karabiner, next to the back bar. If this linking karabiner is clipped in after the rope, when weighted it could push the rope down into the bend of the karabiner brake and cause it to jam. The attachment of the brake to the harness is by a screwgate karabiner, and this should again be orientated so that it will not press the rope against the back bar of the brake and cause it to jam.

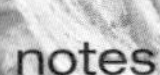

notes

It should be noted that if there is any chance of the abseil rope touching the webbing connecting the lower karabiner to the climber's harness during the descent, this should be replaced by a screwgate. If the rope were to rub against the tape it would generate heat and cause the webbing to become damaged or even fail completely.

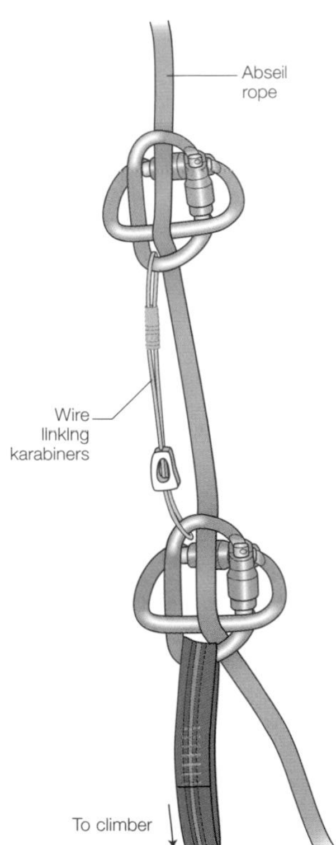

Two karabiner brakes linked with a wire.

KiloNewton

See also: impact force.

A basic understanding of kiloNewtons (kN) is important, as this is the strength rating given to a number of types of climbing equipment.

The Newton is a unit of force used by the International System of Units (SI), which has as its basic qualities mass, length and time. The Newton is equivalent to the force required to produce an acceleration of one metre per second squared on a mass of one kilogram.

A one kilogram mass is given a weight of 9.807 Newtons because of the acceleration due to gravity. This is usually rounded up to 9.81 Newtons. Thus a climber who claims to weigh 80kg (176 pounds) should really express his weight (mass) as 784.8 Newtons.

1,000 Newtons equal 1 kiloNewton, so a piece of climbing equipment with a 25kN stamp on it would have a strength rating equivalent to 25,000 Newtons. As 1 Newton is equal to 101.97kg (225 pounds), this particular piece of equipment would have strength equivalent to 2,549.25kg (5,621 pounds).

Kingpin

See pitons.

Klemheist

See also: escaping the system, French prusik, prusik loops, ascending the rope.

The klemheist is a very useful knot, sharing some similarity with the **French prusik**, although with one major difference. While the French prusik can be released when under load, the klemheist cannot, an important property for a number of situations. Indeed, the two knots complement each other to the extent that they can be used alongside each other on certain hauling and rescue situations but have entirely opposing purposes. Also, the klemheist is omni-directional, unlike the symmetrical French prusik. One further advantage is that the klemheist can be tied using a sling, which is advantageous when dealing with techniques such as **escaping the system** with the anchor points out of reach.

The knot is best tied from the top downwards. A small eye of the **prusik loop** or sling is held against the climbing rope and the rest of the loop is neatly wrapped around the rope downwards. The number of wraps depends upon a variety of factors, such as whether one or two climbing ropes are being

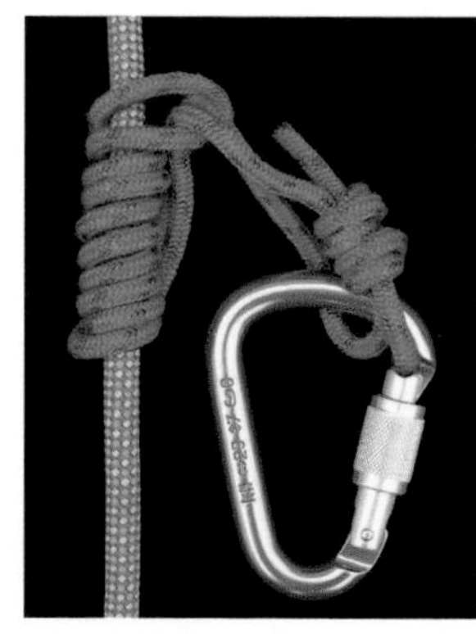

A klemheist.

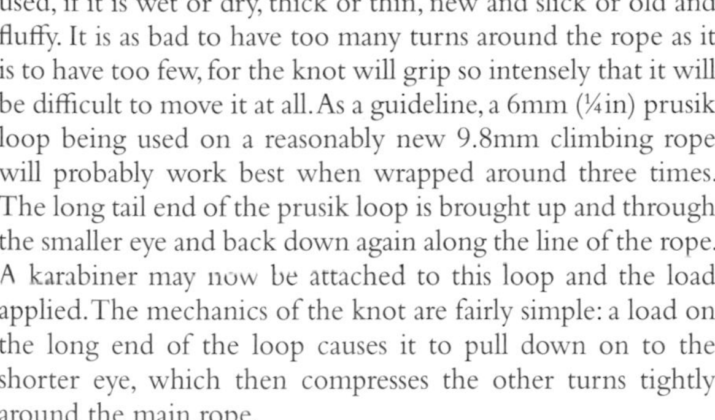

used, if it is wet or dry, thick or thin, new and slick or old and fluffy. It is as bad to have too many turns around the rope as it is to have too few, for the knot will grip so intensely that it will be difficult to move it at all. As a guideline, a 6mm (¼in) prusik loop being used on a reasonably new 9.8mm climbing rope will probably work best when wrapped around three times. The long tail end of the prusik loop is brought up and through the smaller eye and back down again along the line of the rope. A karabiner may now be attached to this loop and the load applied. The mechanics of the knot are fairly simple: a load on the long end of the loop causes it to pull down on to the shorter eye, which then compresses the other turns tightly around the main rope.

The knot cannot be moved at all when loaded and sometimes, even when the load is released, it can still be tricky to shift. This can be easily rectified by pushing the eye part of the loop back on itself a little so that the subsequent wraps can loosen; the knot should then move without difficulty. It is this moving of the upper eye of the knot that will allow a smooth ascent when **ascending the rope**.

notes

Like any of the prusik knots, shock-loading of the system should be avoided at all costs otherwise catastrophic failure may occur, with the klemheist slipping a short way and possibly either burning through or stripping the sheath of the climbing rope.

Knifeblade

See pitons.

Lark's foot

See also: clove hitch, sling, cowstail, harness.

The lark's foot is a weak knot that has few uses in modern-day mountaineering, as it is easily destroyed by shock loading. It can sometimes be tied by mistake where a **clove hitch** should have been deployed, but it certainly has nothing like the clove hitch's holding power. The one place where it is of use is when constructing a **cowstail** as a personal safety system. When using a **sling** for this purpose, thread part of the **sling** though the **harness** leg loops and waist belt to create a small loop, then thread the other section of the sling through this, pulling the knot tight. The lark's foot can also be tied directly through the abseil loop instead of around the harness.

A lark's foot on a harness.

Leading through

See multi-pitch changeovers.

Leashes – ice axe

See also: lark's foot, overhand knot.

The use of a leash or wrist loop for an ice axe is very much a matter of personal choice. To use one means that there is support when climbing and security against axe loss when crossing the mountain terrain. However, it also means a loss of dexterity in some situations, as well as the chance of injury should you not carry out an arrest promptly.

Two categories

To split the categories of use into two extremely broad areas, there are general-purpose mountaineers and those seeking steeper, more technical terrain. For all-round use across the broad spectrum that is 'general mountaineering', a wrist loop is a tool in addition to the axe that can be either used or dispensed with at ease, depending upon a number of factors including the type of terrain, the ability and experience of the person involved and the consequences of dropping the axe. Most users at this level will find a simple tape-loop wrist leash to be completely adequate. This is a length of tape with a sewn loop at one end, furnished with a plastic or metal slider. The other end of the tape can be knotted with an **overhand knot** on the bight, and then lark's footed through the hole at the head end of the axe. This means that the leash can be used as normal, but should it need to be removed for any reason it can be swiftly taken off, even when the tape is frozen, with replacement being equally as quick.

General-purpose axes

Some axes come equipped with a wrist loop that is already attached to the shaft by means of a metal oval slider. A problem with these is that if the shaft of the axe ices up in cold temperatures, the slider will be unable to move, thus rendering the system useless.

Some walkers employ a system of attaching the axe to themselves, often to the lower section of a rucksack shoulder strap, with a length of rope or sewn and elasticated webbing leash. This allows for easy swapping of hands when traversing to and fro up and down slopes, but the axe can still be dropped if grip is lost, and in the event of a sliding fall the long leash can wrap itself around the victim, possibly causing harm.

Technical axes

Technical climbing axes, designed for use on steep ground, will often be supplied with a leash to suit the tool and the terrain for which it has been designed. Sometimes a user may choose to fashion their own leash, but most will go along with that decided upon by the manufacturer.

It is very useful for the leash of a tool that has been designed for steep and technical ice or mixed climbing to have the ability for the wrist loop to be quickly detached from the shaft of the axe for a short period of time, whilst being retained around the wrist of the climber. This will normally be for the placing of protection, where freedom of movement becomes important. One of the best systems consists of a 'C' clip held in place by a gate, a little like that employed by a karabiner. This is clipped around a stud on the shaft of the axe and may be removed and reconnected in less than a second.

Some climbers like to connect their axes to themselves with two lengths of rope, frequently in addition to a wrist leash on each. This is so that a hand may be removed from a loop with no fear of the axe or hammer being dropped down the route. Those seeking out technical mixed or iced-up rock routes will often adopt this method.

tip
The optimum length for a leash is slightly different for a general-purpose axe to that for a technical axe. For the former, having the loop adjusted so that a gloved hand can grip the bottom of the shaft with the tape tight would be right. For the latter, the length will often be determined by the shape of the axe shaft, the positioning of the grip, and any fist-stop incorporated into its design.

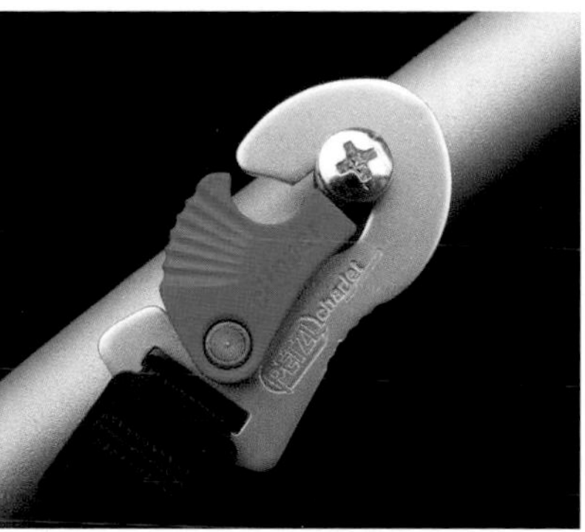

A quick-release mechanism on a leash for a technical axe.

Closure

The mechanics by which the wrist-loop section of the leash closes should be considered, again relevant to the terrain on which the axe and hammer are to be used. A system by which the loop is pulled tight around the wrist of the climber is all well and good, as long as there is a mechanism by which the tightening will stop before it becomes painful, as might happen when all of the climber's weight is committed to it. For this reason, a simple padded wrist loop with an adjustable buckle system will often be seen as being the best, in particular when allied with the fast removable leash system.

tip
It would be very sensible to try out axes prior to purchase with the gloves that will be worn when climbing. Some axe shafts and glove fabric don't mix, resulting in a loss of friction, making the axe very difficult to hold on to and wield under certain conditions.

Leeper

See pitons.

Live rope

See also: belay device, dead rope, direct belay, Italian hitch, waist belay.

In a climbing situation, the live rope is the rope that has the climber on it, that is, the one that travels from the **belay device** towards the person climbing. Once the rope has passed through the belay plate or around the back of the belayer if a **waist belay** is being used, it becomes the **dead rope**. This is also relevant if the belayer is not part of the system, such as when using **direct belay** techniques, perhaps incorporating an **Italian hitch**.

Locking off – belay device

See belay device: locking off.

Lost arrows

See pitons.

Low-stretch rope

See also: abseiling, anchor, dynamic ropes, group climbing, group abseiling, running belay, stopper knot.

Low-stretch ropes, sometimes known as semi-static or static ropes, have modest energy-absorption properties when compared with **dynamic ropes**. They are very useful in situations such as rigging **group climbing** and **abseiling** sessions and for use as fixed ropes, but should never be used when there is any chance of them having to hold a shock load. Although they do stretch to a certain degree, this is not enough to guarantee the safety of a falling climber, and will exert great forces on to both the **anchor** and **running belay** sections of a climb.

Low-stretch ropes tend to be stiffer than dynamic ropes, with the effect that tying knots can sometimes be awkward. If knots are being tied into a low-stretch rope, perhaps when rigging a group session, ensure that plenty of tail is left or that the end is secured by a stopper knot, to ensure that there is little chance of rope creepage and the knot loosening off during use.

Lowering

See also: abseil device, abseil loop, abseiling, belay device, bolted routes – lowering off, direct belays, direct belays – rock, direct belays – snow and ice, figure-of-eight knot, HMS karabiner, Italian hitch, indirect belay, multi-pitch climbing, overhand knot, passing a knot on a lower, screwgate karabiner, slings, Thompson knot, waist belay.

Lowering can take place in many situations and be in many forms. It may be that an instructor or guide has to negotiate a section of descent with their party, and lowering is a swifter and safer option than abseiling. Also, it could be used if a climbing partner is injured on a route and needs to be lowered a distance to the safety of a ledge. In fact, any time when one person is descending under the control of another is termed lowering, be it from a climbing wall or bolted route through to lengthy lowers on mountainous terrain.

Considerations

Lowering can take place using a variety of anchor and belay systems on snow, ice or rock, although it will most usually be carried out with a **direct belay**. The direct belay system means that the person controlling the lower is not being affected by any weight on the rope and is free, within the constraints of the stance and their own personal safety system, to move around the immediate area for the purpose of communication and group control.

If the lower is to take place in a **multi-pitch** situation, there should be no doubt that the rope reaches a safe stance at an appropriate point. This could be measured by dropping the tail of the rope down as a gauge before rigging the system, but care should be taken to ensure that there is no chance of the rope becoming stuck when it is pulled back up. Once the group member/s are down, it is most likely that the leader will have to **abseil** to the same place. It is therefore important that this is taken into consideration when selecting an intermediate ledge on the descent, for if the rope is 60m long and a suitable ledge is chosen 50m down, if the leader is to abseil on a doubled rope they will only descend for 30m, ending up some distance above their group. Having two ropes will help this, although there may well be a benefit in this situation in tying the ropes together to make the lower much further and thus the overall descent quicker. However, there would still remain the question of the safety of the leader if they are to abseil.

The Italian hitch lower

The following sequence assumes that one anchor point is used, and that an Italian hitch on an HMS karabiner is the controlling method chosen.

METHOD

- The HMS should be clipped into the anchor with the gate opening upwards and the wide end of the karabiner away from the anchor, so that the hitch will sit in the correct orientation.
- Preparation of the rope should take place, with it being flaked out in a neat pile at a suitable place near the anchor. The rope that is to lead to the person being lowered should come out of the top of the pile.
- The person controlling the lower should be on the downslope side of the system, and tied in to the anchor if appropriate.
- The end that is to be attached to the person going down can have a **figure of eight** on the bight tied into it, and a **screwgate karabiner** clipped in. This will be used to clip into their **abseil loop**.
- Clip the Italian hitch into the anchor HMS.
- Clip the screwgate into the abseil loop of the person being lowered.
- The lowering can commence, with the system being slowly loaded until it is taking all of the weight. Lowering should still take place at a slow rate, as it may be difficult for the person going down to maintain their footing if the descent is too rapid.

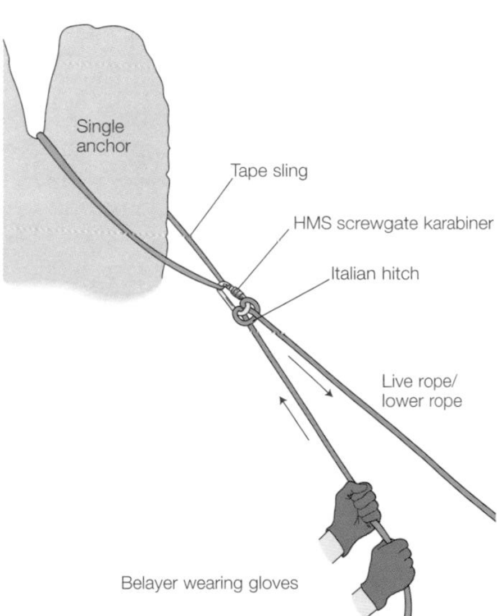

Lowering using an Italian hitch.

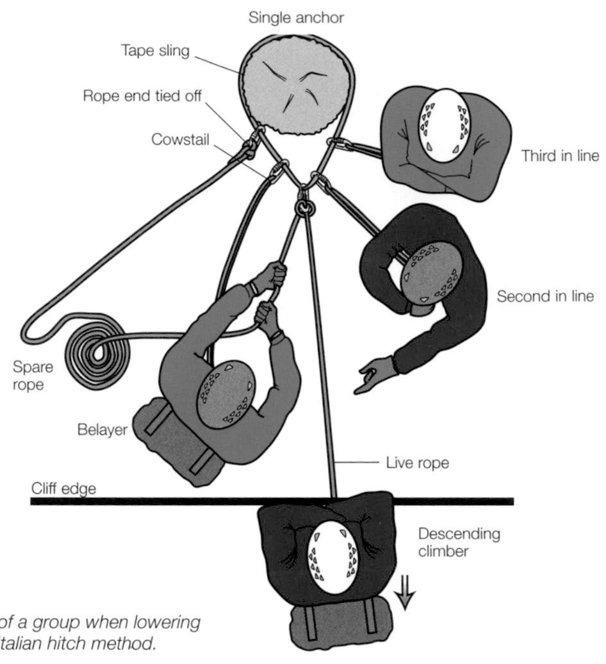

Security of a group when lowering with the Italian hitch method.

Using a belay device

The Italian hitch is an excellent lowering method over short distances or if there is no extra equipment available, such as a **belay** or **abseil device**. However, if one of these is available it may be chosen as it will tend to twist the rope less than a friction hitch. The main difference is that the person controlling the descent needs to rig the system so that the dead rope is running back from the device to allow for the correct friction to be applied. This would not be possible if the Italian hitch rig mentioned above simply had the hitch replaced by a belay device, as the positioning of the belayer would mean that an effective braking style would be impossible to attain. However, a slight adjustment to the rig will allow this to take place.

METHOD

- The system is rigged as normal and brought down to one point.
- An **overhand knot** needs to be tied into the anchor **sling** approximately 30cm (12in) from its end.
- The belay device is clipped into the loop at the end of the sling.
- A screwgate karabiner is clipped into the sling just above the overhand knot.
- The rope from the person being lowered is brought up, through the belay device, back through the second karabiner, and down to the belayer.
- The belayer can take up position on the down slope side of the system, as the additional screw-gate will ensure that the dead rope is always being directed into the belay device at the correct angle for maximum braking.

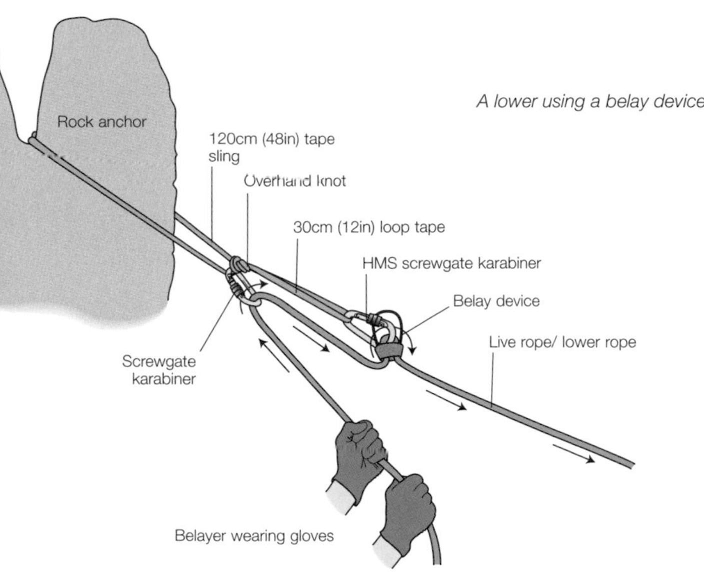

A lower using a belay device.

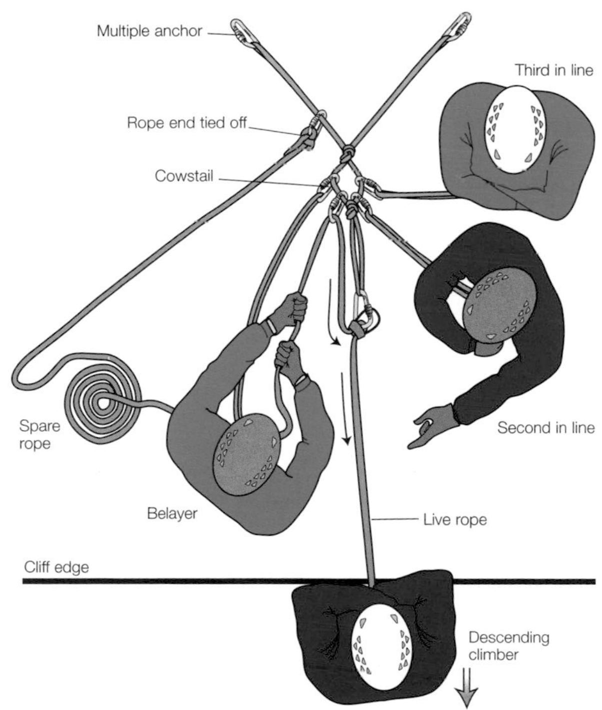

Security of the group when lowering with a belay device.

Lowering

A Freino karabiner and belay device rigged for a lower.

tip

If to hand, a Freino or similarly designed karabiner will perform a similar job to the system above. This style of karabiner has an extra captive section through which the rope can run, allowing the dead rope to be held in the correct position.

Two person lower

Although a lowering system will normally be used for a single person, it is quite possible for two to be lowered together, thus speeding up the overall descent. This may simply be to save time, or it might be required if one of the group members has an injury or medical need, which precludes them from making the descent alone. If this is the case, the system is set up in one of the variations above. The only difference will be the attachment to the rope of both parties. This can be done in one of two ways:

METHOD 1

- A figure of eight on the bight is tied into the end of the rope.
- A 240cm (96in) sling has an overhand knot tied into it at its midway point, and a screwgate karabiner attached. This is clipped on to the figure of eight on the rope.
- The people descending clip on to an end of the sling each, using screwgate karabiners.

A second method, using just the rope, is as follows:

METHOD 2

- At the lowering end, approximately 3m (10ft) of rope is doubled back on itself.
- An overhand or figure-of-eight knot is tied around 1.5m (5ft) along, to make a large loop with a long tail coming out from the knot.
- One person clips themselves on to the loop with a screwgate karabiner.
- The tail end has a figure of eight tied in it and the second person attaches themselves to this.

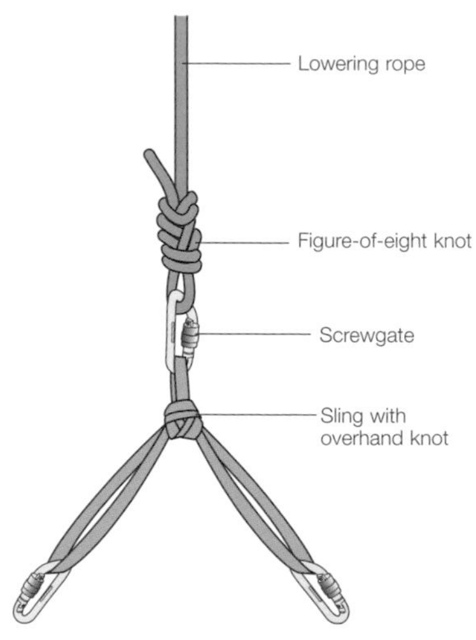

Using a sling to attach two people to a lowering rope.

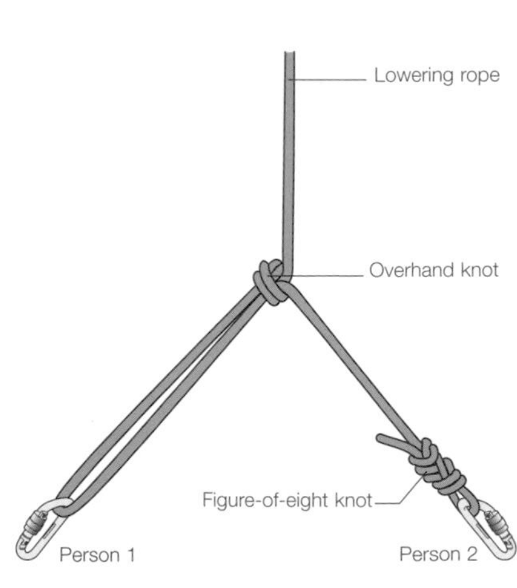

Tying the end of a lowering rope in the 'V' system.

- There is some leeway in the positioning of the two people, as the central knot can be adjusted to allow them to descend in the optimum position.

Lowering with no equipment

In some situations, very little equipment may be to hand with which to construct a technical lower. This will often occur in a hillwalking situation where just a rope is being carried for use in emergencies but there is no intention of using it. If the situation arises where it needs to be deployed, such as if a party came across a short but steep drop, possibly only of a few metres in height but which is unavoidable, a lower could still be organized. As harnesses are unlikely to be carried, this would entail the use of a **Thompson knot** to provide comfort for those descending. Although the system could be set up as a direct belay with the rope running around the back of a suitable boulder or tree, which is a far more sensible proposition as far as the comfort of the belayer is concerned, it is more likely that the lack of equipment will mean that an **indirect belay** system is used, utilizing the **waist belay** as the controlling method. It should be noted that this is not a comfortable method of lowering for the belayer, and if used should be rigged in such a way as to make the most of any padding which can be provided by rucksacks, spare clothing and the like.

METHOD

- The belayer ties on to the anchor, arranged so that they are in a good position near the edge of the drop from where they can communicate with the person being lowered, but not so close that rope-stretch will cause them to be pulled forwards and over the edge. Ideally, this position will be higher than the point at which the lowered person will be committing their weight to the rope.
- The loop that is tied around their waist is adjusted to accommodate the width of a rucksack. This should be worn for the lower, with the shoulder straps being loosened so that it sits low down on the belayer's back.
- The rope from the Thompson knot is arranged in a waist belay manner. The rope at the back of the belayer should be at the same level as that coming in from the anchor, and should sit so that it is running across the rucksack to save it rubbing across the belayer's lower back.
- Padding, such as a spare fleece jacket, can be placed in front of the belayer under the anchor rope around their waist. This helps to lessen the discomfort felt when being pulled forwards on to the anchor rope.
- The lower can start, and should be carried out in a slow and careful manner for the benefit of both parties. Gloves and long sleeves on the part of the belayer are essential.

notes

For all lowers, it cannot be overemphasized how important the solidity of the anchor must be. If there is any doubt whatsoever about its properties it should either be backed up or another one chosen. For an anchor to fail, especially if a group is using it for their own security as well as for the lower, would be catastrophic.

notes

If using the direct belay method for a simple lower using the Thompson knot, care should be taken that the belayer is in no danger of being pulled towards the anchor, losing control of the lower in the process. This could possibly happen if the direct belay was around a tree that afforded little friction. Also, any direct rock belay should be inspected to ensure that it is not only safe but that there is no chance that the rope could get caught in a crack during operation and result in the lowered person being suspended simply by a rope jam, a very difficult situation to rectify.

tip

On rocky ground, once the person has been lowered and is on safe ground, they may need to completely untie any knots in the end of the rope before the belayer pulls it up ready for the next person. If a knot is left in, the rope could jam and become irretrievable.

Lowering

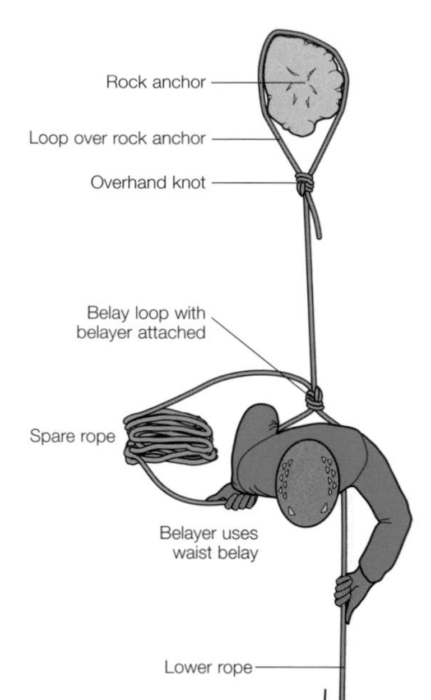

An indirect lower.

notes

On certain types of terrain, it may be necessary to provide some padding over which the rope will run during the lower. This may be because the rope is in danger of being damaged by a sharp edge of rock, or because it will cut into the edge of the ledge, as in the case of snow, and possibly jam. This protection can be easily provided with a rucksack, ice axe or ski pole, ensuring that there is no chance that whatever is used will drop over the edge and be lost and possibly injure the person being lowered.

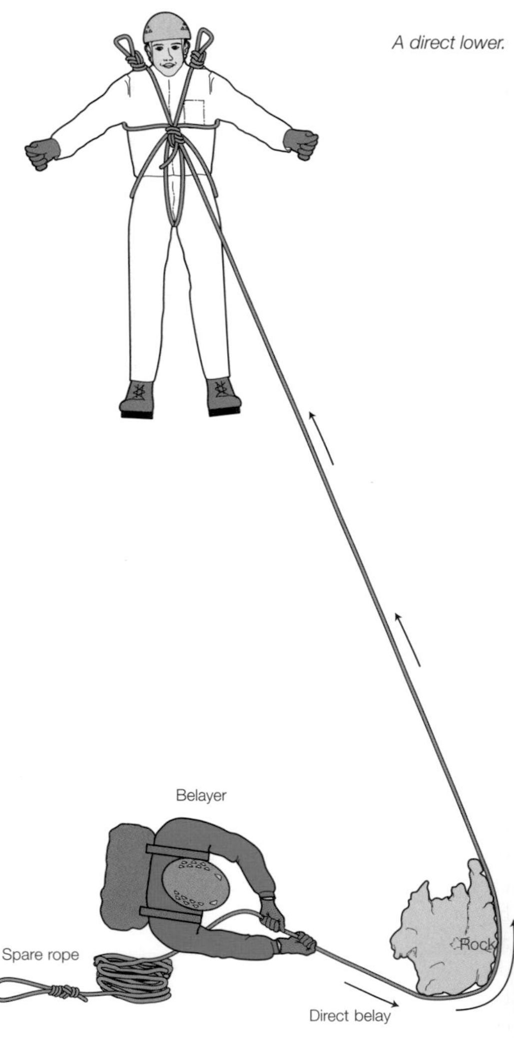

A direct lower.

Lowering off

See also: bolted routes – lowering off, protection, shock loading.

Lowering off is the term usually reserved for a retreat from a route, often simply carried out by a second who lowers their leader back down to the start of a route or pitch. This will most likely be because the pitch is very hard and the leader needs a rest before continuing, or so that the leader and second can swap over. It may also be because the route has been completed and to be lowered off is the standard means of descent.

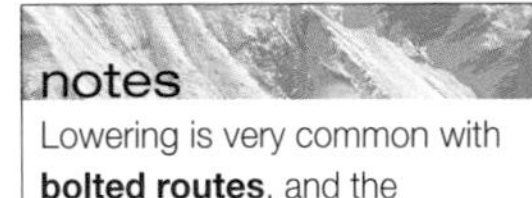

notes

Lowering is very common with **bolted routes**, and the mechanism for safely achieving this is covered under its own heading.

Loading on top runner

An extremely important factor to remember when lowering off from a route is the force being placed on the final piece of equipment through which the rope is running in order for the lower to take place. For instance, it is fairly common for a leader to need to be lowered off a route if they are unhappy about the **protection** that they are placing, the feeling being that it would not be strong enough to hold their weight should a fall occur. The lower would then take place through the last piece of protection. It should be remembered, though, that when the climber commits their weight to that piece of protection it has to not just hold their weight but also that of the belayer, a combined load that may be enough to cause the placement to fail. If this happens and the previous placement was also not as secure as it could have been, the subsequent shock loading could be enough to strip both it and all following pieces of gear from the route.

Placement security

If a leader needs to be lowered off for the reason of poor placements, they need to be certain that the highest point from which they will be suspended is of good quality. If not, backing it up with a second piece would be prudent. Down-climbing would most likely be the best course of action, although care should be taken insofar as the further down the route the leader climbs, the more rope there is up to the last placement and, should they slip on to the rope at some point and the piece fail, this extra rope may be enough to cause them to hit the ground.

Thus, lowering off from a route should only be undertaken if there is no question as to the holding properties of the protection through which the rope will run. If down-climbing is to be carried out, it would be sensible to place a back-up piece of protection as soon as possible below that already being used. If this new placement is very good, the decision may be made to re-ascend a short distance, remove the poor piece, climb back down a way and then be lowered off from the safer point.

Moving together

See also: abseil loop, cowstail, crevasse rescue, harness, nuts, overhand knot, protection, screwgate karabiners, self-arrest, self-belay, slings, tying-off coils.

This is the process by which two or more people move at the same time across either technical or non-technical terrain. This may be on the flat, such as encountered in glacier travel, or on steeper ground such as a snow or rock ridge at altitude. It may also simply be the process by which a climbing party moves from a safe gearing-up spot to the bottom of the climb that they are to attempt, perhaps a distance of no more than a couple of hundred metres but entailing the ascent of a slope. As such, the two most common methods of moving together are:

- On a short rope.
- Climbers close together.
- Hand coils possibly being carried.
- Uncomplicated or non-serious terrain.

Along with:

- Increased rope distance between climbers.
- No hand coils being carried.
- Runners being placed whilst on the move.
- Awkward or technical terrain.

It should be emphasized that moving together is a recipe for disaster if it is not done in an appropriate fashion on relevant terrain, and if it has not been fully discussed and practised beforehand. However, it is a very swift method of moving across a variety of types of ground and is crucial for the safe completion of many alpine and high mountain routes, where to stop and climb each pitch in turn, with the resultant loss of time, would almost inevitably result in benightment or failure.

The distance apart that climbers arrange themselves will depend upon the terrain over which the ascent, or descent, is to take place. The following table is given as a guideline but the actual distance decided upon will obviously be the choice of the climbing party, taking into account such influences as numbers, experience, equipment available and the like.

	Number of climbers	Distance apart
Snow slope	two or more	3m (10ft)
Snow ridge	two or more	6m (20ft)
Rocky ridge	two or more	9m (30ft)

For any of the following examples, it will be assumed that the climbing party is a rope of two people, and that coils have been taken and **tied off** in an appropriate fashion.

Moving together on a snow slope

Ascent of a snow slope will see the climbers arrange themselves to be in the region of 3m (10ft) apart. This allows for a safe distance to be attained between the two, but not so excessive as to create a problem if a slip occurs. When moving up or down the slope, it is the role of the lead person to set a pace that is appropriate to both, and a constant, rhythmic pace will be better than short bursts of speed.

It is for the second person to match the leader's pace, and also to ensure that they never close up to the extent that the rope sags and touches the surface of the snow. If it is allowed to do so, it would mean that there was slack in the system and if a slip occurred the person remaining in control would obviously be shock-loaded with greater force than if there were no slack at all.

Conversely, the second's pace must also be regulated to ensure that they are never tugging the leader backwards with the rope, as this would not only be irritating and tiring for the leader, but could also upset their balance.

Distance

This method of ascent is frequently used for the rise from a gearing-up area to the start of a climb. The preparation of equipment may have taken place on a flat safe area at the bottom of the cliffs, but the climb starts on the steeper ground above. In this situation, once the stance has been reached where the first belay is to be constructed, both climbers can clip themselves into it with a **cowstail**. They are then safe and free to uncoil the ropes from around themselves and prepare to climb in the normal manner.

Moving together on a snow ridge

The negotiation of a sharp snowed-up ridge presents a different problem to the climbers, as the possibility to stop and take a conventional belay may be less than on a wider ridge or one with rock protrusions. The distance between the climbers is thus adjusted to be in the region of 6m, maybe with a couple of hand coils being carried, with the extra rope allowing for an unconventional, if effective, remedy to a partner slipping off one side.

If the leader falls off to the left of the ridge, for instance, the immediate reaction of the second should be to throw themselves to the right. This results in a counterbalance situation with the weight of the climbers supporting each other and the rope cutting into the snow and helping to create some friction. Re-ascent to the ridge should be made as soon as possible, with coordination of the final couple of metres being essential so that the weight of one climber does not pull the other over the opposite side.

notes

The first line of defence will be a swift and safe execution of a **self-belay** or **self-arrest**, and these skills should have been well practised before taking to the hills.

tips

If negotiating a wide snow slope and both climbers are of equal ability, there is no reason why they should not ascend or descend side by side, remembering the above notes about keeping the rope clear of the snow. However, if there is a more experienced climber in the group they would be best taking the lead so that, should the lesser skilled person take a slip, there is no slack rope in the system and the slip is more easily controlled.

Moving together

Moving together on a rock ridge

The ascent or descent of a narrow rocky ridge, or indeed any rocky terrain where moving together would be appropriate, will often allow some measure of more conventional security to be introduced into the system. At its most basic level, as the person leading passes a suitable rock spike or block, they can either flick the rope over it or alter their route slightly so that they are weaving in and out of a number of these. The idea is that, should a fall occur, the rope will be held by the rock and the distance fallen will be minimal. A length between climbers of about 9m (30ft) is optimum (although this could be lengthened for steeper ground), as it is long enough to allow for the rope to be used around spikes and blocks en route, but not so long that excessive friction or jamming occurs.

Using protection

A more technical approach can be made on this type of terrain in that the leader places **protection** of some description, maybe simply a **sling** over a spike or a **nut** in a crack, and then clips the rope through it so that it runs freely. This protection will then act as a stop in the event of a fall. Any protection placed should be extended a suitable distance to negate the chance of either party pulling it out when moving close by, and stops can be made at relevant points so that the gear collected by the second can be returned to the leader. Alternatively, the second could lead through and alternate leads take place.

notes

When dealing with technical ground, thought should be given to the safety of the leader. If the second falls off, and this need only be a short slip, the leader could be pulled back and off from any move that they are currently making, with the high possibility of them falling and sustaining injury. The leader may therefore decide to place a series of small rope clamps to any intermediate protection points to help negate this, so that should the second slip the clamps grip the rope and the second's weight is held by it and not by their partner. This is, however, a technique that requires a lot of judgement and experience to accomplish swiftly and safely, and the time taken for an inexperienced party to think through and rig this process on even a short section may have been better spent by them in resorting to conventional pitching.

An overhand knot rethreaded at the harness.

Dealing with larger parties

If more than two people are to be included on the rope, they need to be incorporated into the system using the distances suggested above. Their attachment is best achieved by tying an isolation loop, usually through the use of an **overhand knot**, on the rope giving a loop about 1.5m (5ft) long. The end of this loop is then attached to the harness by an overhand knot rethreaded, the short end of which is then clipped back into itself with a screwgate karabiner for security. When they are moving with the team, it is important that they stay behind the knot on the rope so that any slip that they may take will have a minimal shock-loading effect on those ahead of them.

If others are to join the team for a short distance on snowy terrain, for instance when making their way up from a gearing-up area to the start of a climb, the isolation loop should be tied a lot shorter. Measuring about half a metre, the attachment can be made directly with a screwgate karabiner into the harness strongpoint, most likely the **abseil loop.** However, if the group is to negotiate any awkward ground the extra climbers should tie in with the overhand knot system, a process that only takes a few seconds longer but provides far greater security.

notes

If this technique is being used on steep ground, consideration should be given as to whether it is appropriate given the terrain and associated risks. If there is any question, a different approach should be adopted, which may well be the more conventional pitching of sections until any difficulty is bypassed, and moving together is once again appropriate.

Multi-pitch climbing

See also: belay device, belay device orientation, clove hitch, direct belay, double rope techniques, escaping the system, fall factors, live rope, moving together, overhand knot, protection, running belay, screwgate karabiner, self-locking belay device, twin roping.

Multi-pitch climbing demands a great deal more thought and structure of approach than single-pitch routes will often require. The entire process of climbing, anchoring and either keeping the same leader or leading through means that methodical organization will make the difference between safety, success and disaster.

Climbing styles

Two basic processes can be identified in multi-pitch climbing. The first is where the lead alternates, such as with two climbers where each person climbs on and completes a lead, and then brings up the second who collects gear from them and in turn becomes the leader. This is the norm for an informal climbing team. The other is where one person does all the leading. This may be because it is an informal team but their companion is a novice, or because the leader is being professionally employed to take others climbing, on a mountaineering course or a guided trip.

Leading through

The mechanics by which each variation is completed rely very much on the ability, experience and skill of the person or persons organizing the climb, as well as that of those taking part.

For the first example, it will be taken that the two climbers are on an informal trip and that the intention is for them to lead through, that is, to alternate the lead. It is immaterial as far as these techniques are concerned whether they are on rock or snow, although here we will assume snow, as the leader will make their axes safe by clipping them to the anchor.

Multi-pitch climbing

EXAMPLE 1

- From the lowest stance, the leader makes their way up the first pitch and belays themselves. They should note the direction that the next pitch takes and position themselves accordingly.
- Care should be taken that, when belaying the second up, the dead rope does not fall down the route.

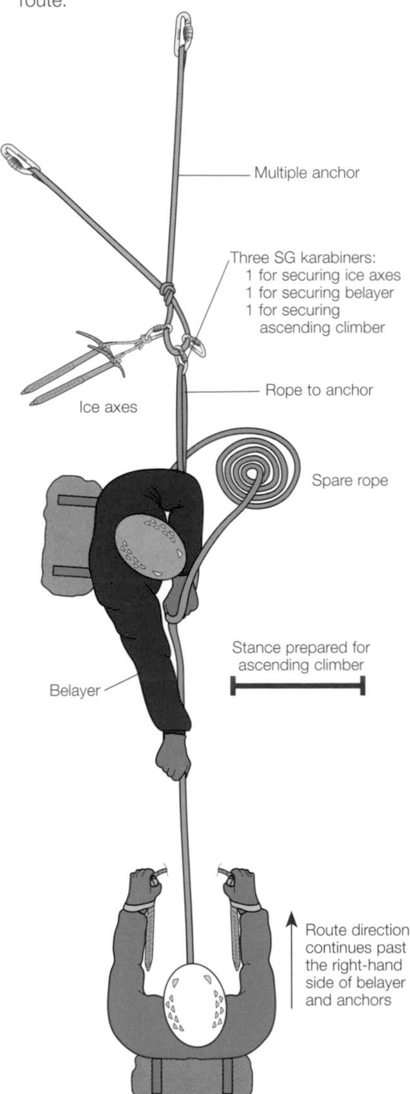

A basic leading-through belay system.

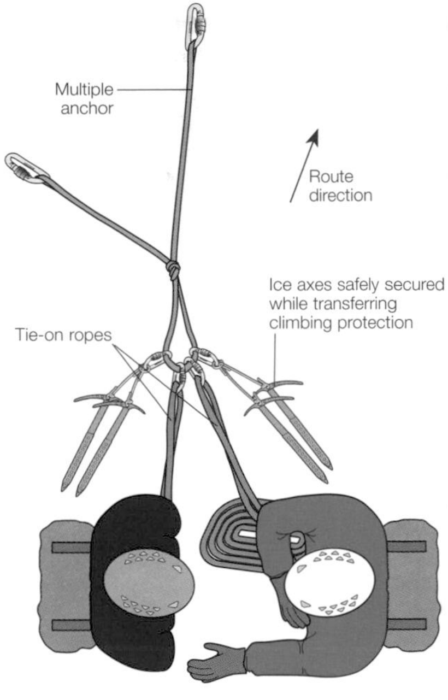

Both climbers at the stance on a leading-through system.

- When they arrive at the stance, the second can make themselves safe by clipping into the anchor using a **screwgate karabiner** and a **clove hitch** taken from either the **live** or **dead rope** just in front or behind of the **belay device**.
- It is very likely that the belay device will need to be **re-orientated**. This is a step that is often overlooked as it is felt that it is unnecessary. However, an incorrectly orientated belay device taking the force of a fall, with the possibility of the rope within the device crossing over and jamming, should not be treated lightly, as it would result in both members having an extremely difficult time extracting themselves from the stuck system.
- The equipment is passed across to the new leader, taking care that none is dropped.
- The new leader can, once the belayer is ready, unclip themselves from the anchor and continue.

Improved leading-through system

This is a very basic method of the management of leading through on multi-pitch routes, with only the re-orientation of the belay device requiring much thought. To markedly improve on this system, a little extra time should be given to the construction of an anchor rig that greatly eases the transfer of second to leader.

EXAMPLE 2

- Once the leader reaches the stance, they anchor and secure themselves.
- At the base of the next section of the route, they place a piece of **protection**. This will in effect become the first **runner** of the next pitch.
- The leader takes in the rope as normal and clips it through the protection above, then down to their belay device.
- When the second arrives at the stance, they can be made safe by the belayer tying a large **overhand knot** on the bight directly in front of the belay device.
- Once the equipment has been transferred, the second can now become the leader and continue up the route.

Advantages

The advantage of this method is that once the original leader has constructed the anchor system as described, no re-orientation of the rope or other part of the system has to take place. The second simply arrives, picks up the spare kit, and climbs on. It also has the advantage that the leader, belaying from above, has the assistance of the high runner to take the weight of a fallen second, rather than all of the weight being taken in a downwards pull as would be the case with the basic rig. Having a pre-placed runner to lower the possible **fall factor** when the leader leaves the stance is also a definite advantage.

> **tip**
> It may be prudent in some situations to have part of the anchor system able to take an upward pull in case escaping the system becomes necessary.

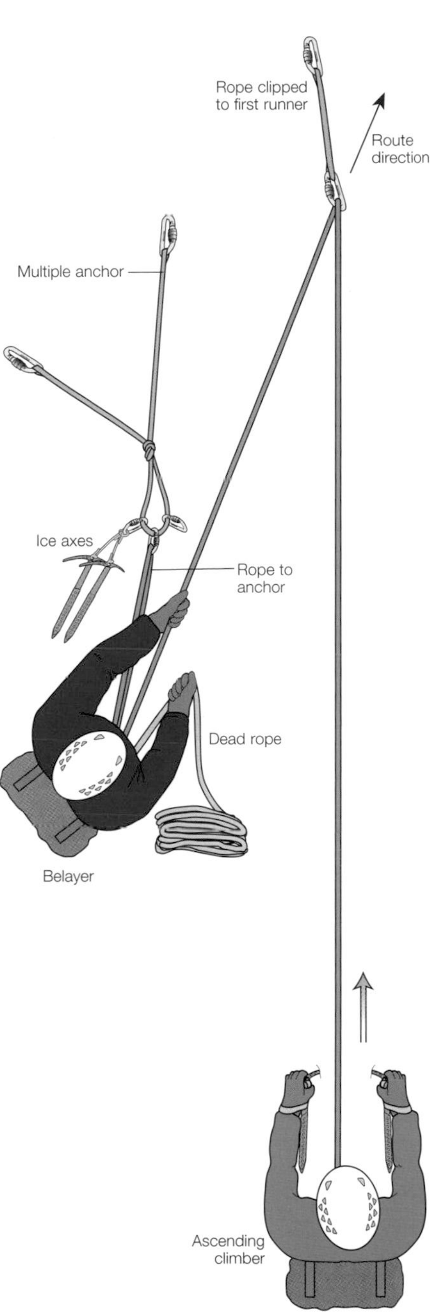

The improved leading through anchor system.

Leading two seconds

The management of two seconds makes for more complicated belaying, but overall should not present too much difficulty to a leader who is used to climbing multi-pitch routes. This method is often the one utilized by a leader who is working with clients and will lead the entire route. A suggested way of dealing with this is as follows, and in this case the leader is climbing with two ropes, one to each second, and the belaying method is a **self-locking belay device** on a **direct belay**.

METHOD

- The leader is tied on to one end of each of the ropes. Once they arrive at the stance, they create an anchor system and clip in.
- Two screwgate karabiners are placed on the anchor, in readiness for the arrival of the two seconds. In snow, stances could be cut for them.
- Once at the stance, the seconds are made safe by clipping them into the screwgates on the anchor with clove hitches from an appropriate point of either the live or dead ropes. The two should be positioned in the order that they are to climb the next pitch, and should be placed to the inside of the direction that the leader needs to take.
- The belay device can be removed from the anchor and the slack taken in through the clove hitches if required.
- Both of the dead ropes need to be run through, so that the rope to the leader is coming out of the top of the pile. This is important to avoid any chance of tangling, something that may be difficult for a novice second to efficiently rectify, especially on technical ground.
- The leader then continues.

This is a very simple method of managing the situation. Either one or both of the seconds can then belay the leader. If both are belaying, it means that they are occupied and are learning as they do so. It also means that the leader has a little more leeway in the rope system that they decide to use, as **double roping** may be their choice. However, this is often more awkward for the seconds to manage,

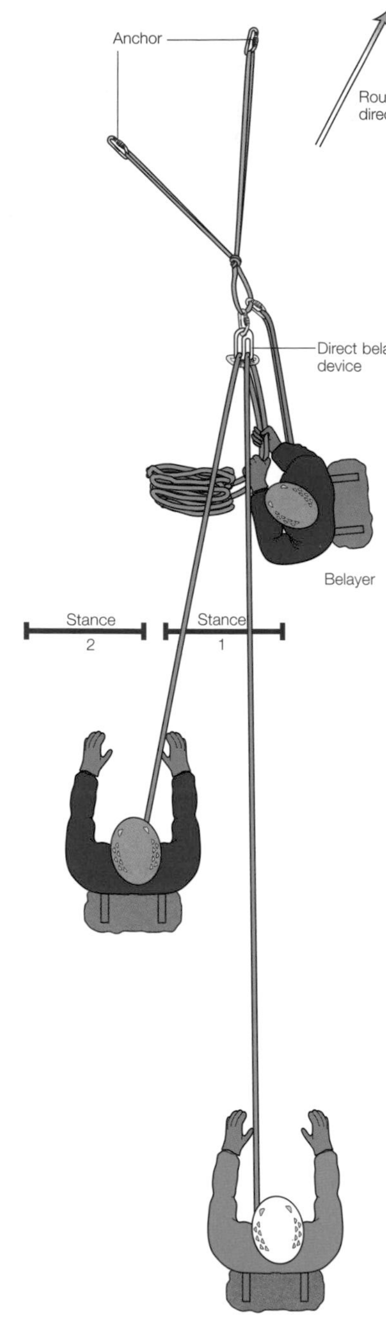

A leader bringing up two seconds using a self-locking belay device.

and if they are not belayed in a line one above the other there is a concern that the rope from the inner second to the leader will be running awkwardly around the other person. Therefore, a better method may be for just one of them to be belaying, which will be the person on the side nearest the leader, and the other to manage the ropes by paying theirs out hand over hand as it is needed.

Two seconds climbing

As far as the climbing is concerned, the seconds can either climb side by side, which has the advantage that they will not be dropping any debris on the other in a loose mountain or winter situation (awkward, however, to maintain, as one person will almost always be climbing faster than the other), or one behind the other if space is restricted, such as on a defined route or winter gully. It may be that the leader brings one second up and allows them to belay the third person, very much dependent upon the required outcome and learning structure desired for the trip.

If a single rope is being used to bring up two seconds, the set-up at the anchor will differ only slightly. For attaching the extra person to the rope, see the relevant diagram and description under **'moving together'**. The distance between the person on the end of the rope and the one attached ahead of them will be in the region of 2–3m (6–9ft). In winter, it is important that there is no way that the crampons of the second person can reach the head of the third person in the event of a slip. Once they arrive at the stance, they can be clipped into the pre-placed screwgates as before, but this time the rope between them can be used for the clove hitches. They should again be placed in an appropriate position, with the leader on the side of the system from where they will be moving up the next pitch of the route. Once the rope has been run through, it will be the person nearest to the leader who will belay.

Multiple seconds

It is quite possible to bring up three or four climbers on two ropes. This should only be contemplated on ground where a slip will not result in a major problem, and will often be reserved for use by the most competent of leaders on ground requiring a fast ascent, such as moderate rock or snow terrain. Although a very quick way of climbing with a large group, poor management at the stances will result in any time advantage being wasted away with sorting out positioning, rope tangles and the like. The following method is a method of bringing up three seconds on two ropes, again using a self-locking belay device with a direct belay.

notes

The double and **twin rope** systems are quite popular and relevant when climbing on technical routes. If leading with two ropes, it would be a good idea to use just one to tie in to the anchor as the second rope, not part of the system, can be used in case of emergency.

notes

On routes in winter, or when on shattered ground, as may often be encountered on mountains, care should be taken when positioning the stance. Consideration must be given to the direction of the subsequent pitch, as any debris knocked off by the leader could fall and injure those left at the belay.

tips

Whenever there is someone other than the belayer at the stance, it would be sensible to involve them in any rope work that needs to be carried out. In particular, they could be running their rope through in preparation for the next pitch, to save time when the others arrive. Helping to re-rack and sort equipment would also be a time-saver.

Multi-pitch climbing

METHOD

- The stance and anchor system is prepared as normal, again with two spare screwgate karabiners in preparation for the arrival of the seconds.
- The seconds ascend in the pre-arranged order.
- The person on their own on the rope is clipped into a position nearest the leader.
- The two climbers on the same rope, once they have reached the stance, are clipped into the other screwgate. This could be in a manner that means they are counterbalancing each other, with the rope between them being simply clipped through the screwgate. If thought necessary, a clove hitch could be used to provide extra security.
- The ropes need to be run through so that the ropes to the leader are coming from the top of the piles.
- The single person nearest the leader now belays them as they climb the next pitch, the next nearest, most likely the higher of the two on the second rope, pays out their rope hand over hand to ensure that no tangles or snagging occurs.

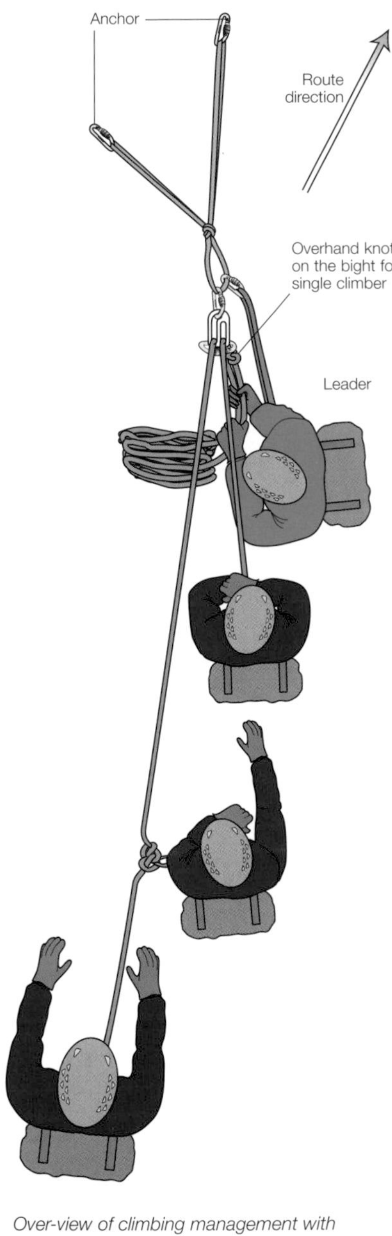

Over-view of climbing management with three seconds.

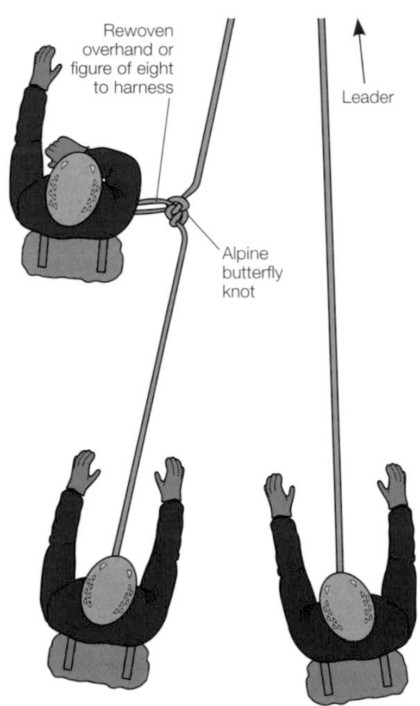

The attachment of three seconds.

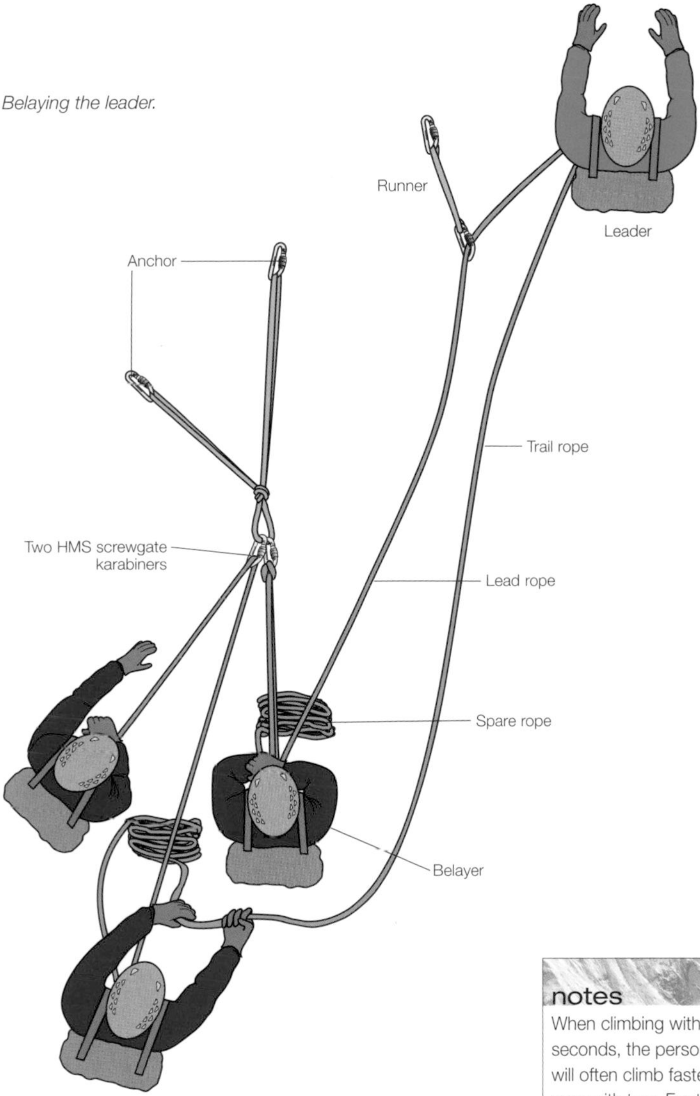

Belaying the leader.

Runner

Leader

Anchor

Trail rope

Two HMS screwgate karabiners

Lead rope

Spare rope

Belayer

notes

When climbing with three seconds, the person on their own will often climb faster than the rope with two. For that reason, this may be the person who is briefed to ascend first.

Munter hitch

See Italian hitch.

New Zealand boot-axe belay

See boot/axe belay.

Newtons

See kiloNewtons.

Nuts

See also: running belays.

This is the generic name given to a variety of metal wedges fixed to the end of wire, rope or tape extensions, ranging in size from very small to extremely large. They are used for placement on the lead as **running belay**s, as well as for anchor construction. Many manufacturers have their own versions, and climbers often display loyalty towards their own favourite design.

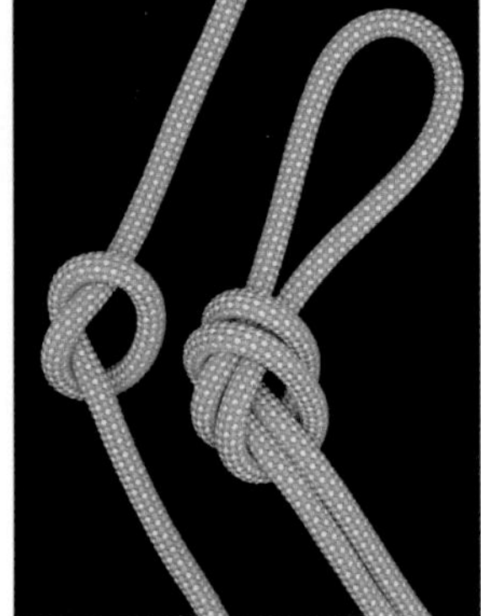

An overhand knot and an overhand knot on the bight.

Overhand knot

See also: bowline, equalizing anchors, figure of eight, slings.

The overhand knot has its place as both a **stopper knot** and as a method of attachment in its own right. If it is being used as a stopper on a **figure of eight** or **bowline** for instance, it should be tied so that it is snug against the main knot when it is tightened. It can also be tied on the bight to provide a quick and simple loop for either belaying with or fixing around the waist.

A third common use for the overhand knot is when using **slings** to **equalize anchors**

Opposition placements

See also: nuts, running belays.

These can be useful if conventional placements, for either **running belays** or anchors, would not be suitable due to the direction of loading. They can be placed in any plane from horizontal to vertical, and a number of variations are possible. The simplest of these is for the connecting rope of one nut to pass through the karabiner attached to another. A load applied will then have the effect of pulling the two placements closer to each other, but with the understanding that they will also be pulled slightly outwards as well. If an opposition placement is needed in a vertical crack to stop one piece of protection from being pulled upwards by the rope, for instance, the lower opposing nut could be secured to it by way of an overhand knot on a sling, tied so that the connecting section is pulled snug.

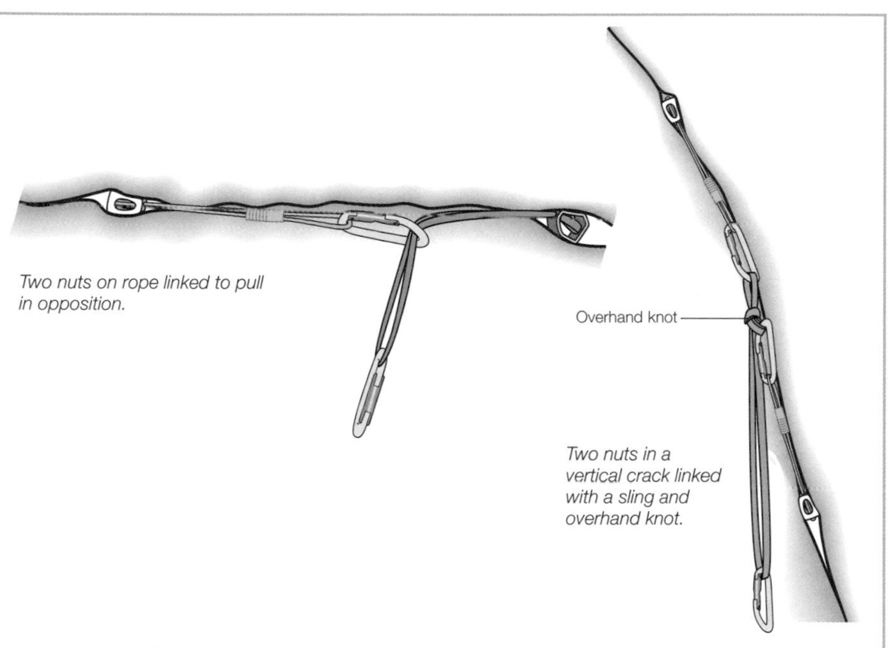

Two nuts on rope linked to pull in opposition.

Two nuts in a vertical crack linked with a sling and overhand knot.

Parisian baudrier

See also: French prusik, lark's foot, sheet bend.

This is an effective method of improvising a chest harness, and can be most useful if working with a casualty. It can be tied with a single 240cm (96in) sling, or with two 120cm (48in) slings joined with a **lark's foot.** The knot with which it is tied is a **sheet bend**, and care should be taken that this is tied correctly and that the knot cannot slide tight, causing injury to the wearer.

In an emergency situation, it may be necessary for the rescuer, having descended to an unconscious casualty and placed a Parisian baudrier around them, to connect it to the support rope in a releasable fashion. This could be attained by using a French prusik, which means that the support to the casualty's chest could be swiftly released if the rescuer needed to clear their airway in a hurry.

A Parisian baudrier.

Passing a knot on an abseil

See abseiling past a knot.

Passing a knot on a lower

See also: anchor, abseil device, belay device, French prusik, HMS screwgate, Italian hitch – locking off, overhand knot, passing a knot on an abseil, prusik loop.

The reasons for having to pass a knot on a lower are very similar to those for **passing a knot on an abseil**. You may need to lower an injured companion a long distance down a mountainside, so the ability to tie two or more ropes together will greatly speed up the descent, as the distance that can be lowered from each individual stance will be increased. Alternatively, mechanical damage to the rope may have occurred, with the offending section having been isolated with a suitable knot.

Methodical set-up

A methodical set-up at the stance is important, and there are a number of variations possible. The system described here uses **Italian hitches** clipped into **HMS screwgates** as the controlling devices, as this method uses the minimum amount of equipment. To replace one or more of the Italian hitches with a **belay** or **abseil device** of some description would be perfectly acceptable. For this purpose, we will also assume that the **anchor** is coming from a single point.

Communication

If the terrain over which the lower takes place allows the person descending to take their weight off the rope, then the time taken to complete the bypassing of a knot is greatly speeded up. It is important, however, that there is clear communication between the person being lowered and the person who is in control at the stance. Should there be any question that commands and calls are not being clearly heard and understood by either party, it is important that the controller takes over the running of the entire system and does things at his or her own speed.

Initially, we will assume that there is good and clear communication between the two people and that the terrain is such that the person being lowered can unweight the rope. Cutting a ledge in the snow or using suitable rock ledges to stand on may well achieve this.

METHOD

- As the knot in the rope is nearing the Italian hitch, the person being lowered will be prompted to make him or herself safe. This will ideally be at a point where the knot is in the region of 60cm (24in) from the karabiner into which the Italian hitch is clipped.
- Once the call has come from down below that your partner is safe, it would be very tempting simply to undo the karabiner, take the rope from the other side of the knot, tie a new Italian hitch there, clip that into the karabiner and continue lowering. However, such a decision should not be taken lightly, for if the person below loses balance or is for some reason knocked off their feet, perhaps by a snow slide or strong wind, the consequences would not only be severe for them but would also involve a huge loading on the anchor system, which may then fail. This could result in the loss of the rope at least, worse still the loss of the belayer if they were also clipped in. To avoid this, **lock off the Italian hitch**, tie a second Italian hitch in the lowering rope on the opposite side of the knotted section, clip this into a second karabiner, release the first one and take it out of the karabiner, then continue lowering. The person being lowered will have to step carefully down the initial metre or so until their weight is back on the rope in order to avoid shock loading the system.

Opposite: *The Great Prow, Sa Gubia, Mallorca*

P

Passing a knot on a lower

Advanced lower

If the lower is down terrain where the lowered party cannot get any purchase on rock or ice to aid them in bypassing of the knot, or if the casualty is unable to assist due to injury or unconsciousness, then the process will have to be carried out with the system loaded throughout. We will again assume that a single point of attachment for the anchor is being used, although this could, of course, either be one anchor, or two or more that are brought down to one point.

METHOD

- At the attachment point, most likely formed by a sling, clip in two HMS screwgates alongside a third screwgate containing a **prusik loop** on a 120cm (48in) sling.
- Into one of the HMS karabiners goes an Italian hitch, formed on the rope to the person to be lowered.
- The prusik loop is tied as a French prusik on to the live rope. This is not so much a back-up in case the rope should slip too fast through the friction hitch, although it may well serve this purpose, but more as a preparation for the procedure to follow.
- Lower the person until the knot in the rope is around 60cm (12in) away from the Italian hitch, then let the French prusik take up the weight, easing the weight of the lowered person slowly on to it.
- A second Italian hitch can now be tied on the opposite side of the knot in the rope and clipped into the second HMS, taking care not to let go of the dead rope during this procedure. A little practice in advance will result in the slick tying of an Italian hitch with one hand.
- Once the hitch has been tied, ensure that the knot in the rope is butted up against the HMS.
- The first Italian hitch can now be unclipped, again ensuring that you do not let go of the dead rope in case the French prusik should slip and the rope start to run.
- Still holding firm to the dead rope, pull upwards on the French prusik to release it, taking care to do this slowly, to allow the load to come on to the second HMS.
- The prusik can now be unclipped and taken off the lowering rope. You may wish to replace it as a back-up, otherwise leave it hanging while you continue the lower.

If there is more than one knot in the lowering rope, it is prudent to tie off the Italian hitch to allow the replacing of the French prusik in preparation for the next time it is needed.

Peg

See piton.

Peg hammer

See also: piton.

A peg hammer is carried when the placement of **pitons** is intended. You might not need to carry one on a long winter route if an ice hammer is being carried, as this will adequately perform the job.

A variety of designs are available, but a standard hammer will have a rubber grip, a head with a striking surface on one side and a spike to aid the cleaning of cracks as well as piton removal on the other, and an eye or similar point at the end of the shaft for attaching a cord, which can clip to the climber's harness for security in case the hammer is dropped.

The most usual way to carry a hammer is in a purpose-designed holster clipped on to the harness. However, if it is to be used frequently, such as when aiding a difficult pitch, it may be more convenient to have it attached to the harness and suspended below the climber. The rope from which it is suspended need not be longer than the distance of a full arm stretch above the head.

Opposite: *Hard but well protected climbing on granite.*

Pendulum

See also; pendulum traverse.

A pendulum is the name given to a swing across a rock or ice face, performed either intentionally or not. To perform a pendulum intentionally usually means that it is being used to aid progress: see **pendulum traverse.** An unintentional pendulum is to be avoided at all costs, as it often means the uncontrolled swinging of a climber or abseiler, possibly into a wall of rock or other obstruction.

Pendulum traverse

See also: ascending the rope.

A pendulum traverse is a method by which blank areas of rock can be bypassed in order to gain easier ground. In its simplest terms, it involves the leader swinging backwards and forwards across the rock, often running in order to gain momentum, until purchase can be made some distance away. It is best completed with two ropes, one to support the pendulum and the other as a safety rope that can be clipped into runners or an anchor, once the ground has been covered. The use of two ropes also ensures that the second climber is safeguarded as they make their way across, either by penduluming from the same suspension point or maybe by **ascending the rope** to the stance taken by the leader.

Recovering the rope

Thought should be given to the recovery of the rope, and it may be that the leader pendulums from a bight of rope through an anchor point which is then pulled through once the manoeuvre is complete, allowing the second to then progress with the second rope.

Great care should be taken when organizing a pendulum traverse that the rope will not be abraded by the action of it rubbing on the rock as the leader makes their series of swings. It would be prudent not to make a pendulum traverse directly from an anchor system, but to place protection, which may have to be sacrificed, from which the technique can then take place.

Piton

See also: clove hitch, extender, peg hammer, protection.

A piton, or peg, is a piece of pre-shaped metal that is forced into a crack with a **peg hammer**, for use as protection or a belay. In particular, they are sometimes used as protection when aid climbing on technical routes, either crag level or expedition big walls. However, local ethics will dictate whether they are acceptable for use or not, and many areas do not welcome them due to their propensity for scarring the rock into which they are placed. They come in many shapes and sizes, from very small (often called RURPs, standing for 'Realized Ultimate Reality Piton') which have blades measuring only a millimetre or so in thickness, through to bongs, large pieces of folded metal, designed for placement in cracks several centimetres wide, with their name derived from the noise that they make when driven in.

Types of piton

Pitons can be loosely categorized into two types: those that present a flat surface to the rock when driven in, and those that present an angle, as a fold in the metal is part of the design and manufacturing process, often a 'V' in section. Into the first category fall RURPs, knife blades, kingpins and lost arrows; the second category includes the likes of angles, leepers and bongs.

Generalizing for all piton placements, they should be capable of being placed into a crack for 50 to 75 per cent of their length, depending upon type, be driven in until the eye is flush with the rock, and produce a note that steadily rises in pitch – a good measure as to how well the rock is gripping the metal. A far better placement will be obtained if the piton is placed into a crack capable of accepting it, and not into a crack that will need the piton to be pounded almost out of shape in order to make it fit. A horizontal placement will usually be stronger than a vertical one.

Tying off pitons

If a piton cannot be driven all the way in, care should be taken that the eye is not clipped and then loaded, causing a high amount of leverage to be taken by the placement. A short loop of sling can be tied in a **clove hitch** and placed over the eye of the piton, and then inverted and pushed down until flush with the surface of the rock. A karabiner can then be clipped into this sling, with any subsequent load being exerted on to the point that the piton enters the rock. In some circumstances, if a kingpin or lost arrow is being used, it may be prudent to insert the piton eye-uppermost to avoid the chance of the sling slipping off. For all other piton types, where the eye should be placed at either the lower or side of the placement, clipping a spare karabiner into the eye will help prevent the sling from dislodging completely.

Stacking pitons

In some situations, the crack that is presented may be wider than the width of a single piton. In this instance, it is quite acceptable to stack two or more pitons together and drive them in, to achieve a secure placement. Some combinations of pitons sit together well, for instance two angles stacked up, or an angle with a leeper. Other combinations are not as effective, in particular arranging a lost arrow along with a bong can be particularly awkward. If stacking pitons, treat one of them as the 'real' placement, with the others doing the work of holding it securely into the rock. When they have been driven in, a placement of stacked pitons should be tested by hand to ensure that, even if they are secure in one plane, they do not slide against each other and slip out if loaded in another.

Removal

Most designs of piton can be removed by successively tapping each side of its head a couple of times. This wears a channel in the rock and aids extraction. As the piton loosens, there is a good chance that it will drop out on the final blow and be lost. To help prevent this, an old karabiner or piece of rope can be threaded through the eye so that the piton is held should it fall from the crack. Using the spiked section of the head of the **peg hammer** as a lever will aid this removal.

notes

A piton should never be hit whilst the extender is still clipped into it, as this is likely to result in damage to the connecting karabiner. If some connection is needed to ensure that the piton is not lost during removal, a designated small accessory karabiner – one that has been retired from climbing – can be clipped in with a length of cord attached.

Stacked pitons.

A piton tied off to reduce leverage.

notes

It is the removal of pitons that creates damage to the rock, and this is why they are frowned upon in many areas of the world. The hitting from side to side of the placement to produce a gap wide enough to allow them to slide out, creates a channel from which the piton can be removed but which damages the rock irreparably.

Piton hammer

See peg hammer.

Piton brake

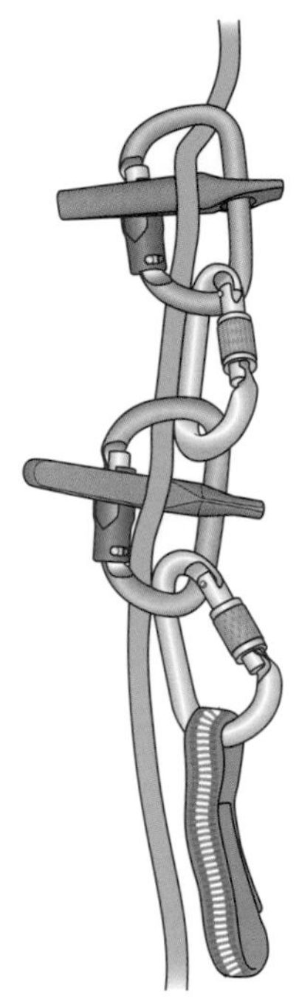

A piton brake, with a karabiner being used to extend one group of pitons above another.

notes

It should be noted that if there is any chance of the abseil rope touching the webbing connecting the lower karabiner to the climber's harness during the descent, this should be replaced by a screwgate. If the rope were to rub against the tape it would generate heat and cause the webbing to become damaged or even to fail.

See also: abseiling, extenders, karabiner brake, lowering, piton, wires.

The piton brake is a method by which the rope is run through one or more **pitons** in such a configuration as to provide sufficient friction to hold bodyweight, usually in an abseiling situation. This method of descent is seen as being all but obsolete for most modern mountaineering circumstances. However, it may still have its place when friction in excess of that which can be provided by modern devices is required, such as when **lowering** or **abseiling** with a casualty on slick ropes.

Equipment

The number of pitons used depends on the amount of friction required: the more pitons, the more the friction. Large-angle pitons are the best to use, as they will fit across a karabiner and remain reasonably stable. Kingpins are a good second best. Each piton should be placed on a separate screwgate karabiner, with the back bar of each karabiner being as straight as possible to allow the piton to sit squarely. 'D'-shaped karabiners are well suited to this process.

Linking brakes

If successive karabiners with pitons across them need to be linked up, they can be attached to each other in a variety of fashions. The least desirable is to link them together using tape, such as short **extenders**. This will do the job for a short while, but there is a high chance of the tape melting through during an abseil descent, with the system failing after only a short distance. The best method is to connect them with either a screwgate karabiner between each set, or to use **wires**. If using a wire, one end of it can be clipped in the normal manner, with a second loop being created by pushing the body of the wire up slightly so that the head of the wire slides down a little, exposing enough area in which to clip the other screwgate.

With either of these methods, ensure that the part of the linking screwgate or wire that is taking the load is at the closest point to the back bar of the karabiners holding the pitons. If not, and the rope was next to the back bar with a supporting karabiner or wire next to it, when the system was loaded the link could force the abseil rope against the back bar, causing it to jam.

Protecting an abseil

See: abseil protection.

Protection

See also: bolts, nuts, SLCDs, wires.

Protection is the generic name given to equipment placed in the rock, snow or ice, designed to safeguard the climber or abseiler. It can take a variety of forms, from permanent **bolts** through to equipment placed on the lead by a climber such as **SLCD**s, **wires** and **nuts**, which will later be removed as their second follows them.

Prusiking

See ascending the rope.

Prusik knot

See also: klemheist.

The prusik knot, devised by the Austrian Doctor Karl Prusik, is now often overlooked in favour of the klemheist. It can be prone to jamming in certain circumstances, for instance on wet ropes, and thus be difficult to move when speed is a factor. However, it has its place in some situations, particularly as it is possible to tie it with one hand.

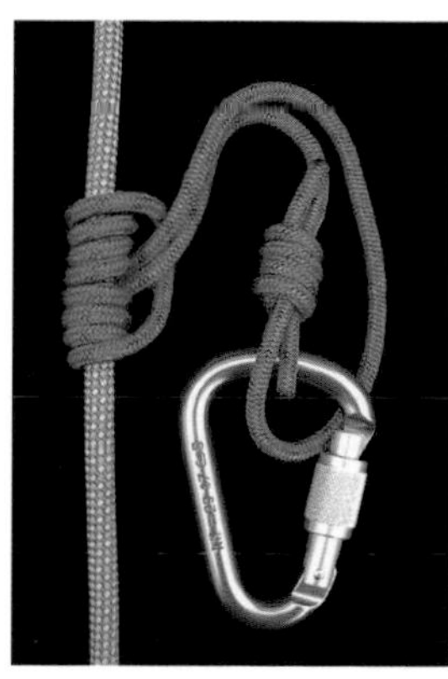

The prusik knot.

Prusik loop

See also: accessory cord, autobloc, double fisherman's knot.

The prusik loop is the generic name given to a length of **accessory cord**, the ends tied together (usually with a **double fisherman's knot**), which can be used to construct a variety of prusik knots and **autoblocs**. Two loops are often carried, and they can prove very useful in all climbing situations. The length of these loops is up to personal preference, but it may be found that a length of 40cm (16in) when tied, will be about right. The diameter of the accessory cord from which the loops are made is quite important, and 6mm cord will most likely be found to be the most suitable. Much less than this and the cord will tend to bite in tightly to the climbing rope when loaded, especially when wet; any thicker and the loop is less likely to grip effectively.

Pulley

See also: hauling, hoisting, self-belaying.

Pulleys come in a variety of shapes and sizes, although all are designed to perform a similar job, primarily that of reducing friction in a hoisting or hauling system. They can be simple in design, such as a basic and lightweight swing-cheek pulley useful for techniques such as crevasse rescue, through to those that incorporate a system of automatically locking off the load when the operator requires it to do so. Pulleys of the latter type can also be used, in some situations, as self-locking devices, which enable a climber to **self-belay** up a rope whilst still being protected.

A selection of pulleys.

Pulley systems

See hauling.

Punter knot

See tying on.

Quickdraws

See extenders.

Opposite: *Challenging ground in the Nepalese Himalaya.*

Rapelling

See abseiling.

Reef knot

See also: abseil rope: joining, coiling the rope.

The reef knot has a number of uses. It is most likely to be used for tying the rope around the waist of the person carrying it, once it has been coiled at the end of a route. It is also utilized as part of the knot system when joining two ropes together, when organizing an abseil.

A reef knot joining two ropes.

Reinforced buried axe

See also: buried axe anchor, clove hitch.

This belay method has the advantage over the standard **buried axe anchor** in that it provides a degree of extra security in softer snow conditions. The preparation is exactly the same as for the buried axe anchor, up to and including the point where the horizontal axe is placed into the slot.

METHOD

- Using a second ice tool, place it just back from vertical into the top of the vertical slot so that it is just touching the shaft of the horizontal axe.
- It should be pushed down between the two sides of the sling coming from the inverted **clove hitch**.
- Care should be taken that it does not disturb the horizontal axe, pushing it up and away from the downslope face of the slot.
- The vertical axe should be pushed down as far as possible, stopping at a point where its head reaches the level of the shaft of the horizontal axe.
- The anchor sling should be tugged, keeping it level with, or below the level of the ground, to ensure that the set-up is sitting correctly.
- The rest of the process is as for the buried axe anchor.

The reinforced buried axe anchor.

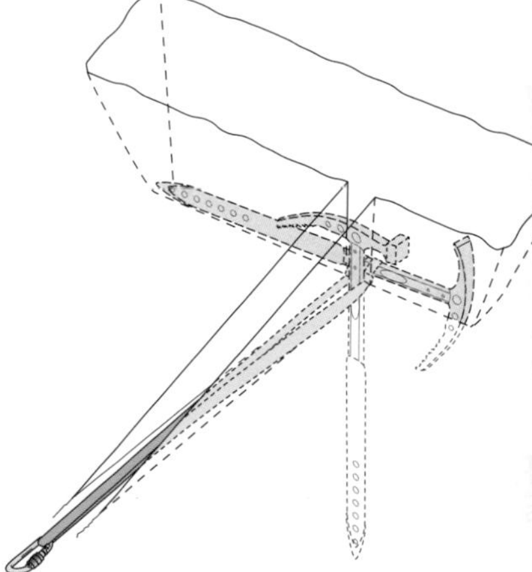

Releasable abseil

See also: abseil devices, group abseiling.

A releasable abseil is one where the abseil rope can be loosened in the event of it becoming necessary to do so, such as if hair or clothing become jammed in the abseil device. It is a very common method of setting up an abseil rig when dealing with group sessions, and as such the rigging of the system is covered under the **group abseiling** entry.

Rigging rope

See low-stretch ropes.

Rope drag

See also: double rope techniques, protection, running belay.

Rope drag is most often a product of a climber's own error, most prominent when climbing with a single rope. It can be dramatic and will affect a leader in a number of ways. It can render the rope unmovable, as the friction created by it zigzagging between running belays or across rock bulges will defeat attempts by the leader to pull it through. Also, if the runners are not in line, it can very easily exert an upward pull on the first piece of **protection**, lifting it out of place and rendering it useless. The lifting effect will then be transferred to the second piece of protection, and so on.

Simply looking down the line of the rope every so often when leading will go a long way to reducing rope drag or, if the route is one that does not allow a straight line to be taken, consider using **double rope techniques** to help solve the problem.

> tip
> The second, belaying from below, is often in a very good position to spot any potential rope-drag problems occurring before they become apparent to the leader, so it will often fall to them to point it out before the situation deteriorates.

Rope protector

See also: bottom rope systems, rigging rope.

Rope protectors, whether bought commercially or home-made from sections of carpet or canvas, have a dual purpose. They will save damage to the rope in certain situations, such as when using bottom rope systems, and also save erosion to the crag environment.

> tip
> Making a rope protector is very simple. Excellent protectors can be made by obtaining 30cm (12in) squares of carpet, such as those often used as samples by carpet showrooms. Through a hole made in one side, pass an old sling or piece of tape and attach it with a lark's foot. This can be used to hold the protector in place, either by tying it to the **rigging rope** or clipping it to a piece of protection.

Rope retrieval

See abseil rope retrieval.

Ropework – basic skills

notes

The simplest form of anchor system will be one utilizing the open loop method. This is simply a single large loop that contains both the belayer and the anchor. It is essential that the belayer is seated and braced correctly, being both tight on the anchor and in line.

See also: bowline, figure of eight, overhand knot.

There are a number of techniques by which a rope alone can be used to safeguard group members when on steep ground. This may be because the rope was simply being carried as an emergency piece of equipment and has had to be deployed due to a problem arising, or it may be that the team are travelling lightweight and the rope is there purely for use on short sections of awkward ground.

Whatever the reason, the basics of anchoring without the use of karabiners, slings and other paraphernalia are skills essential to all mountaineers, and a variety is covered below. For the majority of techniques, an **overhand knot** in its various forms is all that is needed. Attaching to an anchor can be achieved in a variety of ways, depending upon the anchor type and method of use.

METHODS

❶ For a thread belay, the rope is secured around it using an **overhand knot** rethreaded. A loop is then created further down the rope by tying an overhand knot on the bight, into which the belayer will place themselves.

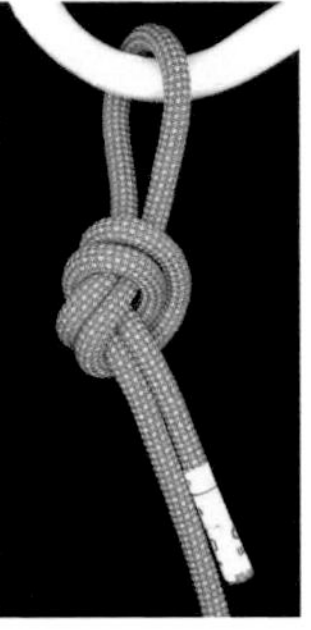

An overhand knot rethreaded.

Overhand knot

To climber

Belayer in here

The rethreaded overhand knot system on a tree.

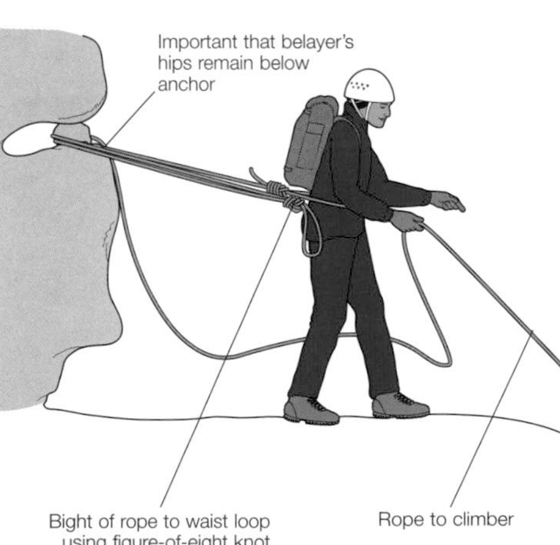

A threaded bight to a waist tie-in.

tip

When tying on using methods 1, 3 or 4, it takes quite some practice to get the rope length correct between the anchor and the belay position. To get round this, it may be useful to allow excessive rope between the stance and the anchor, then taking in the slack by tying off with an overhand knot on the bight. If this method is used, the loop from the overhand knot should be at least 20 cm (8in) long in order to avoid any risk of it undoing.

❷ Also for a thread, the belayer can be tied on to the end of the rope and pass a bight through the constriction. This is then tied around the waist tie-in loop with either an overhand or figure-of-eight knot on the bight.

❸ If a spike anchor is being used, a loop can be tied in the end of the rope and dropped over it. The belayer can then tie a second loop at an appropriate distance from the edge and use this to secure themselves.

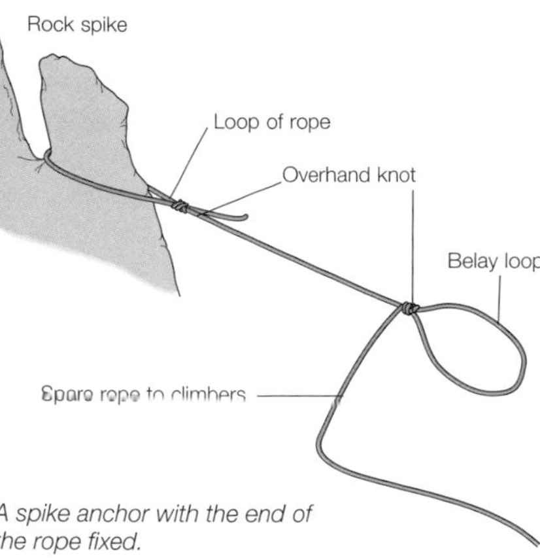

A spike anchor with the end of the rope fixed.

❹ Another method of attaching to a spike can be used if the belayer is already tied in to the end of the rope. A loop is created at the correct distance down the rope, and this is then placed over the spike to complete the system.

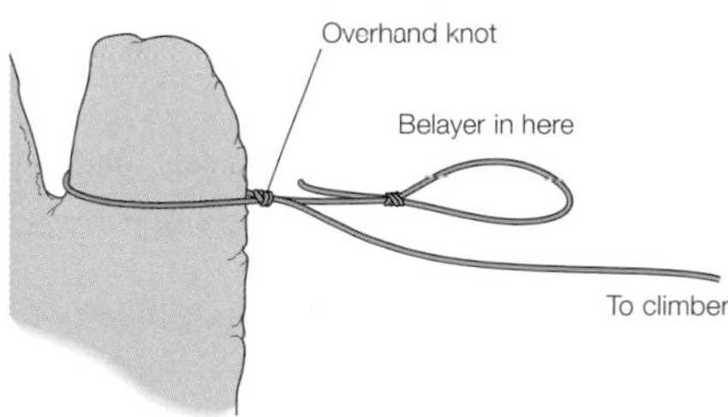

A spike anchor with a loop dropped over it above the waist tie-in point.

❺ A system that deals with both spike and thread anchors is called the 'spider knot'. This also has the properties of being easy to tie the correct distance in relation to the edge each time, and as such has an advantage over the previous methods, all of which take a little more practice. The main disadvantage is that it takes up quite a lot of rope to complete. Once the rope is around the spike or through the thread, the end is folded back from the edge of the cliff allowing extra for a loop into which the belayer will fasten themselves. An overhand knot is tied at this point, which not only secures the rope around the anchor but also ties the belayer's loop.

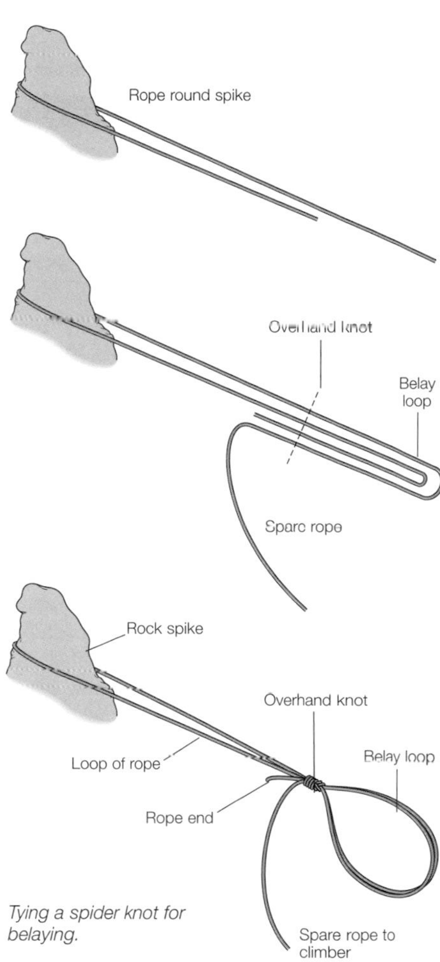

Tying a spider knot for belaying.

notes

The overhand knot is an extremely useful knot in this situation, but should not be used to the exclusion of others such as the bowline and the figure of eight. The deciding factor as to which knot is used will often be up to the experience of the individual.

Runners

See running belays.

Running belays

See also: protection.

Running belays, or 'runners', are the pieces of protection placed by the leader whilst climbing on the route. The intention is that, should the leader fall, they will be held by one of the running belays and so not be injured by falling any great distance.

Great skill and experience is required to place secure runners, and it is one of the fundamental areas in which novice climbers need to become proficient to progress to leading routes.

Running belays – climbing past

See also: abseil loop, belay device – locking off, dead rope, harness, HMS karabiner, Italian hitch, screwgate karabiners.

In some circumstances, and not just when climbing with novices, there is a chance that the second person may become so involved or overwhelmed by the climbing itself that they accidentally climb past a running belay and end up being pulled downwards by the rope in what may well be a rather insecure position. It should be noted that the main cause of this problem is very often inattentive belaying, and an alert leader is not likely to have to face solving this problem too often because the rope to a novice second should be reasonably snug.

The simplest solutions, as ever, are often the quickest and most appropriate. Can the second down-climb the move they have made? If not, can they reach down and unclip the protection from above? Will the protection pull out of its placement from where they are standing? However, should the answer to these question be 'no' it may be time for a more pro-active response. Below is set out a simple method of safeguarding the second from above, to ensure that they do not take a fall of any distance.

METHOD

- The **belay device** needs to be **locked off**.
- A **screwgate karabiner** is clipped on to a loop of **dead rope** coming from the anchor.
- This loop is lowered down to the second, and they clip it into the **abseil loop** on their **harness**.
- The belayer clips an **HMS karabiner** on to their rope tie-in loop. Into this goes an **Italian hitch**, formed on the section of rope coming up from the second.
- The belayer can now undo the locked-off belay device, keeping hold at the same time of the dead rope coming from the Italian hitch. The second is now supported from above, and can either continue up or, more usefully, be lowered a little so that they can retrieve the runner and then climb.

Running belays – climbing past

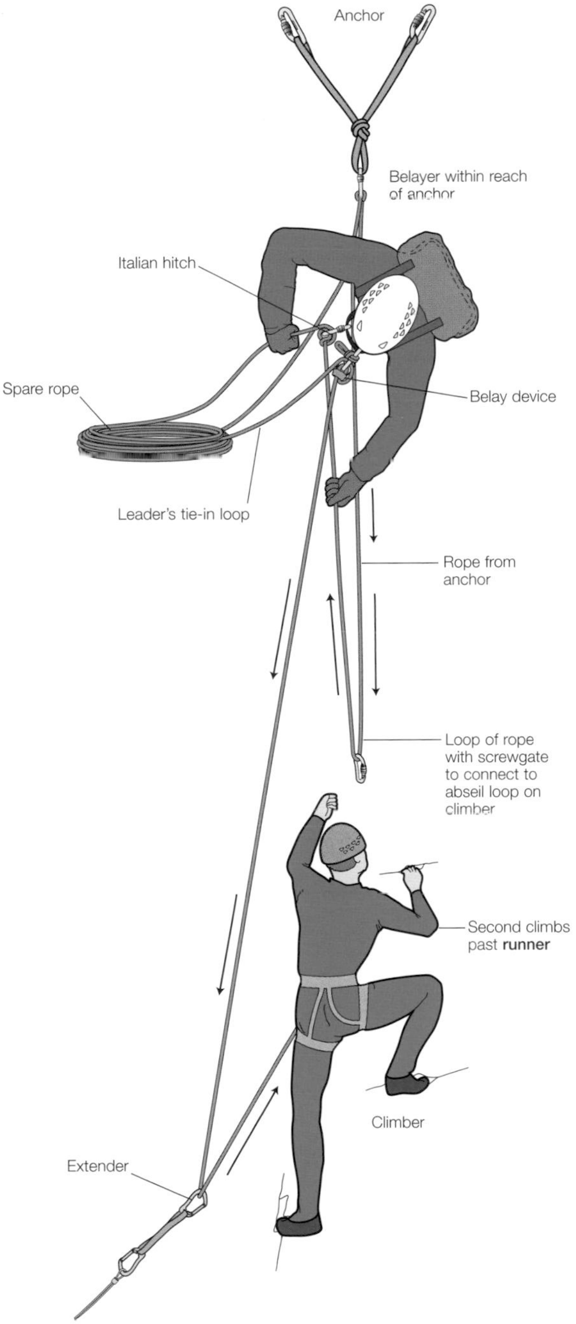

Anchor

Belayer within reach of anchor

Italian hitch

Spare rope

Belay device

Leader's tie-in loop

Rope from anchor

Loop of rope with screwgate to connect to abseil loop on climber

Second climbs past **runner**

Climber

Extender

Solving the problem of a second climbing past a runner.

notes

It should be ascertained before committing to this procedure that the second is indeed able to take a hand off the route for a brief moment. If they are on extremely precarious ground or unwilling to let go with one hand to perform this manoeuvre, it will be necessary for the leader to go down to them. This may give rise to another solution to the problem, depending on whether the route is multi- or single pitch, such as a Y-hang abseil.

notes

If the second is lowered to retrieve the runner, which is the recommended course of action, the belay device need not be unlocked. Once they have gone down the required distance and released the runner with the protection of the rope loop on the Italian hitch, they can revert back to being belayed conventionally with the belay device. The rope loop can be unclipped and pulled back up. The advantage here is that there will not be a length of the climbing rope trailing down the route, through the runner and back up to the climber, as this would have to be paid out by the belayer as they take in the new rope on the Italian hitch.

Following pages: *Coire an Lochan, Cairngorms.*

Sack hauling

See hauling.

Screwgates

See also: bottom rope systems, HMS karabiners, kiloNewtons, screwgates – jammed, snap-gate karabiners.

Screwgate karabiners are fundamental in constructing safe and solid anchor and belay systems. The ability to secure the gate closed means that the protection that they provide is considerably more than that given by simple **snap-gate karabiners**, and they should be the first consideration for systems requiring complete security.

Screwgates come in a variety of shapes and sizes, from small 'D' shapes through to larger **HMS karabiners**. The gate securing mechanism can also vary, and may include an auto-locking device. This device keeps the sleeve secured around the gate by means of a spring. When the gate needs to be opened it is manually twisted to allow entry. Often treated with caution by climbers, the better versions are designed to require two manoeuvres to open the gate, such as depressing a ball before twisting the sleeve. This goes some way to alleviate the fear that, in the event of a sideways loading, the rubbing action of the rope on a simple sleeve auto-lock would cause the gate to open and the rope to become unattached.

notes

'Gate creep' is a situation where the effect of vibration through the rope causes the karabiner gate to unscrew in certain circumstances. This would be particularly noticeable when running a **bottom roping** session, where the top pulley screwgate has been arranged with the gate opening at the upper end. A sensible precaution would be to arrange the system so that the gate opens at the lower side, so any vibration from the rope will cause the gate sleeve to tighten itself into place.

Screwgates – jammed

See also: abseil loop, protection, screwgates, snap-gate karabiners.

It is not uncommon for the sleeve of a **screwgate karabiner** to become jammed tight, and this can obviously cause a number of problems. The jamming will most often occur because the sleeve has been twisted too tightly shut and the metal of the sleeve has ridden up over the nose of the karabiner and distorted. This is not an unusual occurrence when working with novices, as they are often under the misapprehension that the tighter the sleeve is turned the safer the system will be. To solve this problem, a tight grip on the sleeve of the karabiner will be needed, possibly also the use of multi-tool pliers. If this is not practical, however, there are a few other remedies available.

tips

Problems can occur if the gate is screwed up tight, as the rotating sleeve can often jam on the nose of the karabiner, making it difficult to undo. This problem is particularly associated with novice climbers and abseilers, who hold the false belief that the tighter a gate is done up the more secure it will be. A guideline would be to do the gate up fully and then release it a quarter of a turn. It will still be secure but will be less prone to becoming stuck.

METHOD

- Tap the sleeve of the karabiner with another. This may be enough to help it to move, or to dislodge any debris that has become trapped.
- Stretch the karabiner. Although this may sound strange, karabiners have a certain amount of 'give' in them. Pulling them along their axis,

for instance with one end clipped to an **abseil loop** and the other to a piece of **protection** and applying bodyweight, will often stretch the karabiner sufficiently for the gate to be turned freely.

- In winter or at altitude, a screwgate can freeze solidly shut. It is best not to blow on it, as this will merely deposit more water vapour on to it from your breath and, even if it solves the problem in the short term, the karabiner may not be usable afterwards due to the consequential ice build-up. Also, there is a chance of your lips sticking to the super-cooled metal. Placing gloved hands around it may be the best answer, again taking care to protect bare skin. If freezing is a possibility, it may be better to use **snap-gate karabiners** back-to-back for anchors and critical placements.
- If there is no chance of the screwgate undoing, final options depend on where in the system the problem lies. Perhaps the knot that is tied around it can be undone, the piece of protection to which it is clipped can be lifted out or, if it is attached to a harness, even the harness taken off while the problem is fixed.

Self-belaying – continuous ascent

See also: clove hitch, cowstail, impact force, low-stretch ropes, overhand knot, protection.

This technique allows the climber to make a solo roped ascent of a route. It should be stressed from the outset that this skill is very time-consuming to organize, and will place the climber in a position where any fall that occurs may continue for some distance, should a slip or other reason cause them to lose contact with the route. It is essential that this technique be practised before both deciding to use it and committing to it on a route of any great length. It should also be remembered that the climber is in danger of hitting the ground during the first few metres of the route, either when leaving the ground or when leaving a subsequent ledge.

A number of methods are possible, of which two are detailed here. These are the 'loop' system and the 'series' system.

> **notes**
> The lower of the runners needs to be able to sustain an upward pull. As each runner will in turn take on the role of lower runner, and thus be pulled upwards, this technique can only really be recommended for use on bolted climbs where the loading on the attachment points can be multi-directional.

Loop system

The loop system is the least effective, as the climber is guaranteed a fall of some distance before their weight is taken by the rope. It also relies on the integrity of just two or three anchors, so is not suitable where some placements could be considered as being marginal. However, it is fairly simple to arrange and does not require the carrying of large amounts of equipment.

- A short length of dynamic rope is tied into a loop, the length of which is determined by a number of factors such as the severity of the route and the availability of **protection**. This loop may be around 5m in circumference or more.

Self-belaying – continuous ascent

- The climber ties on to the loop at the point where the ends meet, to ensure that the loop runs smoothly and to avoid the chance of the joining knot snagging.
- As the climber starts to ascend, they clip the runners until the rope loop has run out.
- Using the rope, they descend to the bottom runner and unclip it.
- They now climb back up the rope and continue up the route, clipping the next available runner.
- They descend again, and the process is repeated.

Series system

The series system allows for a more continuous ascent than the loop system, but again will result in a long fall should a slip occur during the earliest part of the climb following a tie-on changeover. It is often seen as a better method for mountain ascents, such as winter routes where frequent ledges can be utilized to help with the tie-on changeovers. A full length climbing rope can be used, which negates the need for frequent descents, and also helps to reduce the **impact force** on the system should a fall occur. A second rope would often be carried, which will be used for descending and re-ascending the route to aid retrieval of the climbing rope and equipment. This second rope could be of a **low-stretch** construction.

> **notes**
> It may be tempting to make the connection from the climber to the rope with a clove hitch via a karabiner. However, this technique introduces a number of weak links into the system and is not to be recommended.

- A bottom anchor is arranged to take an upward pull, and the climbing rope tied on to this.
- The climber ties on to the rope around 5–10m from the anchor, depending on the terrain. This tie-on would most likely be achieved using an **overhand knot** on the bight through the harness with the tail clipped back in to stop it from undoing.
- As they ascend, the climber places protection conventionally.
- Once they have got to the end of the initial rope length they secure themselves, either by using a ledge or by clipping in to a piece of protection using a **cowstail**.
- Pulling through a second length of the climbing rope, most likely equivalent to that used at first, they tie it on to their harness, once again with an overhand knot on the bight.
- Once the climber has secured themselves, the first overhand knot is released. This will introduce slack into the system and they can continue the ascent.
- The process is repeated until they reach either a suitable point on the climb or the end of the rope.
- The rope is then secured to an anchor and tied off. It will save time in the long term if this anchor is also arranged to take an upward pull in preparation for the next stage of the ascent.
- The second rope is secured to the anchor and the climber descends to the original anchor. This is then dismantled and the rope ascended, with the climber stripping out the protection as they ascend.
- Once at the high point, the climber secures the climbing rope to themselves and continues up the route as before.

Self-belaying – fixed rope

See also: abseil loop, rope protectors, screwgate karabiner.

Self-belaying with a fixed rope will often be the choice of those wishing to climb a route for either enjoyment or training purposes. The process allows the climber to ascend the route free, but with the safety of a rope should they slip or tire. A number of devices are available to allow self-belaying to take place, and here we shall consider the use of a Petzl 'Basic' ascender as a benchmark. It is assumed that an ascent will be made of a steep single-pitch rock route.

notes

With most mechanical self-belaying devices, it would be prudent to tie a series of knots on the rope at suitable points during the ascent in case a slip occurred that was not arrested by the device.

METHOD

- A rope is arranged to hang down the line of the climb, well anchored at the top. The point at which the rope hangs over the edge should be padded with **rope protectors** if appropriate.
- The bottom of the rope is weighted in some manner, to assist the device to operate smoothly. This can be achieved by tying a loop in the rope and clipping spare equipment to it, or simply by tying a few coils together so that they hang free.
- The self-belay device is attached to the rope, and then to the **abseil loop** of the climber's harness by means of a **screwgate karabiner**. Ensure that any guidelines given by the manufacturer of the self-belay device are adhered to. This is especially important in the case of devices that have a number of possible attachment points. For a climber to connect themselves to an incorrect point when self-belaying may mean that the device fails to work when loaded.
- Once connected, the climber should ascend a metre or so and then weight the system to check that all is in order.
- When the ascent starts, care should be taken for the first few metres to ensure that the rope is running smoothly through the device.
- If a rest is needed, the climber should lower their weight on to the device gradually, rather than shock loading it. Although the device will take a shock load should the climber inadvertently slip, a gentle transfer of weight if possible will save excessive loading on all parts of the system.
- Ensure that, at the top of the climb, personal security is not compromised once the relative safety of flatter ground has been reached.

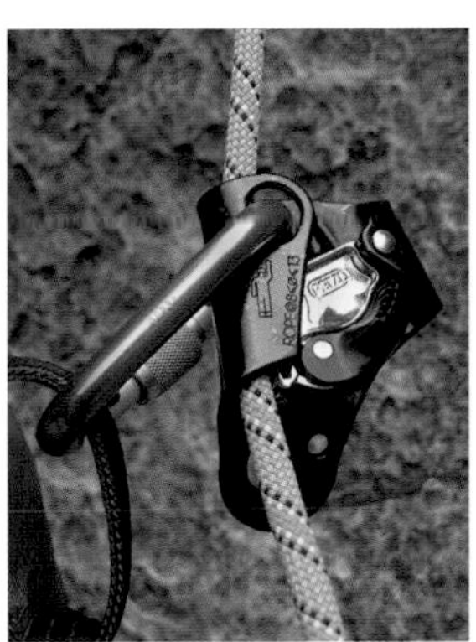

The connection of a self-belaying device (Petzl Basic) to the climbing rope.

Self-locking belay devices

See also: abseil devices, belay devices, multi-pitch climbing, self-locking belay devices – releasing under load.

This description is reserved for the family of **belay devices** that will automatically lock off the rope when a load is applied. It is something of a misnomer, as although the weight of a climber can easily be held they are not generally designed as 'hands off' devices, with few exceptions. Indeed, should the rope start to slide through one and the belayer not be attentive, a fall could be as difficult to stop as with a conventional belay device.

A passive self-locking belay device.

notes

A major drawback of many of these devices is the difficulty with which the load can be released and rope paid through. For this reason, those designs that will suffer from this problem can only be recommended for routes where there is little chance of the climber hanging free, as they would usually need to gain some purchase with the rock or ice in order for rope to be paid out from above.

A common type of active self-locking belay device, the Grigri.

These devices can be split into two broad areas, passive and active. A passive belay device will be one where the belayer adds the locking mechanism, most usually by clipping a karabiner into the rope once it has passed through the device. An active unit will usually use an internal camming system, sometimes like that used on car seat belts, where a load causes the internal mechanism to move and tighten on the rope.

Considerations

Many passive and active units are designed with more than one purpose in mind, and will often be capable of being used as an **abseil device** as well as for conventional belaying. Passive devices in particular will normally have the ability to accept two ropes, and as such are frequently used by instructors or those guiding on routes. This means that a variety of techniques can be used, and on multi-pitch routes allows a good deal of variation to occur in the climbing order of clients. Used in this manner, self-locking belay devices lend themselves particularly well to being used on direct belays when bringing up seconds.

Self-locking belay devices – releasing under load

See also: belay devices, belay methods, dead rope, Italian hitch, self-locking belay devices, slings.

If a **self-locking belay device** (one that does not have a releasing system as part of its design) has been used in a situation where the following climber has fallen and is unable to regain contact with the route, a technique needs to be put into place whereby the locking mechanism of the device can be released sufficiently in order to allow rope to be paid out. This is very awkward and time-consuming to do, and if there is any possibility of the rope being loaded in this manner then a more suitable **belay method** should be chosen from the outset. Should this technique be needed, it may be in a situation where the device was being used to secure two climbers. In this instance, extreme care should be taken that the person still in contact with the route is not endangered in any way by the releasing process. For the procedure below, it will be assumed that there is only one climber being protected by the device.

METHOD

- Once the device has self-locked, the **dead rope** is attached to a belay method on to the harness of the belayer. This could be through either a belay device or an **Italian hitch**.
- A sling is either clipped in or looped through the karabiner providing the lock at the back of the self-locking belay device.
- The sling is taken up and through a suitable point on the anchor system, usually by means of a second karabiner, and back down to the belayer. It is then clipped into their harness with another karabiner.
- Holding tight to the dead rope coming from the belay method on their harness, the belayer now commits all of their weight to the sling, which in turn will cause the locking karabiner to rotate and be pulled in an upward direction.
- The rope may now be released by paying it out through the harness belay.

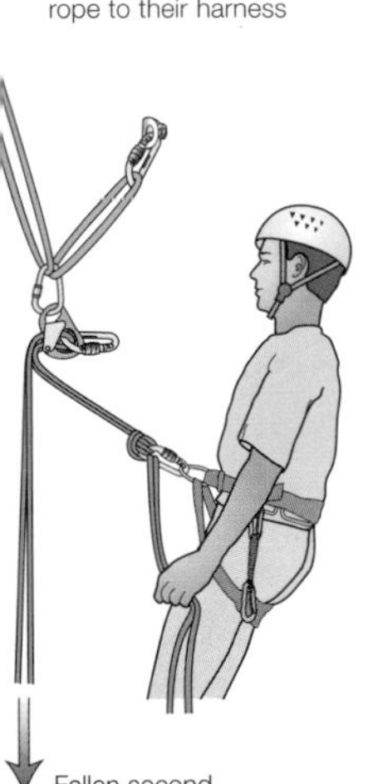

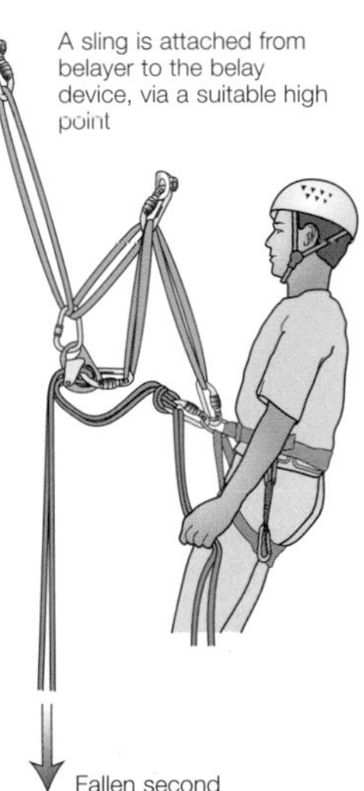

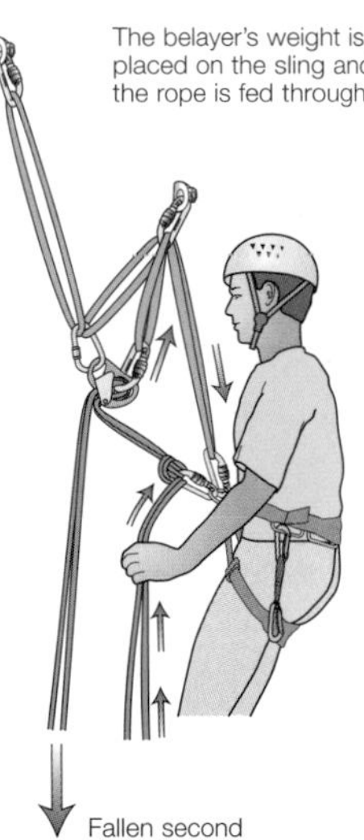

Releasing the load from a self-locking belay device.

Semi-direct belays

See also: ABC, belay device, escaping the system, tying on.

A semi-direct belay is one where the belayer makes up a percentage of the belay system. This is best understood when thought of as belaying conventionally when rock climbing using a **belay device**. The belayer is anchored, the device is clipped into their rope loop created by **tying on**, and any load is subsequently directed via the tie-in loop to the anchor.

The main advantages of the semi-direct belay is that it is quick to set up, the belay device is in front of the belayer and thus easy to operate, and it is simple to provide assistance to a second who is in difficulty by giving a tight rope. The drawbacks include the awkwardness of **escaping the system** and that the belayer is unable to move their position if the climb is taking a long time or repeated falls are being taken.

The **ABC** is critical when using the semi-direct belay, because if the user is not tight and in line they could be hurt in the event of having to hold a fall.

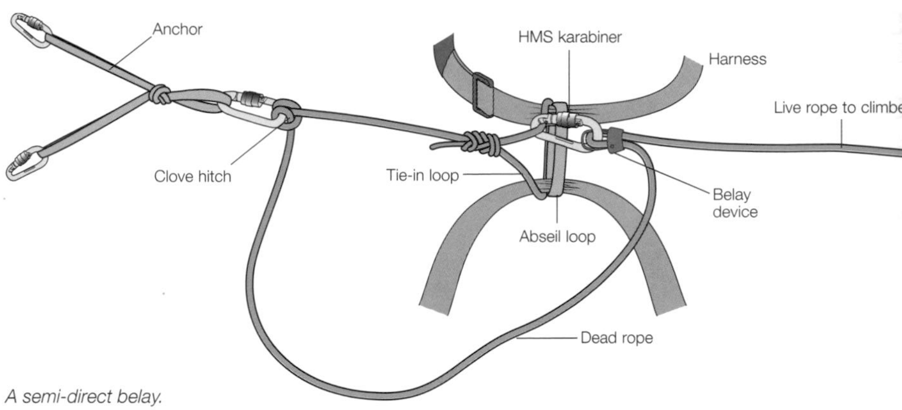

A semi-direct belay.

Sheet bend

See also: Parisian baudrier.

The main use for the sheet bend is in the construction of a **Parisian baudrier**. Care should be taken to ensure that it has been tied correctly and has not been mistakenly fashioned so that it will act as a slipknot when a load is applied. This would obviously be both uncomfortable and dangerous for anyone wearing it, causing compression of the chest and making breathing difficult. The tying of the knot is shown under the Parisian baudrier entry.

Shock loading

See also: fall factors, impact force, vectors.

Shock loading is a very undesirable element, inherent in almost any system being used by a climber. It is one of the major causes of accidents and fatalities in the mountains, as sometimes belay systems and indeed the anchors themselves give way when excessive forces, such as that created by a falling climber, are applied. Although mountaineering equipment is designed to do much to reduce the effect of shock loading, both on the rig and the human body, it still can and does occur with extreme regularity. A knowledge of factors such as **impact forces**, **fall factors** and **vectors**, as well as the shock-absorbing features of the belay system, will go a long way in helping the understanding of shock loading and the effect that it can have.

Shoulder belay

See also: live rope, stomper belay.

This is an almost redundant method of belaying a second, although it is still very relevant for the **stomper belay**. It relies on the rope being brought up the length of the body and over a shoulder to provide the friction. It is important that the **live rope** runs up from behind the belayer and then over their shoulder to the front, because if it were arranged to run up from their front initially they could be doubled up by the load when holding a fall.

Single-pitch climbing sessions

See group climbing sessions.

Sit harness

See harnesses.

Sky hook

Sky hooks are often the preserve of aid climbers, as they can be difficult to use and do not have a place in many areas of mountaineering. They enable extremely small flakes of rock to be used for either protection or, more usually, direct aid, by simply hooking over the top and being held in place by little more than bodyweight. If they are to be used for protection, a technique that is not recommended, they can be held in place with sticky tape. A number of very hard rock climbs have been completed using sky hooks for at least one point of protection, but this will normally have created merely an illusion of safety. The pressure exerted by the tip of the hook on to the small section of rock over which they are placed is equivalent to many hundreds of tonnes per square centimetre, and the chance of the rock failing when loaded is very high. One of the more popular uses is as a point of rest on hard rock climbs, allowing the climber to 'shake out' before continuing the ascent.

SLCDs (spring-loaded camming device)

See also: extenders, slings.

SLCD is the shortened version of 'spring-loaded camming device'. This title covers the range of camming devices from the small to the very large, from few cams to many, and from rigid to flexible stems. They can also be divided into passive and non-passive units, where the passive units are able to take a load through the cams when they are opened out fully and placed behind a constriction.

An extremely useful addition to a climber's arsenal, care should be taken when using camming units and advice taken from the manufacturer's attached instructions.

Generally, camming devices are not recommended for use as part of an anchor

system. This is due to their propensity to shift position through the action of the rope, sometimes called 'walking', although other forces can come into effect to cause this. Any anchor system set up with SLCDs as part of the rig may be affected by this movement, with the consequential altering of the loading on sections of the system.

Extenders

If SLCDs are being placed on the lead and there is a concern that they may tend to move from their original placement due to the effect of the rope moving the stem, they should be extended with the use of a short **sling** or purpose-made **extender**. This should be clipped directly into the sling that is normally sewn on to the stem of the SLCD, and not by clipping a karabiner directly into another karabiner.

notes

Caution should be exercised when using them in winter conditions, as the rock could have ice glazing on it which would not allow the cams to grip properly.

Slings

See also: extenders, slings – shock-absorbing, tape knot.

Slings are available in a variety of colours, shapes, sizes and widths. Although it is possible to buy tape, the material from which slings are made, from a reel by the metre, most users will wish to purchase their slings ready sewn. This gives a greater strength rating when compared to those constructed with a knot, as well as allowing thinner fabrics to be used for their construction. A number of thin modern fabrics are unsuitable for self-tying, as the knots could work loose due to the smooth nature of the construction fibres. The only knot recommended for use when tying ends of tape together, such as when constructing an abseil point, is the **tape knot**.

tip

It is useful to know to what purpose a sling will be put before purchasing, in case the type bought does not fit the requirements. For instance, a sling made of a very thin modern fabric may not possess the abrasion-resisting qualities of a thicker standard tape, thus the thicker type would be more suitable for group activity use or where abrasion is a possibility, such as with the rigging of **fixed ropes**.

Considerations

For most practical purposes, the sizes of general purpose commercially sewn and marketed slings are categorized into 60, 120 and 240cm, or 24, 48 and 96in respectively. These are their lengths measured flat, the system used in this book, although some climbers will refer to them by circumference, often calling them 4, 8 and 16ft. Many variations in length exist, particularly in the smaller sizes, and these will often be categorized as extenders. The widths vary from around 8 to 30mm (5⁄16ths to 1¼in) with the tape itself either being flat or tubular in construction. The flat tape tends to be hard wearing if a little stiff, the tubular type is somewhat more supple and ideal for intricate anchoring purposes.

notes

Sewn slings made from modern fabrics such as Dyneema and Spectra should never be cut and then retied with a tape knot. The nature of the fibres of these materials means that such a knot could easily undo, even under a very small loading.

Slings - carrying

See also: extenders, screwgate karabiners, snap-gate karabiners.

60cm (24in) slings

60cm (24in) slings can be carried over the head and one shoulder, although this makes them difficult to remove and restrictive in some circumstances. A better method is to equip them with two **snap-gate karabiners**, which would most likely be the case if they were to be used as long **extenders**. Holding the sling by one karabiner at the top, bring the lower one up and through the top one. Now clip it around the two lengths of sling loop created lower down and pull it snug. This gives a sling carrying length of around 20cm (8in), which can easily be carried on the harness. When needed for use, unclipping either of the karabiners from two of the three sections of tape they contain will allow the sling to revert back to its original form.

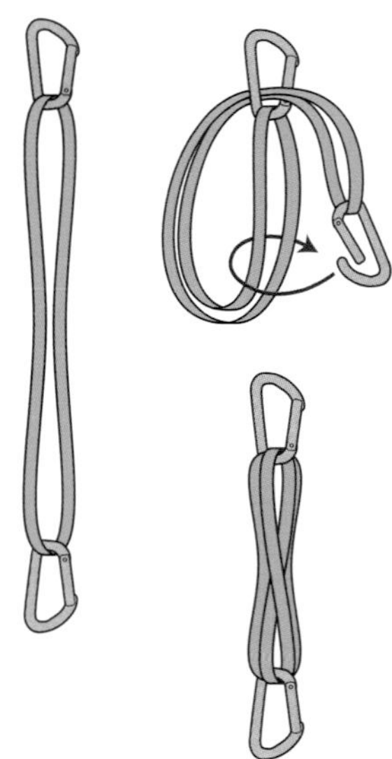

Looping a 60cm (24in) sling through itself for carrying.

120cm (48in) slings

120cm (48in) slings are best carried with the ends being clipped together around the body, using a **screwgate karabiner**. This is useful as the sling will be ready equipped for use with a karabiner attached. The advantage of this method when compared to looping it over the head is that it is easy to release the sling using one hand. Care should be taken that the sling is taken off the body in the same way that it is clipped on, because if it is taken off over the head the karabiner could drop off the sling and be lost.

Another method is to have both ends of the sling clipped into a karabiner, and then twist the sling around a number of times until it is tightly wrapped around itself. The bottom ends are then also clipped into the karabiner. The advantage of this method is that the sling can be carried on the harness and then shaken out when needed. The disadvantages include the chance of the sling falling from the karabiner should an attempt be made to unwrap it in an awkward situation, and the tendency for the sling to remain twisted if left in that state for a long period of time.

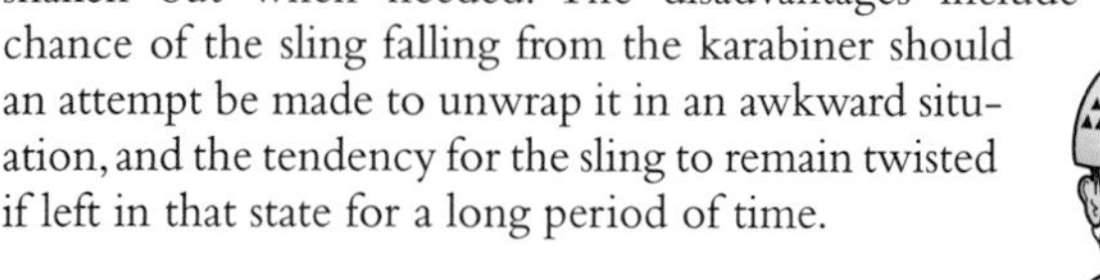

240cm (96in) slings

240cm (96in) slings are best carried by doubling them, so that they are 120cm (48in) in length, and then using the around-the-body system detailed above.

Carrying a 120cm (48in) sling around the body.

Slings – shock absorbing

An energy-absorbing sling, opened out to show the stitching which is designed to fail given a specific loading.

See also: kiloNewtons, running belays, shock loading.

Some slings are designed in such a way as to absorb a proportion of the energy created by a falling climber. This is extremely useful when any equipment being used for **running belays** is poor, such as some ice-screw placements or runners in rock that are not as solid as they could be.

The shock-absorbing properties are created by folding and stitching the sling in such a way as to allow the stitching to rip in the event of **shock loading**, thus taking much of the force away from the anchor. Once the shock-absorbing section of stitching has given way, the sling will revert to performing just like a normal sewn sling.

As a guideline, the stitching on an energy-absorbing sling will fail at a load of around 2.5 **kiloNewtons** (kN), with the overall strength of the sling being in the region of 22kN.

Slings – shortening

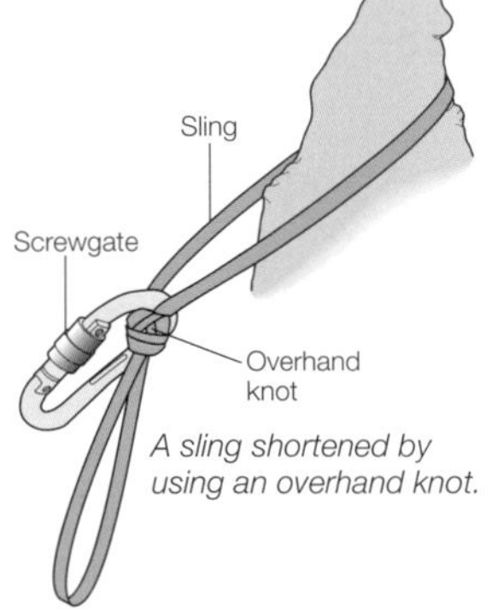

A sling shortened by using an overhand knot.

See also: overhand knot.

There is a variety of ways by which a sling may be shortened to the required length when being used. It can be doubled, trebled and so on, or can be wrapped a couple of times around the retaining karabiner if only a small adjustment is needed. However, the best way to shorten a sling for most purposes is by tying an overhand knot on to it at the point needed for attachment, and to clip the connecting karabiner above this.

Slippery hitch

See also: belay device – locking off, Italian hitch, Italian hitch – locking off.

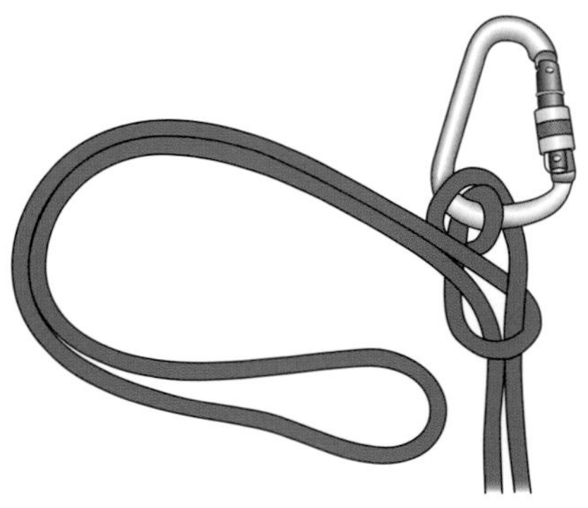

This is mainly used as a formative knot when **locking off a belay device** or **Italian hitch**. Its purpose is to temporarily lock off a load as well as to provide a buffer so that subsequent knots do not tighten excessively. Care is needed when tying and untying the hitch with any part of the system loaded, as some slippage could occur. It should not usually be used in isolation but be finished with the addition of two half-hitches as detailed under **Italian hitch – locking off**.

A slippery hitch being used below an Italian hitch.

Snap-gate karabiners

See also: bent-gate karabiners, bolts, bolts – clipping, extenders, protection, screwgate karabiners.

Snap-gate karabiners, also known as 'snaps' or 'biners', are mainly used when placing **protection** on a lead, although they can also be used for a variety of other purposes. There are a number of designs, and for convenience these can be categorized into straight-gate and bent-gate karabiners.

There is little to choose between the two styles. Bent-gate karabiners generally offer a wider gate opening and are easier to clip the rope into when leading on hard climbs. However, they also present the possibility of the rope unclipping itself with ease if the configuration is not correct, and as such may not be the best choice on routes where the orientation of the equipment into which they have been clipped cannot be guaranteed. See **bolts – clipping** for a diagrammatic explanation.

On bolted routes

When using karabiners in conjunction with an **extender**, as will frequently be the case with both **bolted routes** and those requiring leader-placed protection, many climbers will elect to have one straight-gate and one bent-gate karabiner connected. It is important here that only the straight-gate is used to connect to the protection, with the bent-gate purely for use at the rope end.

If a lot of climbing is to take place on bolted routes at a high technical level with a number of falls subsequently being taken by the leader, it would be prudent to have a set of karabiners that are just used for that purpose. Some types of bolt can damage the inner surface of a karabiner when loaded, causing burrs. If these karabiners are later used in a different configuration in conjunction with software, such as clipping them to a rope or sling, they could cause damage to the fibres.

An extender in a bolt.

Snapgates

Some karabiners are manufactured with wire gates, which negate the need for an internal spring mechanism to keep the gate shut, give less chance of the gate freezing shut in extreme temperatures, and reduce the overall weight of the karabiner.

If, in the absence of **screwgate karabiners,** snap gates were to be used as part of an anchor system, it would be prudent to use two in each section clipped with the gates opening in opposite directions. This will hugely reduce the chance of accidental opening and subsequent anchor system failure.

Snow anchors

See also: buried axe anchor, deadman, deadboy, direct belays – snow and ice, reinforced buried axe, snow bollard, T-axe anchor, vertical axe anchor.

A snow anchor is a method by which the snow itself is used to provide the strength required to render a belay or abseil system safe. This can be provided through a number of techniques, such as a **buried axe anchor**, the placement of a **deadman**, or the use of just the snow itself in the form of a **snow bollard**.

Many variables exist, not least that the effect of the layers of differing hardness within the snow pack may have on the chosen belay system. A thorough knowledge of snow structure and the ability to assess accurately the state of the terrain is essential before effective and trustworthy anchors can be selected, placed and used.

Snow bollard

See also: abseiling, direct belays, spike anchors.

A very useful anchor for a number of situations, the snow bollard has the advantage over other anchors in that no equipment is left behind if it is to be used for **abseiling**. It can take a little while to construct depending upon the hardness of the snow, but once finished provides a versatile and solid point of attachment.

notes

The snow layers should be examined when constructing a bollard. If the surface is very hard and the lower layers soft, there is a chance of the rope cutting through when loaded. It would be worth digging further down to find a more consolidated section of snow pack.

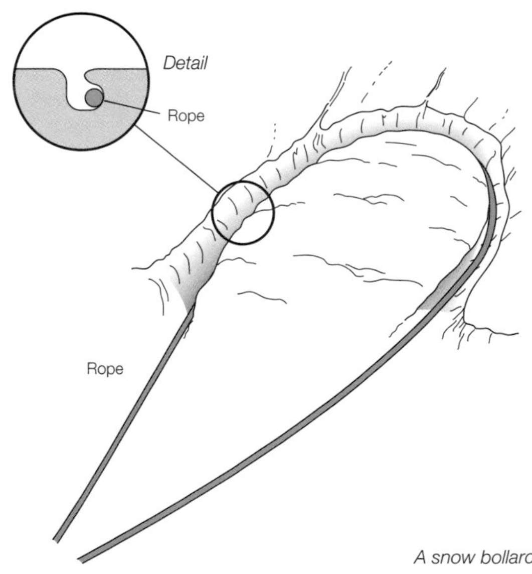

A snow bollard.

The size of the bollard depends on the quality and hardness of the snow, and the width of it can range from 50cm (20in) in very hard snow to 2m (6ft) or more in softer conditions. When choosing an area in which to cut it, care should be taken not to disturb the snow either within the area of the bollard or immediately downslope of it.

The bollard may be used for a variety of purposes, and lends itself to them all very well. Although the method described is for use on deep snow, it is quite possible to fashion a bollard from near-ready material such as a gap between a rock face and the snow pack. Although more resembling a **spike anchor,** this can result in a very strong attachment point.

METHOD

- A horseshoe shape is drawn in the snow with the pick of the axe. This should be symmetrical and have the lower part, where the rope is to exit, tapering in the direction of loading.
- The shape can now be cut around using the axe pick.
- Once the outline has been cut through, the adze of the axe should be used to chop out a trench around it. The depth of this will vary according to conditions, but will most likely be in the region of 15cm (6in) deep.
- The top section of the bollard, at the point that the rope runs round, should be mushroomed slightly so that the rope will sit securely. This can be done with the adze or, in soft conditions, a gloved hand.

tip

A bollard makes an excellent anchor for abseiling, as no equipment is left behind. However, it would be sensible for the last person down to test-pull the abseil rope before abseiling to ensure that the rope has not frozen to the back surface of the bollard, making subsequent retrieval impossible.

Snow mushroom

See snow bollard.

Snow stake

This is an item that is most commonly found on the equipment list of expeditions, although it does have its place in other spheres of mountaineering. At its simplest a snow stake will be a long metal tube or section of either angle- or T-bar that is driven into the snow, and on to which attachments are made. However, purpose-made snow stakes are constructed from very strong materials and designed specifically for the task of anchoring. They will be of a length varying from 50 to 150cm (20 to 59in) long, be manufactured from a lightweight yet strong material, and will have a hole near the top through which attachments can be made. The top of a good stake will also have been reinforced in order to stop deformity when striking, and the lower end will usually be cut at an angle to aid placement in hard snow.

(Continued on p. 198)

Overleaf:
Scottish gully climbing.

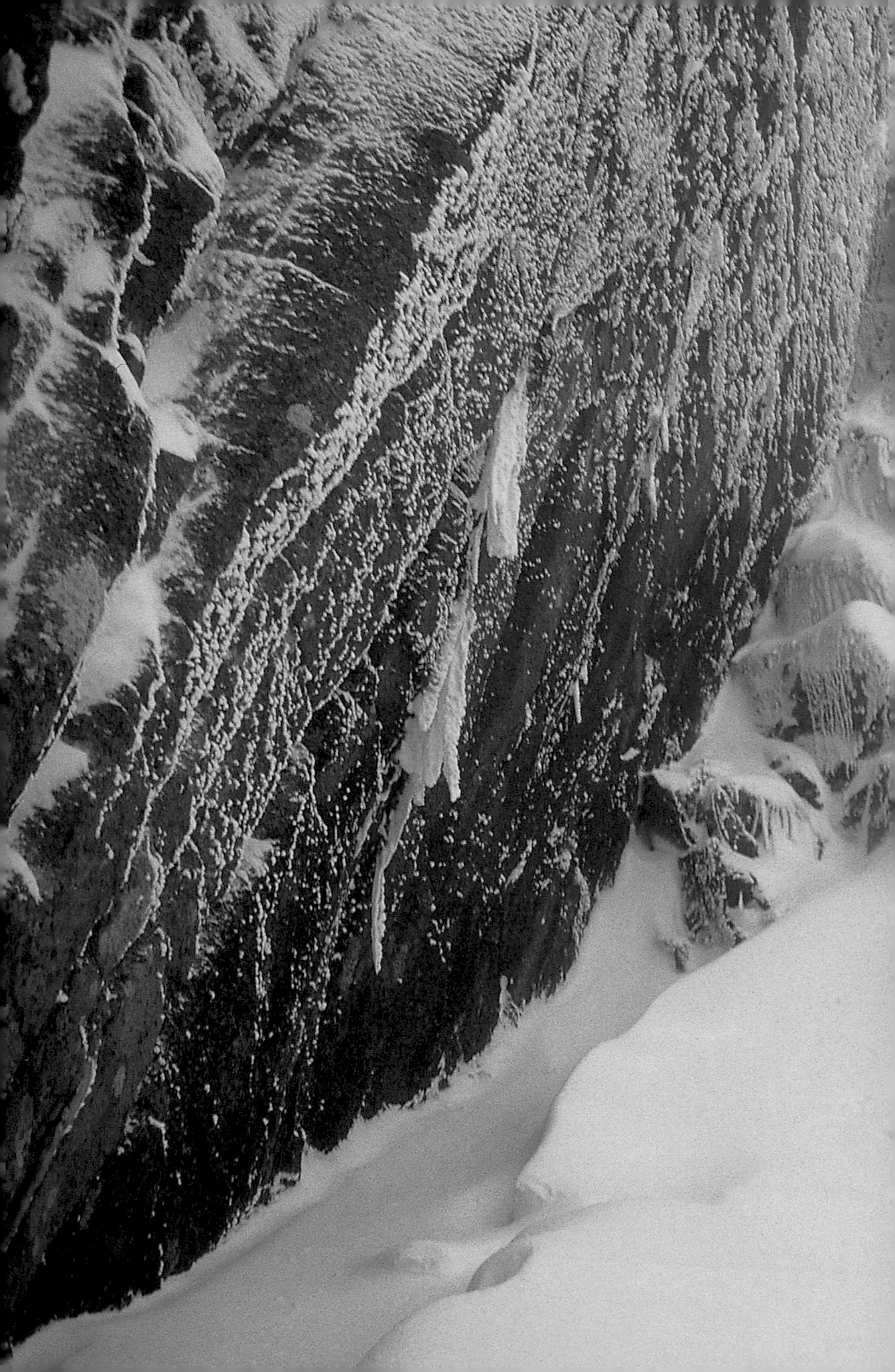

As well as being placed vertically, a stake can be buried in a similar fashion to an axe anchor and used for similar purposes.

As with all snow anchors, the placement will only be as strong as the snow pack surrounding it. Stakes need to be placed carefully because if the top section is in soft snow and the lower part is in hard snow, it could easily pivot out if loaded. Similarly, if the stake cannot be driven in fully, attachment of any system should be done as close to the surface of the snow as possible in order to avoid leverage.

Spider knot

See ropework – basic.

A spike anchor.

Spike anchor

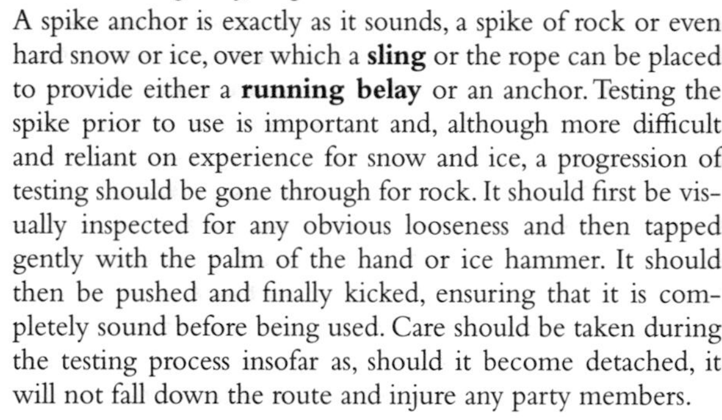

See also: running belay, slings.

A spike anchor is exactly as it sounds, a spike of rock or even hard snow or ice, over which a **sling** or the rope can be placed to provide either a **running belay** or an anchor. Testing the spike prior to use is important and, although more difficult and reliant on experience for snow and ice, a progression of testing should be gone through for rock. It should first be visually inspected for any obvious looseness and then tapped gently with the palm of the hand or ice hammer. It should then be pushed and finally kicked, ensuring that it is completely sound before being used. Care should be taken during the testing process insofar as, should it become detached, it will not fall down the route and injure any party members.

Stacked abseil

See also: abseiling, abseil devices, abseil rope, anchor, French prusik, harnesses, protecting an abseil.

The stacked abseil is a method of attaching one or more people to the **abseil rope** prior to your own descent, so that you are both happy with the fact that they are attached correctly and so that you can control their descent from below. The reasons why a stacked abseil may be chosen are numerous, but as an example you may be with a couple of less experienced people and the abseil descent, which will be over multiple pitches, needs **anchor** systems to be set up at each descent stance before the party is safe and the rope can be pulled through. For this reason, you may elect to descend first, having stacked your companions ready, and set up the stance before they abseil to meet you.

METHOD

- The order of descent needs to be decided upon. The most experienced person, or whoever is to set up the stance or control the descent, will go down first.
- The group connect themselves to the rope, with the lead person furthest from the anchor.
- Only the lead person needs to protect their abseil by use of a **French prusik** or similar means, the second and subsequent people to abseil do not need to use any form of personal protection.
- Everyone apart from the lead person has their **abseil device** extended by around 30cm (12in) from their **harness**. This extension helps to avoid them getting pulled around by the weight of anyone else abseiling.
- Everyone needs to be close to the abseil rope as the leader starts their descent, otherwise they may be pulled over by the increase in weight on the rope. Sitting down would be a good position to be in and it may well prove to be the most comfortable.
- Once the bodyweight of the first person is on the abseil rope, the others left at the stance will be unable to move and are thus protected from an accidental slip.
- When the leader has reached either the ground or the next stance and has made any preparations necessary, the first of the remainder may start to abseil. Once again, as soon as their bodyweight is on the abseil rope those left behind will be unable to move and will thus be safe.
- The leader, at the bottom of the abseil rope, can protect the person descending by loosely holding the dead end of the rope. Should there be a need for the abseiler to slow down or stop, the simple process of the leader pulling on the abseil rope will provide sufficient braking to stop the descent.
- Once the second person is down, subsequent abseilers can start their descent one at a time.

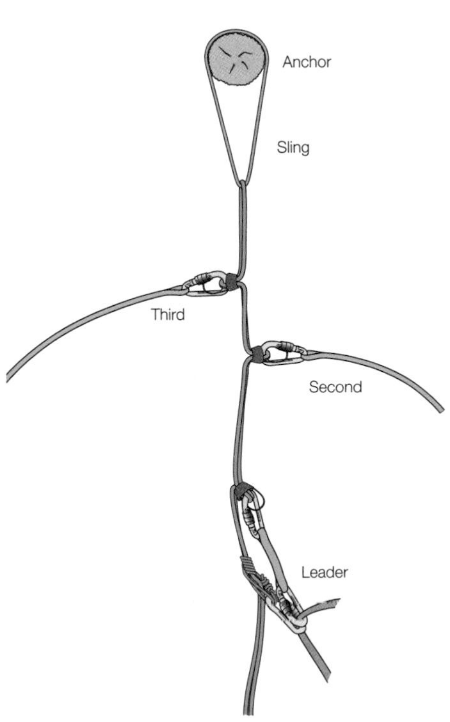

A stacked abseil set-up.

Stance management

See also: multi-pitch climbing.

The efficient management of a stance is something often overlooked by climbers, keen to concentrate on the route ahead of them. However, the small amount of time that it takes to ensure that the ropes are piled correctly and out of the way, that the anchor system has been prepared in a manner suited to the next pitch and the care of any other climbers joining the stance, including the tasks of cutting ledges for both them and their ropes, is tiny compared to the time that it would take to sort out problems arising from slovenly practices.

Keeping the stance tidy

Rope management in particular is often an issue, and the simple process of flaking it over the anchor ropes or using a dedicated rope-tidy clip when working on small or hanging stances will save time trying to retrieve it when a loop becomes snagged below. Simply cutting a ledge for it to sit in when climbing snow will not only stop it from disappearing down the route in a huge arc and possibly freezing to the surface, but will keep it clear of sharp crampon points.

Equipment should be looked after, in particular when on small stances, and anything likely to be dropped should be clipped on to the anchor. This would include ice tools, rucksacks and spare equipment.

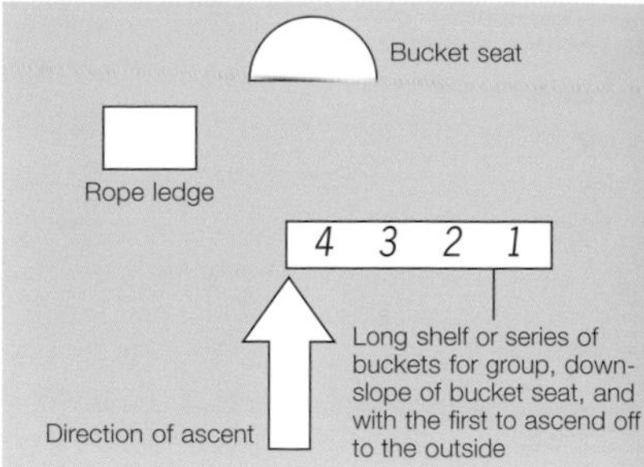

Efficient stance management includes the preparation of ledges for the belayer, the rope and following climbers.

Static rope

See low-stretch ropes.

Stirrup hoist

See also: assisted hoist, clove hitch, escaping the system, extender, klemheist.

This is a method by which a person hanging on the end of a rope can be assisted to ascend, but do so mainly under their own power. This may be necessary if there is insufficient rope to organize an **assisted hoist**, or too much friction is inherent in the system, making a conventional hoist impossible.

METHOD

- A free end of rope is required. This can be the end of a spare rope, or the original rope if the belayer has **escaped the system**.
- The free end, with a loop tied in it, is lowered down to the level of the stuck climber.
- It is secured to the anchor with a **klemheist**, backed up with a **clove hitch**.
- The original climbing rope is also connected to the anchor in the same way. The actual connection method depends upon the situation at the belay, but will normally be made through a klemheist, with the back-up clove hitch being clipped in once some slack has been introduced into the system.
- The two ropes should be arranged so that they are hanging close to each other, to assist the stranded climber with their ascent. If the second rope is hanging a short distance away, it can be clipped to the stranded climber's harness to be free running via a karabiner or extender to keep it near.
- With their foot in the loop on the second rope, the stranded climber pulls up on it. The belayer takes in the slack on the original climbing rope, via the klemheist.
- The climber sits back in their harness and unweights the second rope. The belayer takes in the second rope through the klemheist so the foot loop is again at a suitable height.
- The climber repeats the pull up on the second rope.
- This process continues, with the belayer taking in through the back-up clove hitches at suitable points during the procedure.

The stirrup hoist set-up.

Stomper belay

See also: abseil loop, boot/axe belay, HMS karabiner, Italian hitch, shoulder belay.

The stomper belay is an excellent method of safeguarding a climber who is either ascending or descending snowy terrain below the point of the belayer. It is most important from the outset that it is understood that this method is not designed to take a shock loading, such as may be created by holding the weight of a falling leader. If such a loading occurred the system would almost certainly fail. That said, its uses are many. Quick and simple to set up, it can be used to safeguard a partner investigating a possible cornice obstacle when searching for a descent route, it can be used to bring up a second on moderate to steep ground, or can be used for lowering one or two people at a time if a speedy descent is called for.

Considerations

An over-riding factor to be considered when selecting this method is the safety of the person operating the system. There is no direct attachment for the belayer to the stomper, and as such it should only be used on terrain where the belayer is happy that there is no chance of them either stepping off the stance, which will negate the mechanics of the system, or being blown off their feet by the wind and falling downhill themselves. Also, some knowledge of the snow pack is important because, if the system is set up across layers of widely varying hardness, there may be a propensity for the axe, once placed, to lever out.

METHOD

- If on level ground, ensure that the snow beneath your feet is compacted and able to hold an ice axe pushed in vertically. If you are on terrain that is sloping, either cut or stamp a ledge into the snow, inclined slightly back into the slope. This ledge should end up wedge-shaped, just wide enough for you to stand with your feet together. If possible, make the ledge deep enough so that the snow on the up-slope side supports the backs of the calves, helping with stability. Standing on the ledge and kicking back with your heels will help to shape the back wall to fit your leg shape.
- Having had your feet in position on the ledge, step out to one side and place the spike of the ice axe at a point just in front of the depression left by your heels. Push the axe straight into the snow at an angle of 90 degrees for about half to three-quarters of its length and then pull it out again.
- Clip the rope running to the person being safeguarded into an **HMS karabiner** and do up the gate. The rope should be at the narrow end of the karabiner and emerging from the bottom side of it. Place the

notes

If the person belaying is not tied on to the end of the rope, it is essential that some method is used that will alert them that the end of the rope is near, otherwise they could let the full rope length slip through their hands. A large knot at the very end, with a smaller overhand knot a metre or so from it, would be a sensible precaution.

tips

If wearing a harness, the belayer could use a belay device or **Italian hitch** on the **abseil loop** to control the descent or ascent. This works well as long as the harness is well fitting above the hips. However, in some situations such as in cold conditions where extra clothing is worn, the harness may feel as though it is being pulled down over the hips. In this case a shoulder belay would be the best option.

The **boot/axe belay** is a complementary technique, and can be used where the stomper is inappropriate, such as in high winds.

The stomper belay set-up.

Stomper belay

notes

The suggested method of running the karabiner up the shaft of the axe is preferred, as the alternative of clipping the karabiner through the eye of the axe causes the head riveting to be strained, the rope to twist and difficulty in getting the karabiner to sit flush with the snow.

tips

Gripping the rope tightly with the hand that is down by your side is a way to relieve any discomfort felt due to the rope rubbing across the shoulder of the live-rope arm.

On sloping ground, prepare a ledge for the rope to sit in to avoid any chance of it slipping off down the slope and becoming either an obstruction or snagged.

shaft of the axe through the karabiner and slide it up to just below the head.

- Place the axe in the previously prepared hole, making sure that the axe head is running across the slope, and push it right down so that the head is flush with the surface of the snow. It may need to be stamped into place if the snow is hard. Ensure that the rope can run through the karabiner smoothly.
- Step back into the slot with the heels against the back wall, ensuring that all bodyweight is on the head of the axe. Taking the weight off the axe head when the system is in use would completely negate the strength of it.
- For a right-handed belayer, the rope runs up through the left hand, which is held down alongside the left leg, behind the back of the left shoulder, down over the front of the right shoulder and gripped by the right hand. There should be no need to take a twist around this arm, as there will be a lot of friction already created in the system. Reverse this process for left-handed operation. The rope is then in a position to be used as a **shoulder belay**.
- In operation, there should never be any slack rope between the belayer and the person being safeguarded. If there were to be slack rope in the system, even though the person is below the stomper, the shock loading created by a slip could be enough to cause the axe to rip out through the snow pack. For this reason, a person being lowered should also always be below the level of the axe head before putting any weight on to the system, otherwise it will be loaded in an upwards and outwards direction and could pull out. If a climber is being belayed up, they should stop just below the axe-head level, unless it is set up on flat ground at the top of a route. If dealing with less experienced climbers, and the system has been set up on sloping terrain, it would be a good idea to prepare a ledge or bucket seat below the level of the belay for them to stand or sit in.

Stopper knot

See also: double fisherman's knot, figure-of-eight knot, overhand knot.

This is the name given to any knot used to lock off the end of the rope once a main knot has been tied, for instance when using a rethreaded **figure of eight** tied on to a harness. When completed, it should be snug against the main knot, with a tail of around 5cm (2in) left free.

Opposite: *Route-finding at high altitude in the Himalaya.*

T-axe anchor

See also: bottoming out, bucket seat, buried axe, clove hitch, direct belay, reinforced buried axe, slings, snow stake.

This is a variation of the **buried axe** and **reinforced axe** anchors, and has the advantage that a little less excavation is needed in order to prepare the axe slot. Another plus point is that almost anything can be used in place of the horizontal axe, such as a **snow stake** or trekking poles. The main disadvantage is that a good deal of experience and judgement is needed to avoid placing the axe through snow layers of differing hardness. For instance, if the axe is pushed through a hard layer and down into one that is softer, there is a chance that the system will fail when loaded. This is due to the force of a falling climber exerting a levering effect on the head of the vertical axe, causing it to cut through the softer layers and pull out. For this reason, it is often overlooked in favour of the buried and reinforced axe anchors.

METHOD

- As for any axe anchor systems, an area of undisturbed snow should be selected as the site for the anchor. As the strength of the system is in the snow pack downslope of the axe, disturbing this to any extent with footprints or the like could compromise the strength of the system as a whole, and should be avoided as much as is practicable.
- Cut across the slope with the pick of the axe at 90 degrees to the fall line or line of loading, making the cut a little longer than the length of the shorter of the two ice tools. Make a second cut about 15cm (6in) above the first one to the same length. Using the adze, remove the snow between the two cuts. It is important to know the state of the snow beneath where you are excavating, as this will influence how deep you go. In uniform hard snow conditions, the depth of the horizontal slot needs to be a minimum of 10cm (4in), but much deeper than this in softer conditions. The longer of the two ice tools will be the one placed vertically, so once the slot has been part constructed, push the axe shaft down into the snow (a little distance along the slot from where it will

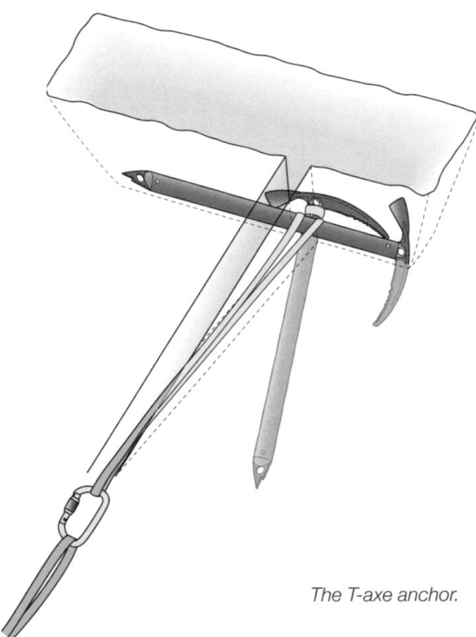

The T-axe anchor.

finally be placed) in order to determine the hardness of the underlying snow pack. If it is difficult to do so, it may be wise to revert to using the reinforced buried axe method, which is not so reliant on the strength of the hidden layers.

- The attachment to the axe will usually be made with a **sling**, although it is possible to use the rope if a sling is not available. This attachment needs to run below the surface level of the snow for most of its length, a slot needs to be cut at 90 degrees to the axe slot, running down towards the stance. Starting half way along the horizontal slot, the width of this slot is also important, and it should only just be enough to allow the sling or rope to sit in it snugly; if it is any wider the strength of the snow pack will be affected. The best method for doing this is to run the spike and shaft of the axe down the snow; if the adze is used it will most likely end up giving a slot that is too wide. This slot should run downslope for approximately 1.5m (5ft) below the level of the snow, before emerging at the position to be taken by the belayer. This would most likely be a **bucket seat** if belaying a lead climber, or perhaps a small ledge cut for using a **direct belay** system.
- Place the axe that is to be horizontal into the slot, pick downmost and with its full length touching the downslope face of the snow. Ensure that the centre point of the axe's surface area, most likely a little towards the head from half way, is in line with the vertical slot.
- Tie a **clove hitch** around the shaft of the axe that is to be placed vertically, and slide it up so that it is sitting snugly against the underside of the axe head. This axe is then pushed into the snow on the upslope side of the horizontal axe at an angle of, or just back from, vertical.
- Push it all the way in until the sling by the head is resting on top of the other axe. If there is a problem with pushing it all the way in, perhaps because it has **bottomed out**, the sling needs to be pushed down the shaft so that it is resting on the horizontal axe, otherwise it would cause excessive leverage. Even so, there are only a few centimetres tolerance, and every effort should be made to get the axes placed in their optimum positions.
- Run the sling down the vertical slot and belay from that as required.

A variation on this is to have the horizontal axe incorporated into the sling by sliding it through before placing both tools into the slot. This would often be most people's first choice, as it connects the two axes together and renders the system more stable.

Tape knot

See also: abseiling, slings, thread anchor.

This is a useful knot for forming **slings** or joining lengths of flat tape together, for instance when constructing a **thread** point for use in an **abseil** situation. It is a fairly weak knot, and cannot be recommended for use in constructing slings for everyday use, especially when heavy use or repeated falls are expected, where a commercially available sewn sling construction is far more suitable. However, for occasional use the tape knot is quite reliable, quick and easy to tie.

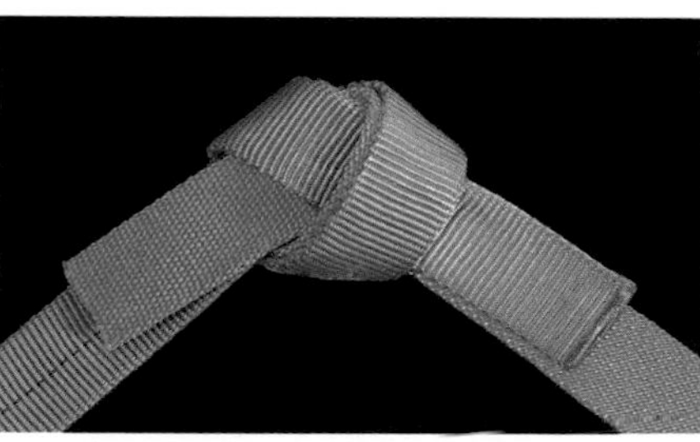

The tape knot.

Tat

This is the name given to any short piece of rope or tape, often carried for use in emergency or retreat situations. Some climbers will carry a couple of 3m (9ft) lengths of tape in their rucksack for use should the situation dictate, or even a length cut from an old leading rope which has been retired.

Tension traverse

See also: pendulum, pendulum traverse.

A tension traverse is a method by which sections of rock, ice or mixed ground, normally for a limited distance, are crossed by means of direct support from the belayer via the rope. To achieve this usually entails the placing of a high runner through which the rope can be clipped. With the belayer keeping the rope tight, the leader can then use its support to lean across the blank section to find better purchase. The higher the runner is placed, the more support the leader will be afforded, and it may be that more than one needs to be used to allow the section of ground to be crossed.

Once the leader is across, the second and any subsequent climbers will need to follow. This may not be a problem if the stance taken by the leader is near to and higher than the traverse, because the second can receive direct support from the rope. If, however, the stance is low down the second may have to self-tension using a back rope from the previous stance until the difficulty is passed.

Care

It should go without saying that great care is needed when performing a tension traverse, as the adhesion to the rock or ice is usually minimal and a slip resulting in a forceful **pendulum** could easily occur. It should also be noted that tension traverses are often easier to perform in one direction than another, and that sections crossed one way may be impossible to reverse, possibly leaving the team stranded if retreat is required. In this case, it may be necessary for the team to climb higher and adopt methods relevant to a **pendulum traverse**.

Thompson knot

See also: overhand knot.

The Thompson knot is a method by which an improvised harness can be made from the rope alone. This is very useful if just a rope has been taken onto the hill, perhaps as a back-up when walking on awkward terrain with a novice group or if travelling lightweight across moderate ground.

Limitations

Although the finished knot resembles a harness, it is important to understand the limitations of it in use. This harness can only be used when lowering a person, and even then only when it will be fully loaded for the entire descent. If there is any chance that the section of descent that is to be negotiated can be down-climbed, a waist tie-on should be used instead of the Thompson knot. This is because as soon as the person wearing it tries to move themselves independently on the terrain, the leg loops in particular will immediately loosen and drop down behind the knees causing the harness to then be positioned incorrectly on them.

The tying of a Thompson knot is carried out as follows:

METHOD

- Use the tallest person in the group as a measure and add about 20cm (8in). Hold together five equal lengths of the rope, measured to their height. There should be four loops, two at the top and two at the bottom.
- Tie an overhand knot approximately a third of the way up the rope when it is held together. Ensure that this has been arranged so that the rope that will be holding the load is coming out from the top of the knot.
- Get the person to be lowered to step into each of the two smaller loops and pull them up snug. They should pull up on the **overhand knot** whilst doing this.
- The position of the overhand knot is critical. It should be positioned at sternum height, any higher and it will be in the way of the person's head, any lower and it may cause them to tip upside down when their weight is committed to the system. If it is not correctly positioned, adjust it so that it sits right when the person is standing upright with the knot being pulled upwards. Independently pulling on all of the sections of rope emanating from it will tighten it into place.
- Place each of the two larger loops over the head and under one arm, crossing over at the back. This crossing is important otherwise the person could fall out of the knot when weight is applied.
- Get the person to hold the overhand knot high and to lean forward slightly. Pull up on each of the crossed-over ropes and tie an

notes

It is possible to tie an overhand knot on each of the leg loops before the person initially steps in, which means that they can be tightened up around their thighs to lessen the chance of them slipping down during the lower. The problem with this is that if the loops do slip down a way, as they often do, it is very difficult for the person being lowered to move them back up again efficiently. With the looser version, at least if the loops do slip down they can be replaced with the minimum of effort.

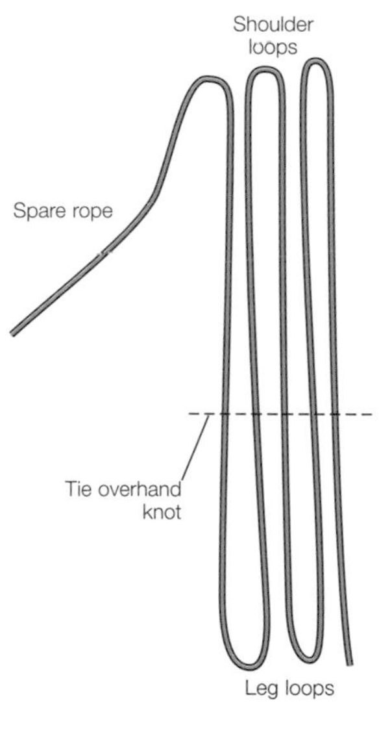

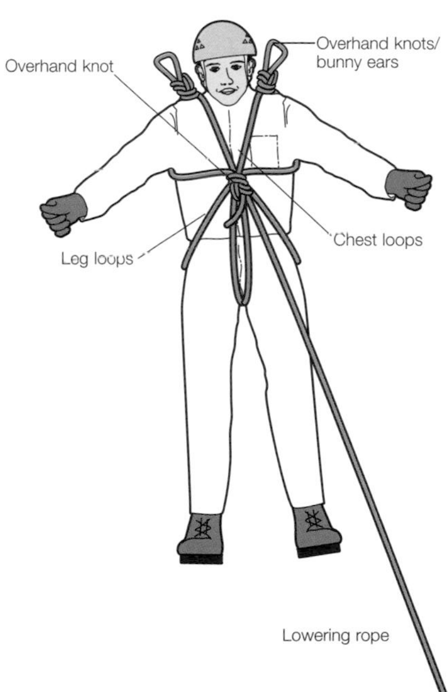

The Thompson knot.

overhand knot on each in order to take out the slack. This knot should be positioned just in front of the top of the shoulders.

- When the person stands upright, the entire rope should be snug around their body. If there are any loose areas, the system should be re-tied.

The reason for choosing the tallest person in the group as the measure for the initial loops is that you have now constructed a harness that will fit everyone once adjusted as mentioned above. This is obviously far quicker than tying a perfectly proportioned harness for each individual group member.

Thread anchor

See also: Abalakov thread, ice threads, lark's foot, sling, spike.

A thread anchor is one where the attachment has to be physically threaded through or around the rock or ice in order to complete the system and make it safe. This may be as simple as passing a loop of a **sling** around the back of a jammed block, and then clipping it into itself again with a karabiner. It may also be used to describe the manufacture of an **Abalakov thread**, as for this a piece of rope has to be physically passed through a couple of holes drilled into the ice. The act of wrapping the rope around the back of a tree could also be categoried as a thread, as it would be impossible in many cases to use the tree as a **spike** by simply dropping a sling over the top of it.

It is important to avoid the temptation to use a **lark's foot** knot when threading slings, as this knot is not only quite weak, but when loaded it will place a high degree of constricting pressure on to the thread, possibly causing anchor failure.

Tie-in loop

See also: belay device, harness.

This is the loop of rope created by tying in to your **harness**. It is important that this loop meets certain criteria, as it will be the central strongpoint from which anchor systems are arranged and belays taken. It should be tied so that it finishes up the same size as the abseil loop on the harness or, if the harness does not have one, as a guide it should have a circumference no larger than fist size. The larger the loop the more difficult it will be to control a **belay device,** as it will be pulled a distance away from the belayer's body when loaded. Conversely, if the loop is too small, for instance tied up very snugly against the climber's harness, it will be very difficult to use it in the correct manner for the attachment of anchor ropes and belay devices.

Tight rope

See also: belay device, dead rope, live rope, semi-direct belay, tension traverse.

A tight rope may be called for at almost any time during an ascent, either to assist the climber by taking some of their weight off their arms, or to hold them in position whilst they take a rest, remove gear and so on. It may also be used as a command when making a **tension traverse**. Providing tension is much easier to do if the belay system is **semi-direct**, with the rope running through a belay device.

Place a hand on the **live rope,** pulling with that hand and using the other, the one on the **dead rope**, to pull through any slack or rope stretch, and then hold it locked off. Doing this a couple of times will get rid of a large amount of the rope's elasticity and provide either physical or mental support (probably both) to the climber.

Top-rope systems

See also: belay device, bottom rope systems, direct belay, group climbing, harness, Italian hitch, Italian hitch – locked off, semi-direct belay.

A top-rope system is one where the belayer is operating from the top. This is as opposed to a bottom rope, where the belayer is running the system from the base of the climb.

Novice sessions

Relevant to climbs of one pitch in length, top roping is the method automatically adopted by anyone who has led a climb and is bringing up a second. However, it also lends itself to a number of other situations where the route has not been led. For instance, those running sessions for novice climbers often adopt it, as it allows the novice to complete a climb from ground up and gain a sense of achievement. It is also often used by friends who are either in training and want to do a number of routes purely as exercise, or by those who are practising specific moves on a hard route prior to a ground-up ascent.

One of the advantages of the top-rope system is that it allows the freedom to adopt a **direct belay** as opposed to a

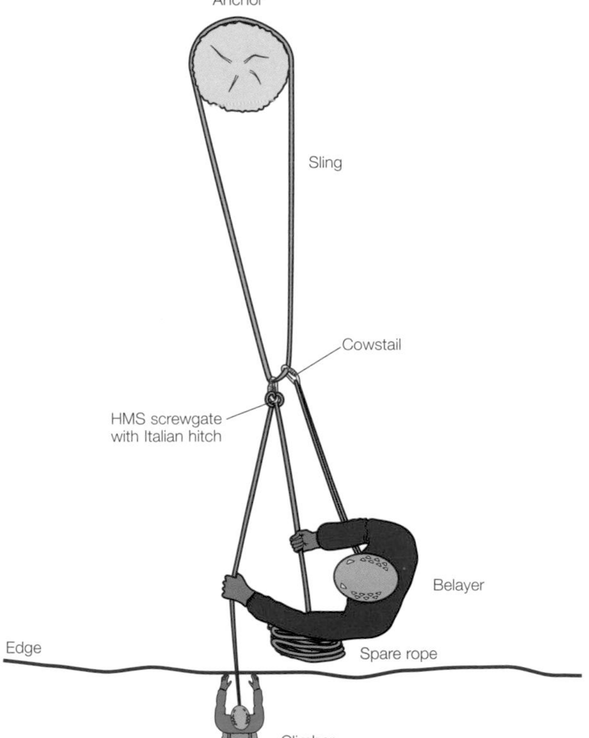

A direct belay system being used when top roping.

notes

It is important, if using the top-rope method with novices, that they all understand what is required of them. They should all be fully briefed before the activity starts, for once it is under way it is likely that the belayer is the sole person in charge and as such they will be at some distance from their group. A secure method of attaching the climbers to the rope should be decided upon, one that is relevant for the abilities of the group. It is also important to have a plan as to what the group are to do once they reach the top. Whether they stay at the top or descend via a path to the bottom should be defined at the outset.

more usual **semi-direct** version. This brings with it a high degree of freedom for the belayer, as well as the opportunity to escape the system easily should the need arise. It also means that, in the event of repeated falls, the belayer is not part of the system and will not be pulled about, as they might be if they are using a **belay device** on their **harness**.

The simplest method of organizing the belay is to use an **Italian hitch**. This can be easily manipulated and can be **locked off** should the need arise. The belayer can be to one side of the system, clipped in either with the end of the rope or **cowstail** clipped on to the anchor.

Traverse – solving a leader fall

See also: abseil loop, belay devices, belay device – locking off, counterbalance abseil, dead rope, escaping the system, Italian hitch, Italian hitch – locking off, HMS karabiner.

Should a leader take a fall whilst traversing, it will often be easy for them to regain the high point. However, in the event that they fall, for instance, into an area of blank rock or under a roof, it will be necessary for the belaying second to provide a means of retrieving them. Here, it is assumed that the leader has ascended a few metres above the stance on a multi-pitch climb, and then traversed out for another 5m (16ft) or so.

METHOD

- The leader should be lowered until they are just above the height of the stance.
- The **belay device** needs to be locked off.
- A loop of rope needs to be passed to the leader. This should be taken from the anchor end of the system. This loop will most likely have to be thrown, so care should be taken that it cannot tangle or get snagged in flight.
- The leader connects themselves to the loop, clipping it into their **abseil loop** or tie-in point using a **screwgate karabiner**.
- The belayer places an **HMS karabiner** on to a suitable point of the anchor system, and clips in the rope coming back from the leader with an **Italian hitch**.
- The belayer pulls in as much slack as possible on the loop rope and then locks off the Italian hitch.
- The belayer now unlocks the belay device and lowers the leader a short distance, maybe just a couple of metres. The actual distance depends upon where the leader is hanging in relation to the stance.
- The belay device is locked off again.
- The Italian hitch is released and the belayer pulls on the rope loop to the leader, moving them across and nearer.
- The Italian hitch is locked off, the belay device unlocked, and the process repeated.

notes

If the loop of rope cannot be thrown to the leader, the second will have to **escape the system** and prusik up and along the rope as far as is necessary to get it across.

If the leader has fallen to a point below that of the stance and the chances of them regaining it under their own steam are unlikely, the belayer will have to rig a hoisting system on the loop rope. This should be set up before the movement of the leader starts, as it would be extremely difficult to stop half way and set a hoist up as an afterthought.

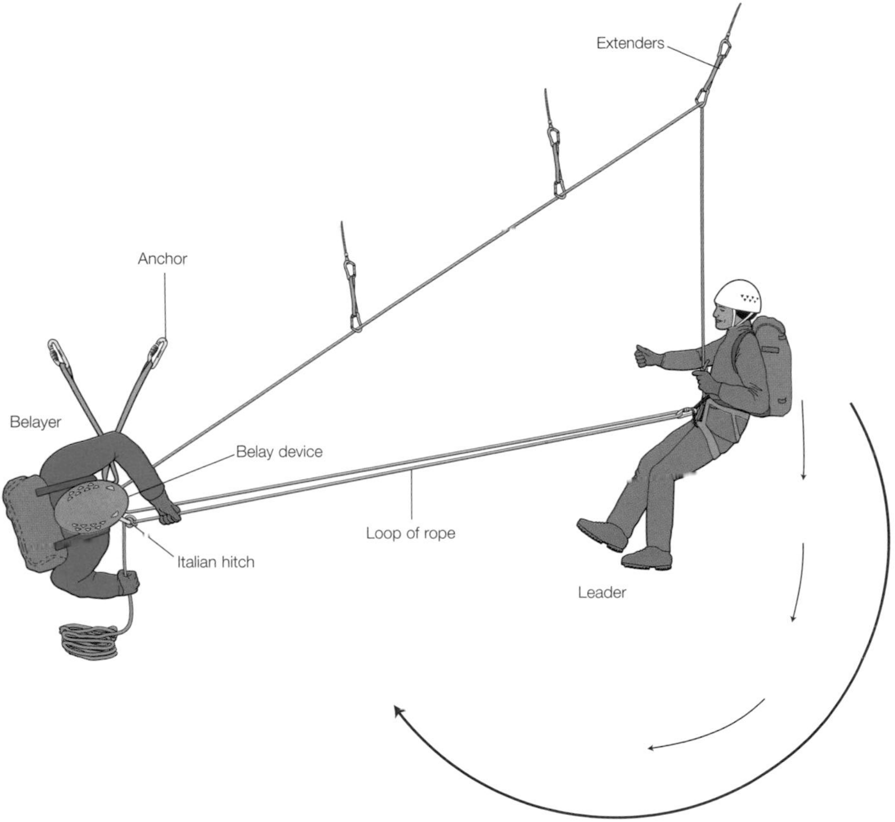

Retrieving a fallen leader from a traverse.

Dealing with an injured leader

It could be the case that the leader has fallen some distance along the traverse and sustained an injury that precludes them from taking an active part in the rescue process. This situation is obviously far more serious than having a fit leader who can assist in their own recovery, and it means that all of the work has to be done by the belayer.

For one person to retrieve the leader and then continue up the climb, hauling them as they go and with no one to provide a belay as they lead, is almost asking the impossible unless the ground is non-technical and the climber very competent. The best process, and the safest for both parties, will be for them to descend. If there is not sufficient rope in the system for this to happen, the belayer will have to go through a process by which plenty of rope is made available.

Traverse – solving a leader fall

notes

The technique used to cross the rope to an unconscious leader, in particular the second time it is done with a back-rope running through the climber's French prusik, needs to be completed in a manner that will not place undue stress or shock on the system. It may be that, should the terrain be difficult, enough rope is paid out at each running belay to allow the climber to lower themselves down to a point where they can prusik directly up to the next runner, and then repeat the process. There is no hard and fast rule as to how this crossing can be completed, as each situation will be different.

METHOD

- Having locked the leader off, the belayer escapes the system.
- They make their way along the rope to the leader, and render any immediate first aid that may be needed.
- The belayer now constructs a new anchor system directly above the fallen leader.
- A French prusik is placed on the rope close to the leader and clipped on to the new anchor. Any slack between the prusik and the anchor is removed.
- The belayer now makes their way back across the rope to the original stance.
- They must now become the back-up for their leader's French prusik, in case it should start to slip before the system is completed. To do this, they place their own French prusik on the **dead rope** coming from the back of the locked-off belay device. Then, to ensure this does not slip, they clip a clove hitch back-up from behind this into their harness as well.
- The belay device can now be unlocked and the weight of the leader gently lowered on to the French prusik at the new anchor.
- The belayer can now remove the belay device from the original anchor system and clip it on to their harness, in place of the clove hitch. Any slack in the rope to the leader should be taken through.
- Although the anchors will have to remain, any spare equipment is stripped out for possible later use.
- The belayer now makes their way back across to the leader and new stance. As they make their way, they will need to feed out the rope through their French prusik.
- Once they arrive at the new stance, they secure themselves to it.
- The climber now backs up the leader's French prusik with a locked-off Italian hitch. This allows them to remove their own French prusik and belay device and pull the rope through.
- The full rope length is now available, and the lowering can commence.

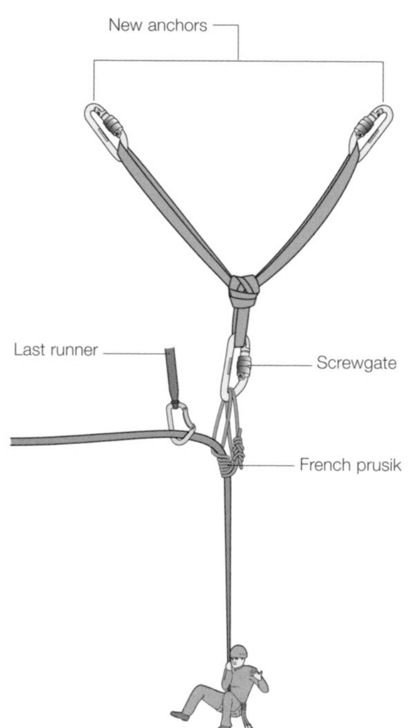

The initial construction of a new anchor after a fall on a traverse.

Intermediate stances

If the full rope length, which is now available, is not sufficient to lower the leader all the way to safety, an intermediate stance or stances will have to be set up. To achieve this, the belayer will most likely be best descending with the injured leader in the **counterbalance abseil** manner, setting up the intermediate stance, pulling the rope through and continuing on down. This will entail the abandonment of a lot of equipment, so anything that can be done to salvage gear in the early stages would be well worth doing.

Twin-rope systems

See also: double-rope systems, running belay.

The twin-rope system has parallels with **double roping**, such as the ability to increase the distance abseiled, the facility to belay in a variety of manners, and the safeguard in case of damage to one of the ropes. However, the main difference is that, unlike double roping, twin ropes are both clipped into the same karabiner on a **running belay**. Because of this, the ropes used tend to be of a lesser diameter and strength rating than those used for either single or double roping, and will often be designated for 'twin'-rope use only. If thicker ropes were used, there would be an undesirable loading on the connecting karabiners and a levering effect which could cause the nose of the karabiner to be forced out of alignment with the gate, thus causing a vast reduction in its breaking strength.

Another potential problem that needs to be considered is that the two ropes may move through the karabiner at different speeds in the event of a fall, possibly causing heat damage to the rope sheath. This would be particularly noticeable if double rope techniques were used for part of the ascent, and as such they should not be employed.

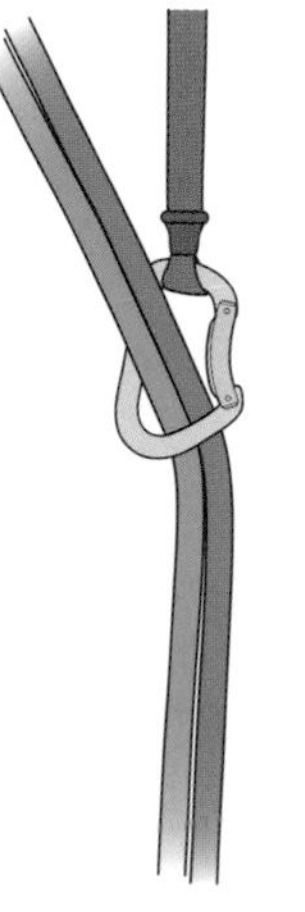

Two ropes running through one karabiner.

Tying in

See tying on.

Tying on

See also: ABC, abseil loop, bowline, clove hitch, equalizing anchors, figure-of-eight knot, HMS karabiner, harnesses, slings, stopper knot, tie-in loop, tying in.

Tying on, sometimes called tying in, encompasses both the process of tying on to the end of the rope prior to climbing as well as the various techniques used when attaching to an anchor. Both of these skills are obviously fundamental to the security of all members of the climbing party, and they should be practised until they become second nature.

Tying on around the waist

The basic method of tying on will be around the waist when a harness is not used. A variety of knots are suitable for this, probably the most versatile being the bowline. This is quick to tie and easy to adjust, although it can be confusing if required by novices. For this reason, the **figure-of-eight** or the **overhand knot**, both tied on a bight and adjusted around the waist once stepped into, would be suitable alternatives.

If a waist tie-on is required when working with a group and

Tying on

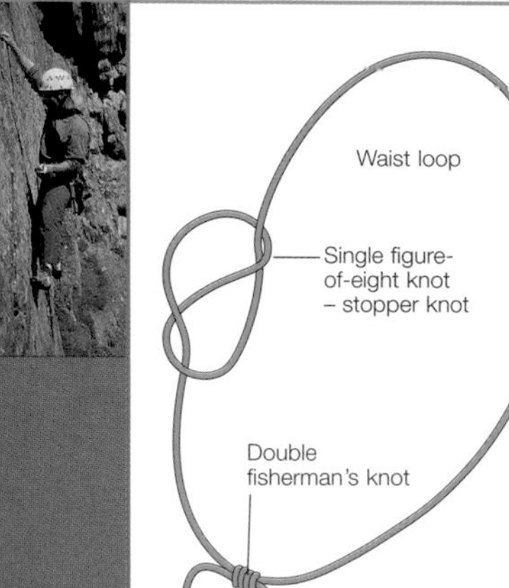

The 'punter' knot.

harnesses are not available, such as when negotiating a short section of steep ground during a mountain-walking excursion, a safe and adjustable loop can easily be fashioned. Called the 'punter knot', it has the advantage that it only needs to be tied once. It is basically a slip knot, but with a stopper on the waist section so that it cannot over-tighten in the event of loading and thus harm the wearer. If the group have vastly differing waist sizes the stopper knot will have to be adjusted occasionally, but otherwise it should be left in a position where it will be snug if the loop is pulled tight.

Tying on to a harness

Tying on to the **harness** can be accomplished in a variety of ways, with the most popular and recommended being the use of a bowline or a figure of eight rethreaded. There is little to choose between them except for personal preference, although they do differ slightly in a couple of ways. The bowline is easy to untie when it has been loaded. This means that it could be the knot of choice for those working a hard route and taking repeated falls, or by those training on a climbing wall to a high standard. The advantage of the figure of eight is that the **stopper knot** is on the outside of the rope, away from the central loop created by tying on. It is into this loop that a number of other knots will be tied, so keeping it clear is worthwhile.

One anchor point	In reach	Clove hitch on to anchor
	Out of reach	Figure of eight on the bight to harness
		Clove hitch on to karabiner on harness
Two anchor points	In reach	Two clove hitches on to anchor, back with figure of eight on a bight to harness
	Out of reach	Two figure of eight on the bights to harness
	One in reach, one out of reach	Figure of eight on bight to harness from furthest anchor, clove hitch to closest
		Clove hitch on harness from furthest anchor, clove hitch to closest
		Figure of eight on bight to furthest anchor, end loop of figure of eight knot into closest
Three anchor points	In reach	Two clove hitches to anchors, back to harness with figure of eight on the bight, back to last anchor with clove hitch
	Out of reach	Three figure of eight on the bights
	Mixture of in and out of reach	Mixture of figure of eight on the bight and clove hitch as suits

When tied on to the harness, ensuring that the recommendations of the manufacturer are adhered to, the central loop so created should be the same circumference as the **abseil loop**. If there is not one on the harness, tying the rope so that the resultant loop is no larger than fist size will be about right.

Tying on to anchors

Tying on to an anchor is obviously an important skill in itself, but equally essential is the ability of the belayer to decide the appropriateness of any given technique in relation to the situation at hand. When tying on to more than one anchor, special care should be taken that the entire system is loaded evenly and that not just one anchor is taking the entire load. As importantly, it should be arranged so that if one anchor should fail, the rest of the anchor system will not be shock-loaded. The table on p. 216 shows a number of possibilities for anchor connection.

It can be seen from the table that once a figure of eight on the bight and a clove hitch are known, the possibilities for tying on to anchors close and distant are myriad. Often the quality of the anchors and the amount of rope available will be the deciding factors.

The contents of the table are clarified below. When tying on to the anchor using any of these it is important to ensure that the belayer has followed the **ABC** and that they are not only tight on to the anchor, but also in line.

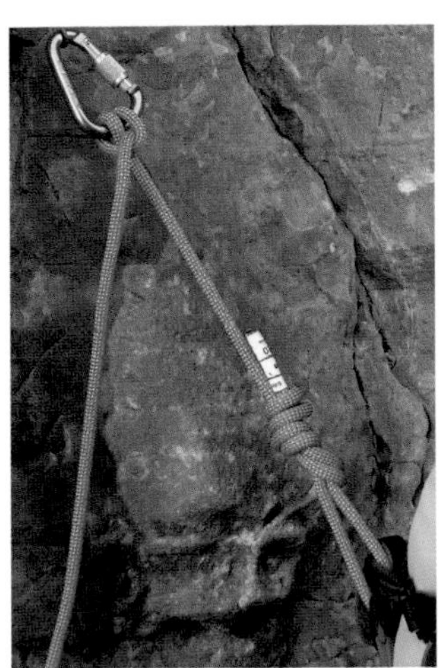

A clove hitch on a single anchor point within reach.

One anchor point

To tie on to a single anchor point means that there can be no question about its integrity. It must have been thoroughly inspected and tested, and if any doubt still exists as to its strength then it should be dismissed and another sought.

If the anchor point is within reach, that is it can easily be reached by hand from the position adopted by the belayer, then the simplest course would be to clip into it using a **clove hitch**. This allows a swift method of attachment and is easy to adjust once clipped into a karabiner, preferably of the **HMS** variety.

If the anchor point is out of reach, there are two options. The first and best would be to use a figure of eight on the bight, which is tied around the central rope tie-in loop at the harness. This is a simple knot to tie, and has the advantage of possessing dynamic properties that allow it to absorb a proportion of a shock load, relieving the anchors of a percentage that they may otherwise have had to take.

A second option is to clip the rope into the anchor, bring it back to the tie-in loop and use an HMS karabiner

A figure of eight on the bight used for a single anchor point out of reach.

tip

A single anchorage point could also be created by the **equalizing** of two or more anchor points using a **sling** or similar method.

Tying on

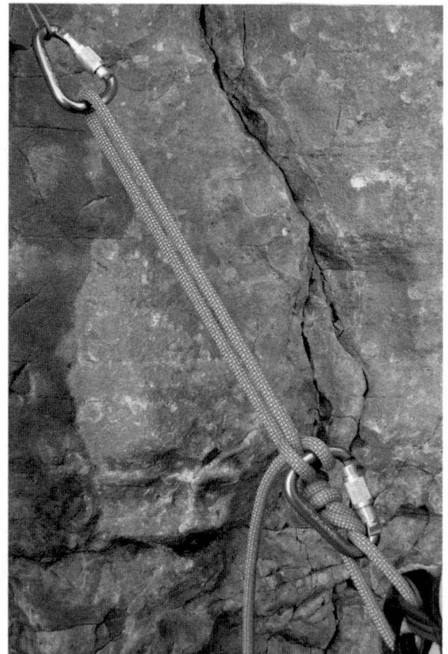

A clove hitch clipped back into the harness tie-on loop.

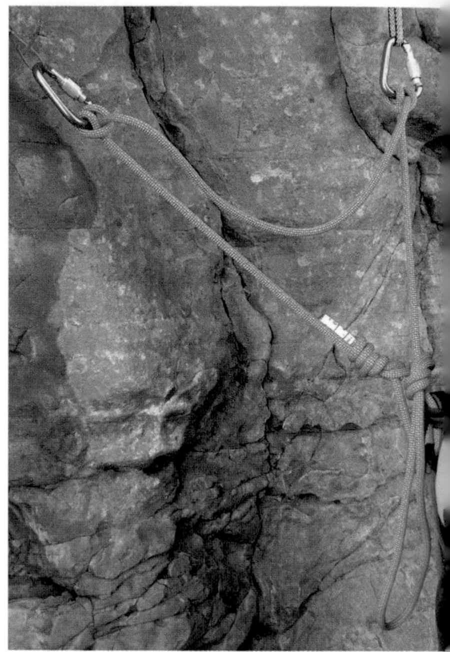

Tying on to two anchors within reach using clove hitches.

into which a clove hitch is placed. Although the anchor is out of reach, the clove hitch is close enough to be easily adjusted. This may be useful when the edge where the belayer wishes to stand is less than perfect and may be badly eroded. It lets them take up a position and then accurately adjust the anchor rope whilst still being protected. The drawback of this is that the clove hitch is not a dynamic knot and will not absorb much energy in the event of a fall, although it may be felt that the advantages outweigh this.

notes

It is also possible to use the clove hitch on the tie-in loop method for two anchors out of reach, but if you do, separate HMS screwgates should be used for each knot, due to the loading dynamics of a clove hitch and the strength alignment of an HMS. The temptation to place two clove hitches into one karabiner should be avoided due to the excessive levering effect they will have on it, as well as the difficulty of adjustment. Because of this, the use of clove hitches for more than one anchor out of reach is not recommended.

Two anchor points

If there are two anchor points within reach, as may be the case on a narrow ledge, these can be tied on to using two clove hitches. For this reason, it would be fortunate if the anchors were equipped with HMS karabiners so that the hitches can sit correctly. From the harness, the first anchor is clipped with a clove hitch. A little slack is allowed, then the second anchor is also clipped with a clove hitch. The rope is now run back to the harness and secured on to the tie-in loop with a figure of eight on the bight. Any fine-tuning that subsequently needs to be made can be done by adjusting the clove hitches.

If there are two anchor points out of reach, these are best tied on to by using two figure-of-eight-on-the-bight knots,

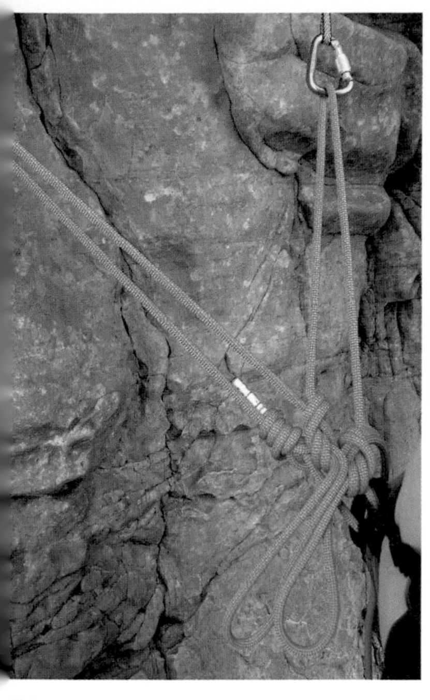

Tying on to two anchors out of reach.

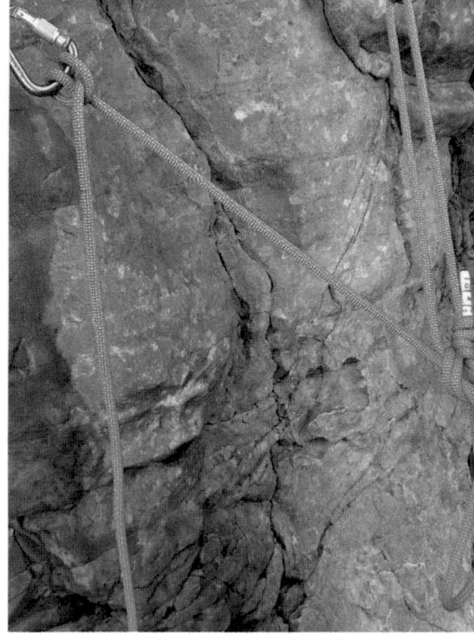

One anchor in reach, one out of reach.

one to each anchor. Once the first knot is tied, the second needs to be secured with exactly the same tension. This is best done by leaning in towards the anchor slightly, tying the knot, and then moving back out into the correct stance position. It may be also prudent initially to clip both anchors and then pull down the rope between them so that both the required sections of rope are to hand, to save having to move off from the stance when the second anchor is needed to be clipped.

If the positioning of the anchor points is varied, such as one in reach and one out of reach, then the furthest is clipped into with a figure of eight on the bight to the harness tie-in loop, and from this point the rope coming from the back of the knot can be clipped into the closest anchor with a clove hitch. It may also be possible that the loop left over when the figure of eight is tied is of sufficient length to clip into the closest anchor, and this may be done. Also, the figure of eight on a bight could be replaced with a clove hitch.

Once the basics of tying a figure of eight on the bight and a clove hitch have been mastered, a climber will be able to tie on to any number of anchors. As shown in the table, three anchors can be dealt with by a mixture of clove hitches and figure of eights, with four or more anchors also able to be dealt with in the same manner.

tip

To ensure that the best position is taken when belaying a second, make certain that the anchor is above hip level. This will help to maintain the ABC and help a downward pull, so as not to cause too much discomfort.

Tying off coils

See also: abseil loop, abseiling, chest harness, crevasse rescue, HMS karabiner, harness.

There are many occasions when the rope needs to be shortened, either temporarily or for an extended period of time. Temporary use may be when, having geared up on a safe area at the bottom of a cliff and ready to climb a winter route, a short section of moderate ground exists before the initial stance is made. In this case taking coils is far preferable to dragging the rope up the slope behind you. An extended period of time may include the traversing of a corniced snow arête at altitude, where the going is slow but the distance between climbers needs to be something less than a full rope length. Another very common reason for taking coils is to allow for the safe and swift movement on alpine or expedition-type terrain, either on a route or across glaciated ground. It is very helpful if you can rapidly undo a number of coils should further rope length be needed if any difficulties on the route are encountered.

	No. of climbers	Distance apart (m)
Snow slope	2+	3
Snow ridge	2+	6
Rocky ridge	2+	9
Glacier travel	2	12
	3	8–10

Considerations

The distances between climbing partners who have chosen to take coils in order to shorten the rope will differ according to the reason for doing so and the terrain upon which they are travelling. A general guide is given in the table at left.

Another factor that has to be decided upon is the method by which the coils will be tied off. There are a number of ways of doing this, two of the most practical are given below, but the terrain over which the ascent or descent is to take place will influence the decision. For instance, if a climber was to tie off in the manner given for scrambler's coils, and they fell into a **crevasse**, there is a good chance that they would invert and end up hanging upside down, as the attachment point is very low. Conversely, if they were on terrain that included a number of short technical pitches interspersed with easy sections, spending a lot of time tying and untying knotted coils would eventually add time to the day, apart from the fact that the knot itself could become frozen in certain circumstances and be next to impossible to undo.

notes

Like so many other techniques, it is important to practise taking coils well before the skill is needed in anger. Poorly prepared coils will either be so long that they keep slipping off the shoulder, or so tight that they restrict the movement of the chest when breathing. If coils are taken in a situation where a rucksack is to be worn, the rucksack should normally be put on before the coils are started.

Scrambler's coils

The scrambler's coils method allows for the slick taking on and off of rope from around the body, and is very secure. It should not be used, however, if there is any chance of the climber becoming suspended free by the rope when wearing a rucksack, as there is a chance that they may end up hanging upside down.

METHOD

- Tie into your harness.
- To make a guide to ensure consistent coil size, place either your left or your right hand (depending on preference – most right-handers will start with the left), pointing out with the palm down, at a point around about hip level. The exact point will depend not only on your physical width, but also on the amount of clothes you are wearing – bulky clothing may well mean that slightly larger coils are required – and whether you are carrying a rucksack.
- Using your right hand (for the sake of this example), bring the rope from your harness up round your neck in an anticlockwise manner, and round your measuring hand, keeping the rope coils snug. Ensure that the coils are all of the same size, and continue until just a metre or so more than the required gap between you and your partner is achieved.
- Put the arm that has been used for the initial measuring through the coils so that they sit on your shoulder in a neat and comfortable manner. The coils should be of a length that doesn't allow them to slide off your shoulder, nor should they restrict your breathing due to their tightness.
- Place an **HMS karabiner** up through the harness, connecting the leg loops and the waist belt, taking exactly the same line as the **abseil loop**. Arrange it so that the gate opens on the outside, and with the wider end of the karabiner on the top. (It should be noted that this is one of the very rare times that a karabiner is connected to the harness in this manner, and it should not be used in this configuration for other techniques such as, for instance, abseiling.)
- Take a bight of rope and pass it through the tie-in loop, up next to your chest behind all of the coils, then through them and back down to the HMS. Clip the resulting loop of rope in, do up the gate, and pull on the main rope to tighten up the coil lock-off loop.
- The system is now ready to use. The friction that is created by the loop round the back of the coils is enough to keep it all snug, and coils are very easily taken off by simply undoing the loop from the karabiner and pulling on the main rope. The lock-off is thus released and rope can be shed as required.

Locking off scrambler's coils.

Tying off coils

Coils for glacier travel

A second method is that used if glacier travel is to be undertaken. This is important if there is any chance of the climber being suspended by the rope. The method of tying off the coils detailed below allows them to act as a simple **chest harness**, helping to keep their body upright should a rucksack be worn.

METHOD

- Take coils and arrange them over the shoulder as detailed for scrambler's coils.
- Making a bight of the main climbing rope, pinch the ropes together about 25cm (10in) from the end of the loop so that you do not lose track of which ropes go to make it up.
- Pass the loop around the back of the coils and up by your chest, then tie an overhand knot on the bight around all the coils, making sure that the resulting tail loop is as short as possible.
- Clip a karabiner into either your abseil loop or tie-in loop, and clip the overhand knot loop into this. If it is tied correctly, you will have to stoop forwards slightly to clip it in and, as you stand up straight again, the loops will be pulled snug around your shoulders as the knot comes tight.

Locking off coils for glacier travel.

Tyrolean traverse – rigging

See also: ascender, dead rope, dynamic rope, HMS karabiners, Italian hitch, Italian hitch – locking off, lowering, low-stretch rope, pendulum traverse, pulleys, screwgate karabiners, vectors.

There may be a variety of reasons for setting up a Tyrolean traverse. One scenario could be that a team attempting to climb a sea stack elects one person to swim across with the rope and secure it, so letting the rest of the party and their equipment cross without getting wet. Another scenario might be that a climbing team needs to negotiate a deep cleft in a ridge on a high peak. One team member could be **lowered**, cross the gap by means of a **pendulum traverse**, then fix a line so that the rest of the team can follow on a Tyrolean. A Tyrolean traverse may also be used as an activity in its own right, rigged to cross between two rock spires, for example.

notes

There are many ways of rigging and executing a crossing by Tyrolean traverse, and the exact method decided upon would be determined by the situation in which it is to be used. However, the basics of the rigging remain the same, no matter what technique is decided upon.

tip

The retrieval of the crossing rope may be an issue if the traverse is part of a journey, and if so the person tasked with rigging it may elect to cross with both ends, allowing it to be pulled through once the last person has crossed.

Anchors

The quality of the anchors must be beyond question, as huge forces will come into effect when the system is loaded, and the section dealing with **vectors** should be referred to for clarification on this. The method by which the rope is attached at each end should also be carefully considered, and the strongest option adopted. If using a Tyrolean whilst on a climb there may be little option but to use the anchor points available within a small area, but the entire operation should be halted if there is any doubt as to their properties. On a larger scale, where the Tyrolean is used more for fun than necessity, the selection of anchors may have been made some time beforehand, and will often be constructed from heavyweight protection material such as large slings placed around trees or similar.

Using dynamic rope

Although **low-stretch rope** should be used wherever possible for Tyrolean rigging, on a climb it is very likely that the rope used for the Tyrolean will be the same one as used for the climbing itself, in other words it will be **dynamic**. This will make the tensioning of the rope a little more difficult as the stretch has to be accounted for. Also, the equipment used will most likely be limited, probably just a few karabiners.

Basic tensioning system

METHOD

- With one end of the rope anchored, tie a figure-of-eight knot on to the rope near to the other anchor. The distance that this knot is away from the anchor is critical, as the rope stretch when the system is tensioned will cause it to move closer. Trial and error may be the only way to get it right for most situations.

Tyrolean traverse – rigging

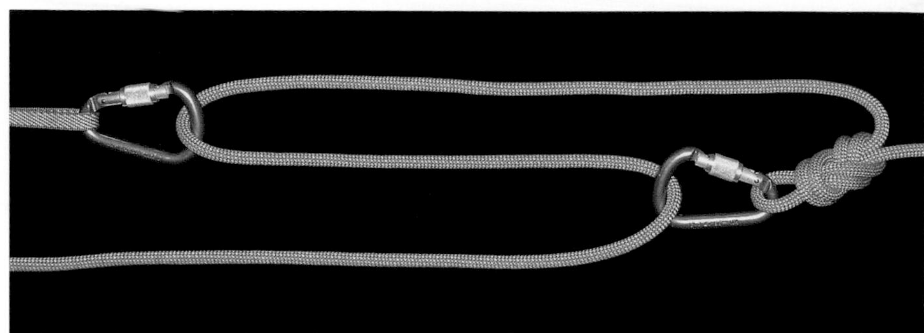

A basic Tyrolean tensioning system.

notes

After the passage of the first person it may be necessary to re-tension the system. This is because the dynamic rope is being elongated by the weight of the person hanging on it and will become slack very quickly.

- Clip a **screwgate karabiner** into the figure of eight.
- Run the rope to the anchor, through another karabiner, and then back and into the screwgate on the figure of eight.
- Pulling on the dead rope will allow the slack to be pulled out of the Tyrolean rope, with extra pulling helping to remove some of its dynamic stretch.
- Once the required tension has been obtained, the dead rope should be secured at the anchor with a locked-off **Italian hitch**.

Improved tensioning system

If a tighter crossing rope is desirable, a slightly different method will help to achieve this:

METHOD

- With one end of the rope rigged as before, tie the figure of eight and clip in a screwgate karabiner at the appropriate point.
- Having run the rope through the anchor karabiner, tie a second figure of eight at a point where, with a karabiner clipped into it, it just reaches the position of the first one under light tension.
- Clip the first karabiner into its own rope running out of the figure of eight and clip the second screwgate into the loop this forms.
- Pulling on the dead rope coming from the back of the second figure of eight will allow tensioning to take place. Secure this with a locked-off Italian hitch to the anchor.

A Tyrolean tensioning system using two screwgate karabiners.

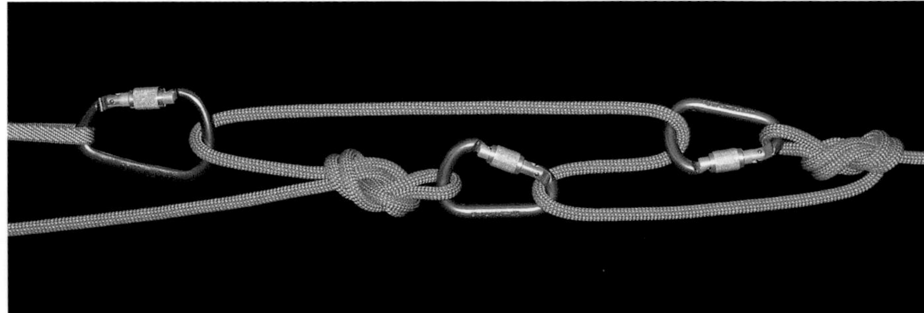

Technical system number 1

If the system is to be set up and used for some period of time, such as the negotiation of a swollen river by a large party when on expedition, a different method of rigging can be utilized. This is best done when a variety of **pulleys** is available, and the rope itself is of a low-stretch construction. This type of rope will make the tensioning easier, and will not give the problems associated with loading a dynamic rope, such as sagging and the time factor involved in re-tensioning.

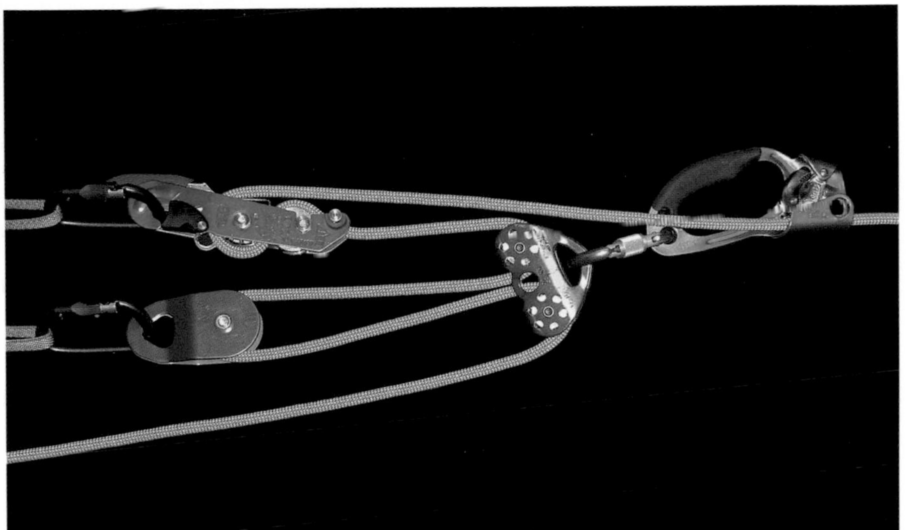

Tensioning a rope using a mechanical device on the anchor.

The first system described is suitable for those occasions when a releasable mechanical device is available to secure the rope once tensioned.

METHOD

- With the far end of the rope tied on to the anchor, it is run through the mechanical device on the second anchor.
- An ascender is placed on to the rope, arranged so that when it is loaded it will pull the crossing rope tighter.
- Either two separate or one tandem pulley is clipped on to the ascender.
- A single pulley is secured to the anchor.
- The dead rope from the mechanical device is run through one of the pair of pulleys, back to the single one on the anchor, then back through the second of the pair.
- Pulling on the dead rope will tension the line, and the mechanical device will automatically take up the slack. Once the ascender has reached the device, the dead rope can be released, the ascender slid back down the crossing rope, and the tensioning can continue.
- Once the correct tension has been obtained, the mechanical device

Tyrolean traverse – rigging

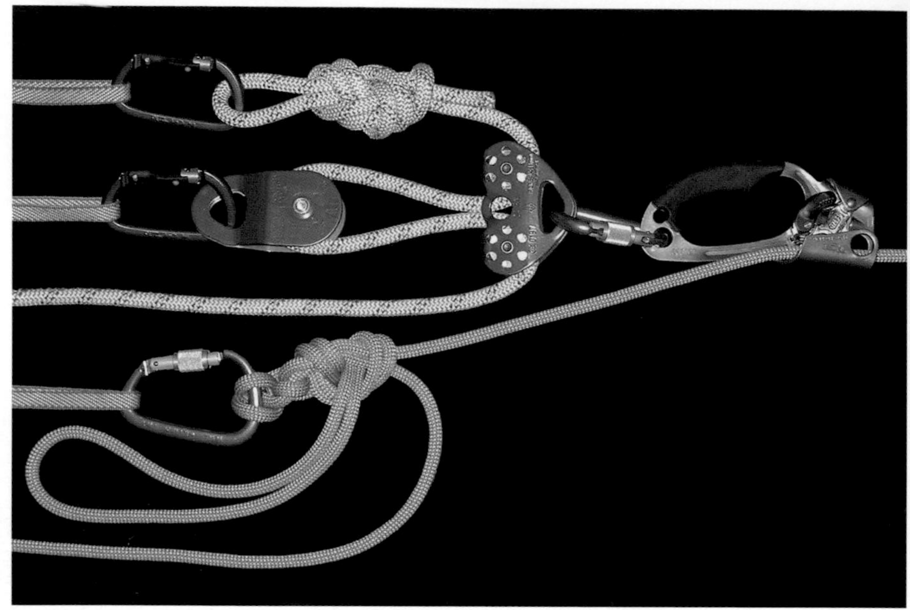

Tensioning the rope using an Italian hitch as the securing method.

should be capable of holding the load on its own. The ascender and related pulleys can now be removed from the rope.

- The device holding the rope under tension should be locked off as per the manufacturer's recommendations, but only in a manner that allows the tension within the Tyrolean system to be swiftly released if the need arose.

notes

It is worth thinking ahead to the stripping out of the system once the traverse has been completed. Because of the tremendous forces that are exerted on the ropes, any knot used needs to be one that can be easily undone once loaded. This most likely means that the bowline will be the knot of choice at the fixed end of the system, as it can be undone with reasonable ease even after significant pressure has been applied to it.

Technical system number 2

If a mechanical device is not available, the end of the rope can be secured by use of a locked-off Italian hitch. It is very useful if two people are involved in the rigging, otherwise the process is extremely difficult to complete. It is as follows:

METHOD

- Having secured the crossing rope to the far anchor, bring it to the second anchor and clip it into an **HMS karabiner** using an Italian hitch.
- Place an ascender on the rope, aligned so that when it is pulled it will tension the Tyrolean.
- On to the ascender, place either two separate pulleys or one tandem pulley.
- A length of low-stretch rope is now needed. This may be a separate piece, or could be the end of the rope being used for the Tyrolean. The end of it should be tied off at the anchor.
- Also on the anchor place a single pulley.

- Run it through one of the pulleys on the ascender, back to the anchor pulley, then through the second of the pulleys.
- Pulling on this rope will now allow tensioning to take place. As this happens, the rope also needs to be taken in through the Italian hitch.
- During the tensioning procedure, if the ascender needs to be moved further away from the anchor to allow more pulling to take place, the Italian hitch needs to be tied off. Once done, the ascender can be moved, the tension taken up again, the Italian released and the procedure repeated.
- Once the correct tension has been achieved, the Italian should be locked off and the ascender and related pulleys removed.

notes

It is important that the end of the rope used to pull the system tight is tied off in some releasable method, such as with an Italian hitch. It should not be secured by a device such as an **ascender**, as this would not allow slack to be released into the system whilst it was loaded, such as may be required in an emergency.

Second rope

As well as the rigging of the main crossing rope, thought should be given to the provision of a second rope, placed with the purpose of providing either extra security, or as a means of moving the person crossing along the rope, or as a combination of both. This may be neither necessary nor desirable in an impromptu mountaineering situation, but should be considered in most other cases.

The tensioning of this second rope should be carefully considered. If it were to be used as a safety line then to have it too slack would mean that the person crossing would drop a considerable distance should the main rope or anchor fail, quite possibly causing them injury. However, if it is to be just used as a means of pulling the person crossing along the Tyrolean or for retrieval of the equipment used when doing so, then to spend a long time rigging and tensioning it may equally be inappropriate. In either case, it is important that this second rope in no way interferes with the workings of the first, and that anyone crossing is aware of its function.

notes

Extreme care should be used when rigging a Tyrolean for use by light people. If the crossing rope is severely tensioned and the take-off point is a little above the landing area, they could pick up speed on the way which would cause them injury if they crashed into either the anchor or the ground on the far side. Consider the use of a safety catchment loop if the rope has been tensioned for large people but there are also lighter people wishing to cross.

Tyrolean traverse – crossing

See also: ascenders, chest harness, dynamic rope, harness, Italian hitch, pendulum traverse, prusik loop, pulleys, sling, Tyrolean traverse – rigging.

The method employed to cross a **Tyrolean traverse** should be considered even before it is rigged. The type of crossing will have a bearing on the equipment used, with the urgency and lack of specialized equipment meaning that the team in a mountaineering situation use little more than a couple of karabiners, whereas a more regimented crossing may use a variety of dedicated apparatus.

Simple crossing

For the simplest of crossings, a karabiner attached to a short **sling** from the **harness** may be all that is used. Great care should be taken to ensure that the sling is arranged to be of a length whereby the person crossing has the opportunity to reach the rope easily with both hands and feet, as these will be the most likely forms of propulsion.

One problem with the rigging of a Tyrolean in a mountaineering situation, where a **dynamic rope** is most likely the only one to hand, is that each person will end up causing the rope to sag during the central part of the crossing, even if the rope is re-tensioned after each person's passage. This can make the progress from the middle of the crossing up to the far anchor extremely difficult, as the closer the climber gets to the objective the steeper the angle of rope they have to negotiate. For this reason, having a **prusik loop** or **ascending** device to hand is advantageous, as it far eases the problem. Placing it in front of the suspension karabiner and having it attached to the harness by means of a sling, it can be moved along at intervals and helps avoid the problem of the climber slipping backwards. Great care should be taken if a prusik loop is used, that it is never over-run by the karabiner as jamming could occur causing major problems. Also, the sling to which it is attached should not be so long that if the climber slipped back a little on the rope they would not be able to reach it, potentially a problem on the steeper section near the end.

Crossing with pulleys

Using a pulley will ease the crossing considerably, and one with a built-in cam is perfect. This allows a smooth crossing to be accomplished, and the camming action ensures that no height is lost when moving along the final section.

For a more organized Tyrolean traverse, other items of equipment may be available. These could include a variety of pulleys, both free running and with an internal cam system, and a second rope for both safety and gear retrieval. Having

tips

If the weight of a rucksack is significant, it can hamper the crossing and make it very awkward. If sending the rucksacks across separately is not an option, each climber can take theirs with them suspended by a sling from the karabiner being used as a pulley. In this manner, the rucksack will not upset the balance of the person crossing as it is connected directly to the rope.

notes

Gloves should be worn when negotiating any type of Tyrolean traverse, as not only could the skin be burnt should it come into contact with the rope when moving fast, but they will also help provide grip during the latter sections of the crossing which may well be on a slight incline.

tip

For some using the Tyrolean, the provision of a **chest harness** may ease their crossing and help them to maintain contact with the rope. This would be particularly important for children or those with a low centre of gravity.

this equipment to hand makes a crossing far easier to manage, and substantially increases the number of techniques that can be employed.

Higher take-off point

The method for safeguarding a person getting on to a high take-off Tyrolean and helping them across is as follows:

METHOD

- Once the crossing rope is rigged, possibly after the chasm has been negotiated by **pendulum traverse**, a second rope to be used for safety and retrieval should also be put into place. This needs to be run through either a karabiner or pulley at the same height as the main rope anchor.
- A pulley is put on to the main rope, with care being taken that it is not let go of during the rigging process, otherwise it may be lost.
- A karabiner is clipped on to this, and a second pulley, one with an internal cam, attached.
- The safety rope is clipped into the cammed pulley. It now runs up from the ledge, through the anchor karabiner or pulley, through the cammed pulley, and back down to the ledge.
- The person crossing is attached to the end of the rope, and is safeguarded as they make their way up to the start of the crossing by a belayer who takes the rope in as they scramble up. The cammed pulley ensures that they will not fall to the ground should they slip.
- Once they are at the desired height, quite close to the crossing rope, they commit their weight to the system and the cammed pulley locks off.
- The person belaying from the ledge can now pay out the safety rope, which will allow the crossing to take place.
- Once they have reached the other side, the person who has just crossed will untie from the safety rope and, releasing the cam, pull enough through the pulley so that when the system is retrieved, sufficient slack rope is allowed so that it will reach the belay ledge from the height of the high anchor.
- If the crossing is part of a journey, the last person to cross can self-belay and the safety rope can be pulled through once they have safely arrived. If both ends of the rigging rope have been secured on the far side it can be untied, pulled through, and the journey continued.

notes

In some circumstances, there may be a need for the take-off point to be considerably higher than the area being used to contain the group. This should not be confused with a 'death slide' type activity, but could occur where a chasm has to be crossed with each anchor section being at different heights, and the start point being a distance above the heads of the group's safe area. It also may be employed to give those crossing an easier run, as if the start is higher than the finish then the section of rope that is predisposed to sagging may be over safe ground on the other side of the obstruction.

A tandem pulley being used with a cammed pulley. A safe system that does not allow the person crossing to slip back along the rope.

T

Tyrolean traverse – crossing

notes

Long hair should be kept well out of the way when using pulleys or similar systems on a Tyrolean traverse. To get hair caught when crossing would not only be excruciatingly painful, but would also most likely result in the system jamming. It should be tied back out of the way or secured under a helmet.

tip

Before departing on a Tyrolean traverse, make sure that nothing is likely to fall from your pockets!

Considerations

For a more usual crossing of a Tyrolean traverse, a second rope will often be employed. If this is to assist the person crossing to the end of the traverse and also to aid retrieval of the crossing pulley, it will most likely be clipped to the top of the pulley by means of a screwgate karabiner. Those controlling the system at either end can then use this rope to move the pulley, loaded or unloaded, wherever they like. An **Italian hitch** at either end of the system will provide the required security and braking force.

For most general-purpose traverses the employment of a pulley on the main rope, combined with a cammed pulley on an upper safety rope, would be the norm. The pulleys could have a retrieval rope attached, and the briefing of each person as to how to release the pulley cam should be carried out. If the traverse is being done more for fun than by necessity, then either each person would have their own set, or the original set could be returned to the beginning after each person has crossed.

Opposite: *Crossing the Tour glacier, European Alps.*

Unassisted hoist

See also: assisted hoist, belay devices, dead rope, escaping the system, French prusik, hauling, hip hoist, klemheist, live rope, screwgates, semi-direct belay, slippery hitch.

The unassisted hoist is a technique that comes into its own should a problem occur on a multi-pitch route that means the second is unable to make their way up a piece of ground and is also unable to help the leader with any kind of hoisting system. Although the **assisted hoist** is the first line of defence, the unassisted version would need to be used if the second was unable to attach themselves to the loop of rope lowered by the leader. This may be because of injury to the second, or simply because they were more than a third of a rope length away and there would not be enough rope to lower down to them. It is similar to some **hauling** techniques, which are covered under their own heading.

Basic unassisted hoist

It should be noted that this system is far easier to operate, especially over longer distances, if you are able to **escape the system** before starting. The following description of the procedure assumes that a single rope is being used, the system has not been escaped, and that a **semi-direct belay** using a standard **belay device** has been taken.

METHOD

- Lock off the belay device.
- In front of the belay device, attach a **French prusik** with enough turns to enable it to grip a loaded single rope.
- Clip the French prusik into the karabiner holding the belay device, using a separate **screwgate**.
- Push the French prusik snugly down the **live rope**.
- Place a **klemheist** on to the live rope, below the French prusik. This should be orientated so that it will lock when taking a pull upwards from the belayer.

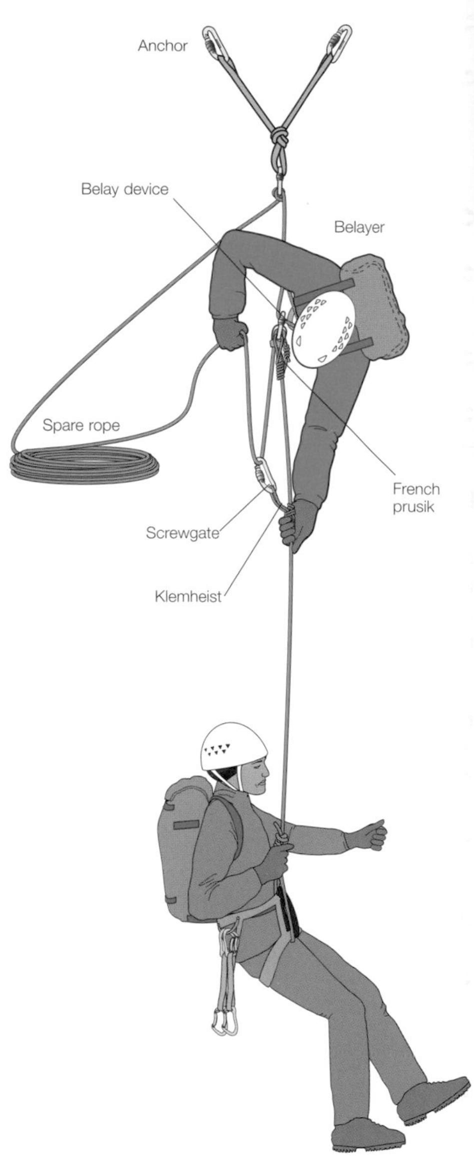

An unassisted hoist.

- Clip a bight of rope from the **dead rope** side of the belay device into the klemheist, using a screwgate karabiner.
- Push the klemheist as far down the live rope as possible. This will probably be best achieved by pushing with your foot.
- Place a couple of wraps of the dead rope around your wrist so that it does not get dropped, wasting valuable time. Untie the locked-off belay device and pull the slack rope through as it undoes. Care should be taken in the final stages that the French prusik is not shock loaded as the **slippery hitch** comes undone.
- Pulling on the dead rope loads the klemheist, which then locks and allows the hoisting to take place.
- When the klemheist has been pulled up to a short distance below the French prusik, push the latter knot down the rope and gently release the load via the dead rope so that it grips.
- The klemheist, which is now unweighted, can be released and slid back down the live rope.
- The procedure is repeated as often as required.

notes

Care should be taken when attaching the French prusik that not too many turns are taken. This can be as bad as taking too few, as the knot will jam up against the belay device as the system is being used and not release, possibly causing a dangerous amount of slack rope to enter the system before the problem is spotted.

Improved unassisted hoist

An improvement can be made and the mechanical advantage increased by the inclusion of an extra karabiner and prusik loop. Once again, it is far easier if the system has been escaped prior to setting up the hoist.

METHOD

- The hoist is set up as before.
- Either the end or a suitable section of the rope is attached to the anchor.
- A klemheist is put on to the rope that would have been pulled with the above technique and a screwgate attached.
- This screwgate is clipped into the new rope from the anchor.
- Pulling on the free end of this rope allows the klemheist to grip the original pulling rope, which in turn grips the live rope, and hoisting commences.
- The system has the weight lowered on to the original French prusik at appropriate times so as to allow the various knots to be re-positioned.

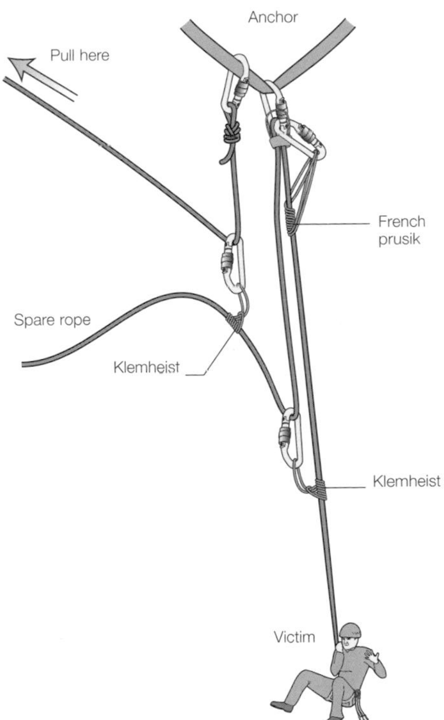

The improved unassisted hoist.

Unassisted hoist

Considerations

It should be noted that there comes a point where the mechanical advantage obtained through the use of extra pulling mechanisms starts to fall away, as the friction created by the system takes its toll. The inclusion of pulleys at key points through the system will greatly aid the technique, and the doubling-up of karabiners will also go some way to help.

Vector

See also: running belays, semi-direct belay, slings.

The vector of an anchor or rigging system can be described as the angle from the outermost limits of the system through to the point of loading. A narrow vector is desirable as it will not only make the operation of a system more comfortable when related to the way in which anchor ropes are tied in to the harness when using a **semi-direct belay**, but also the narrower the vector, the stronger that the system will be. This becomes extremely important when using poor placements in either rock or ice.

The vector angle, for instance, of two **slings** being brought down to a single point, needs to be carefully considered. It would be prudent never to have an angle greater than 90 degrees between the two sides of the system, as the greater the angle, the greater the loading on each individual element.

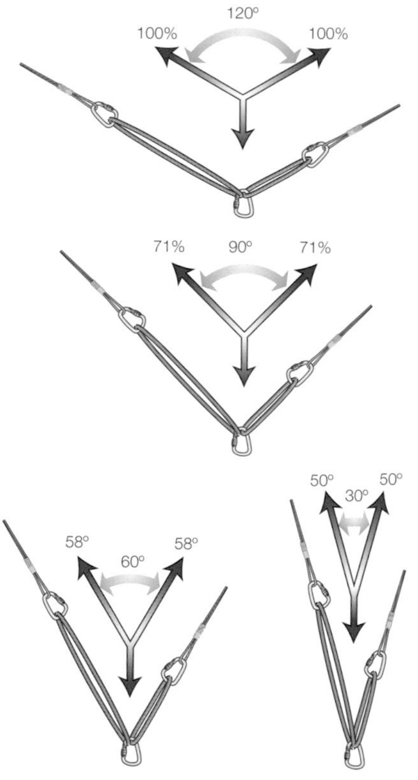

Diagrams showing the relationship between angle and loading percentage.

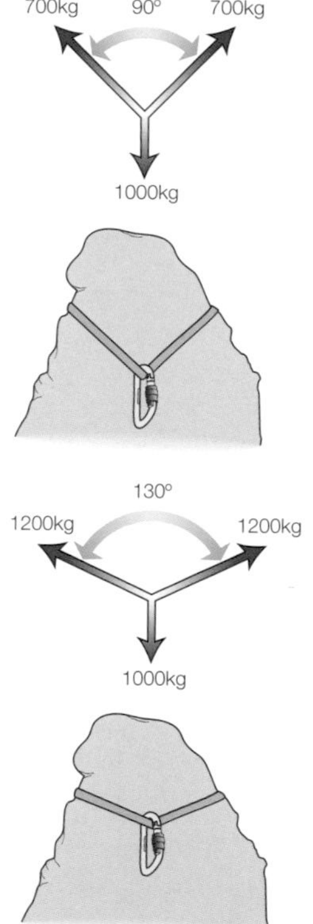

Diagrams showing the relationship between sling angle over a spike anchor and the loading in kilograms.

The following gives the values for a variety of angles. X is the angle between the slings, Y is the percentage of loading transferred to the individual anchor point.

- •X = 120 degrees, Y = 100%
- •X = 90 degrees, Y = 71%
- •X = 60 degrees, Y = 58%
- •X = <30 degrees, Y = 50%

This is extremely important when considering the strength of slings being used as **running belays** or anchors, for instance when placed over a rock spike. The critical failure point can be easily reached with a wide vector at the load area, as the following indicates.

Here, X is again the angle at the load point and Y is the loading on each individual anchor in kilograms. The load applied for this calculation is 1,000kg (2,205lbs), such as that created by a climber who has fallen whilst leading a climb.

- •X = 90 degrees, Y = 700kg (1,543lbs).
- •X = 130 degrees, Y = 1,200kg (2,646lbs).

It can be seen from the above that a wide angle is extremely undesirable, with a load applied to a system set up with a vector of over 120 degrees putting considerably more than the actual load at the central point through to each anchor.

Vertical axe anchor

See also: buried axe anchor, Italian hitch, reinforced buried axe.

A vertical axe anchor is a method of swiftly arranging a belay and safeguarding someone either ascending or descending. However, it is the least secure of the axe anchor systems, so consideration should be given to a variety of factors when choosing to use it. The reason it is less secure than other methods is that the attachment point of the sling, which is either used to clip into or belay from, is just above the surface of the snow. This means that a levering effect could be created in the event of loading, with the axe subsequently pulling out of the ground. The advantage of other axe anchor systems is that the attachment point is below the surface of the snow, thus causing compression of the snow pack as opposed to leverage.

Hard snow

The vertical axe works well in hard snow, although in the hardest it may not be possible to get the full length of the axe shaft into the snow. The axe head may have a hammering plate attached for this reason, and the shaft can be driven deeper in with a few blows from an ice hammer. However, this can cause deformation of light-weight tools and may cause any rubber used as a grip to be stripped from the shaft.

Usage

If the vertical axe is to be used as a belay anchor, a sling can be placed around the shaft, arranged so that it is as close to the surface of the snow as possible. A stance should then be taken some distance downslope of this.

It could also be used as a temporary anchor to safeguard someone over an awkward step. In this mode, a short sling could be arranged around the axe and an Italian hitch clipped in to provide security. This system should only be used where the axe will not be shock-loaded, such as when lowering or belaying a second whilst keeping the rope snug.

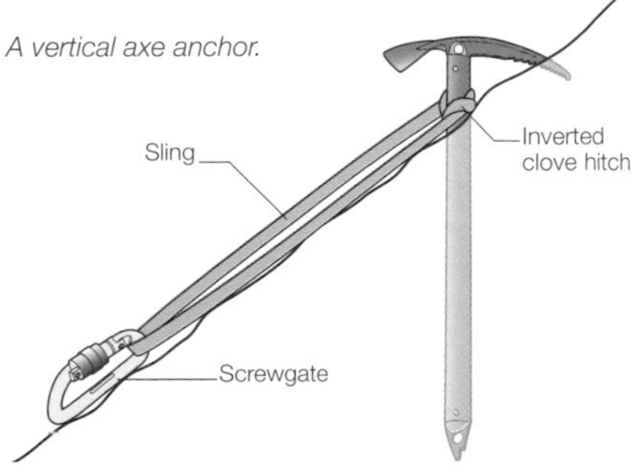

A vertical axe anchor.

Waist belay

notes

When arranging the rope it must go over the head of the belayer and right down on to the anchor rope. Don't step over it and pull it upwards because, when loaded, it could slide out underneath you and be impossible to hold.

See also: ABC, dead rope, escaping the system, indirect belay, live rope, shoulder belay.

Waist belay is usually the term given to an **indirect** belay system, although a **shoulder belay** is in the same category, where the body of the belayer provides the friction needed to make the system work. The simplest type requires the live rope to come from the climber, pass around the back of the body (often cushioned with a rucksack), and out on the opposite side with a twist of the **dead rope** being taken around the arm. When a braking effect is required, the arm holding the dead rope is brought across in front of the body to increase the friction. One of the benefits of the waist belay is that it is difficult to hold any but the shortest fall without letting any rope slip through. Although this may seem contrary to what is desirable, it has the positive effect of greatly reducing the amount of load that is transferred on to the anchor system. It is thus a good choice of belay method should the anchor system be of questionable quality, such as when snow or ice anchors are being utilized. The system may be used to belay a leader, a second, or as part of a lower.

Taking in with the waist belay must be done without the hand holding the dead rope letting go. The process is as follows, and we will assume that the belayer is holding the dead rope in their right hand. Simply reverse the process if you are belaying left-handed.

tips

Wearing a rucksack makes holding a load more comfortable. However, it is important that the rope around the back of the belayer runs low down on top of the rope coming in from the anchor, and is not caught high up on the lid of the rucksack. If this happens, the belayer will be pulled forwards at the moment of loading.

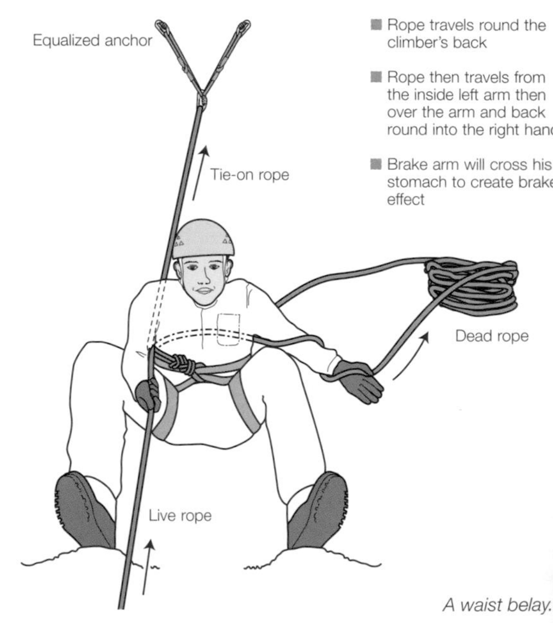

A waist belay.

METHOD

- Have the left hand extended, with the right hand close to the body, a twist of rope around it.
- Pull up with the left hand, at the same time push out with the right. It is important that your hands are co-ordinated, as there should be no slack rope running around your back.
- Releasing the grip of your left hand slightly, slide it back down the rope until it is on the far side of your right hand.
- Using thumb and forefinger of the left hand, grip the rope below the right hand.
- Relaxing the grip of your right hand a little, slide it back up towards your body and grip the rope again.
- Drop the rope being held between thumb and forefinger of the left hand, and repeat the process.

notes

Be careful if choosing the waist belay in a technical situation, as it is extremely difficult to **escape the system** should the need arise. Other techniques should be considered first if there is any question that the belayer may have to move from their stance.

Using a harness

The twist must only be around the arm holding the dead rope. If a twist was taken on the live rope side and a load applied, a broken arm or wrist could result. Gloves and long sleeves should always be worn when using this system, as the rope only has to move a very short distance as it slips through your hands, before severe burning of skin will occur.

When using a waist-belay system with a harness (and so probably tied on at the front) it is essential that the **ABC** of anchor–belayer–climber is carefully considered. If the anchor

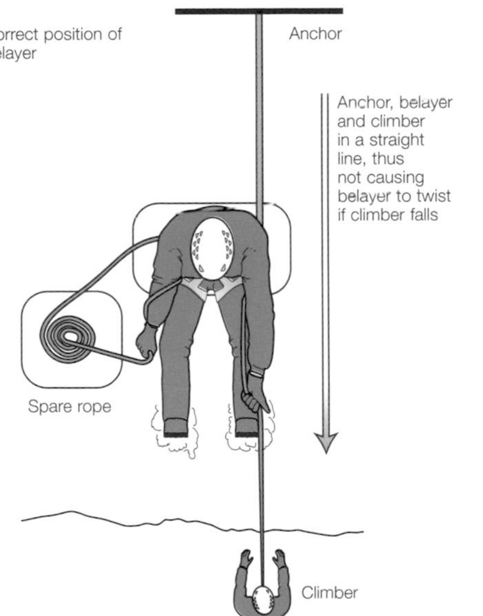

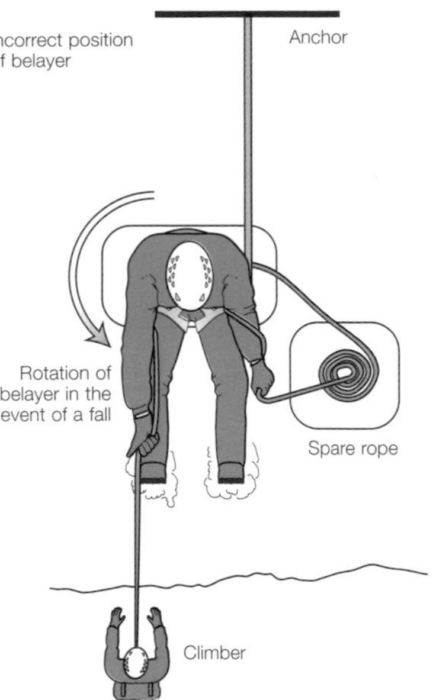

The correct and incorrect orientation of the rope when using a harness and a waist belay.

rope comes to the belayer under their left-hand side, but the live rope to the climber comes out from their right-hand side, should a load be applied there would be a severe twisting motion applied to the belayer as the rope pulls itself into a straight line, ABC. This could easily result in the belayer being pulled from their stance, losing control of the rope and sustaining severe back injury as they are violently twisted around. It is essential that the rope coming to the belayer from the climber is on the same side of the body as the rope coming in from the anchor.

Wires

See also: protection, running belay.

This is the generic name given to the type of **protection** that consists of a metal wedge swaged on to the end of a loop of wire. Wires are generally very technical pieces of equipment, scientifically designed to hold substantial loads by using the shape of the head to hold it in place. They come in a variety of sizes, from a couple of millimetres (fractions of an inch) through to 30mm (1in) or more in width, and it is usual for climbers to carry a selection of up to twenty or more.

Wrist loops – ice axes

See leashes – axes.

Y-axe anchor

See also: bucket seat, buried axe anchor, clove hitch, screwgate.

The Y-axe system of anchoring is useful in areas of shallow but reasonable quality snow cover, such as in shallow accumulations at the top of ice falls where insufficient ice is present to give a good anchor on its own.

METHOD

- Axe and sling slots are prepared in a similar manner to those for a **buried axe anchor**, the main difference being that they are aligned at 45 degrees across the slope. Effort should be made to make the system symmetrical, as it is the pressure exerted by the axes on the snow pack diagonally below that gives the system its strength. For this reason, it is important not to disturb the snow in this area during the construction of the anchor.
- Two 120cm (48in) slings are placed on each of the axe shafts using an inverted **clove hitch**.
- The axes should be placed into the slots with their heads on the upslope sides, and arranged so that the slings, run in the slots, will meet at an angle of no more than 90 degrees.
- A **screwgate** karabiner is used at the point at which the slings meet, and it is on to here that the anchor rope can be clipped.
- This anchor rope will then run down to the belayer at their stance, which would be a **bucket seat** by preference as long as there was sufficient depth to dig one.

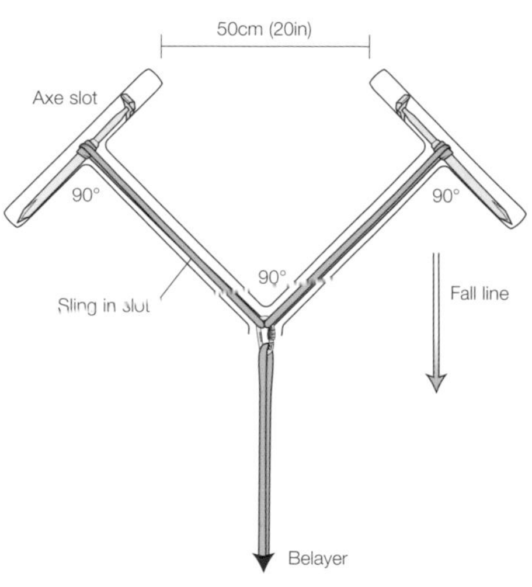

The Y-axe anchor.

Y-hang

See also: abseil device, abseil loop, abseil rope, extenders, HMS karabiner, Italian hitch, larks foot, overhand knot, Parisian baudrier.

The Y-hang is a method by which two people can descend an abseil rope at one time, suspended from a single point at their abseil device. This is particularly useful if rescuing a sick or stranded climber and accompanying them to the ground or some other place of safety.

METHOD

- A 120cm (48in) sling is ideal for this purpose. It should be knotted to provide two attachment points, with the best method being to divide the sling into thirds.
- An **overhand knot** should be tied at the apex, through which a karabiner and the abseil device are attached. This is because it may well be desirable to have the person being accompanied at a slightly different height to the rescuer. This makes the placing of feet easier as there would be less crowding of the available rock. Also, if the person to be accompanied is incapacitated in some way, they may need to be assisted down in a position arranged at 90 degrees across and in front of the rescuer.

Y-hang

notes

If dealing with a semi or unconscious casualty, and they are in the 90-degree position, it could be essential to secure their upper half with a chest harness or a **Parisian baudrier**. This will help to keep them upright and avoid the possibility of them inverting or sustaining a head injury. The attachment of the baudrier to the Y-hang rig should be made so that it can be undone in an instant, in case the casualty's airway needs to be cleared during the abseil.

tips

If there is concern that the weight of two people will be difficult to control, an extra degree of friction can be built in to the system. This could be achieved in a number of ways, such as by clipping an **Italian hitch** on the **abseil rope** in to an **HMS karabiner**, in turn clipped by a short **extender** to the abseil device extender

- The rescuer attaches themselves on to the longer section of sling, either by clipping into the **abseil loop** with a karabiner or, in an emergency, **lark's footing** around the same point.
- The device is connected to the rope and a back-up prusik attached.
- A screwgate karabiner is clipped on to the shorter of the sling ends and it is to this point that the casualty will be attached. If they are able to look after themselves, the two will simply abseil as normal, with the rescuer controlling the rate of descent, taking into account the needs of the other. If, however, the casualty should be unable to take any useful part in the descent, they will be less liable to injury if they are in a position across the front of the rescuer, being fielded away from the rock and any other obstruction. If they are to descend in this position, the rescuer may elect to attach the casualty to them by using a short extender. This will give more control over how the casualty hangs, and will help to avoid any violent swinging motion caused by the terrain over which the descent takes place.

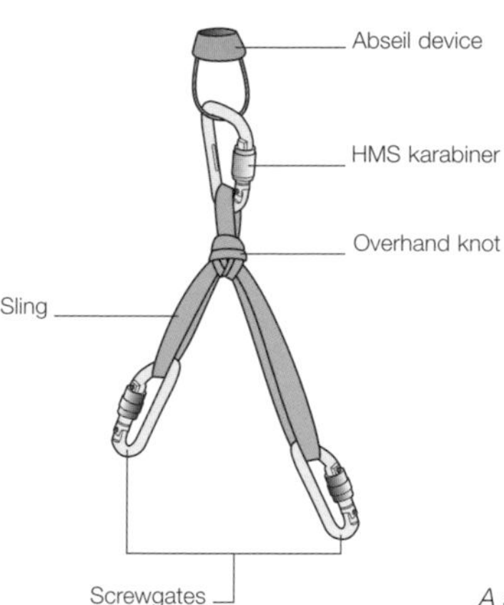

A sling set up for a Y-hang.

Yosemite hoist

See hauling.

Z-hoist

See unassisted hoist.

Opposite: *Difficult and committing climbing in Scotland.*

Index

Opposite: *Typical Scottish winter conditions.*

Opposite: *Committing leading on mica schist.*

Acknowledgments

Opposite: *Sea-cliff soloing.*

Following pages: *Early morning in the European Alps.*

Thanks must go to many people for inspiration and encouragement, essential to the successful completion of any book of this kind. There are too many to name individually, but they all know who they are – it'll be the people I've bought a beer for recently. Cheers all.

Particular thanks go to Paula Griffin for proof reading my initial scrawled attempts, as well as the later drafts, spending many hours burning the midnight oil. She also helped with many of the photographs, often taken in less than clement weather, and for that, as well as just being there, I'm indebted. In addition, Sean Cattanach ran his critical eye over the text and gave me some informative feedback.

I'm grateful to Simon Panton who helped clarify the bouldering grades used in his *North Wales Bouldering Guide*, with particular reference to the V8+ versus Font grades, and his list is included in the relevant section.

A very special 'thank you' goes to Jonathon Preston MIC, BMG, for technically proof reading the final manuscript. Our time together reviewing the latest techniques along with unassociated Pythonesque events has helped to make the book as technically solid as possible – cheers JP.

Thanks must also go to Ethan Danielson for converting my scribbles into some great illustrations.

Much help was begged from, and given by, Lyon Equipment in the UK. Their time and assistance is much appreciated.

Thanks to Beal, who supplied much of the climbing software such as the ropes and slings used during research sessions and in the photographs. I'm also grateful for being allowed to use some of their technical data. They can be contacted via www.beal-planet.com

A good deal of hardware and technical support was given by Petzl and Petzl-Charlet. They were happy for me to use their very useful data resource of technical information re equipment uses and tolerances, for which I am very grateful. They were also happy for me to mimic a number of their very clear diagrams. Their informative website is at www.petzl.com